Watching Media Learning
Making Sense of Media Education

Edited by
David Buckingham

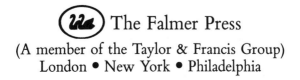 The Falmer Press

(A member of the Taylor & Francis Group)
London • New York • Philadelphia

UK   The Falmer Press, Rankine Road, Basingstoke, Hampshire RG24 0PR

USA   The Falmer Press, Taylor & Francis Inc., 1900 Frost Road, Suite 101, Bristol, PA 19007

First published 1990

British Library Cataloguing in Publication Data
Watching media learning: making sense of media education.
  1. Great Britain. Educational institutions. Curriculum subjects. Mass media.
I. Buckingham, David, *1954*
302.234071041

ISBN 1-85000-652-0

Library of Congress Cataloging-in-Publication Data
Watching media learning: making sense of media education/ edited by David Buckingham.
    p. cm.
  Includes bibliographical references (p.).
  ISBN 1-85000-652-0: — ISBN 1-85000-653-9 (pbk.)
  1. Television in education — Great Britain. 2. Mass media in education — Great Britain.   I. Buckingham, David, 1954-
LB1044.7.W325 1990
371.3′ 35-dc20

Jacket design by Benedict Evans

Typeset in 11/13 Bembo by
Chapterhouse, The Cloisters, Formby L37 3PX

Printed in Great Britain by Burgess Science Press, Basingstoke on paper which has a specified pH value on final paper manufacture of not less than 7.5 and is therefore 'acid free'.

Contents

Part Four: Media Education and the Curriculum

Conclusion

Preface and Acknowledgments

The essays collected in this book have emerged from the work of the Media Teachers' Research Group, based in the Department of English and Media Studies at the University of London Institute of Education. Over the past three years, the group has served as a regular forum for experienced media teachers in secondary and further education to share and discuss their own work.

Despite the current constraints on educational innovation, media education has continued to expand throughout the past decade, and is increasingly becoming a part of every teacher's work. Yet while there is a growing number of publications concerned with the area, none as yet has provided a detailed description or evaluation of classroom practice. This book represents an initial attempt to fill that gap.

Our aim, therefore, is not primarily to make the case for media education, or to provide teaching materials or strategies. Rather than offering glowing accounts of 'good practice', we have sought to acknowledge the difficulties and contradictions of teaching about the media, as well as its considerable achievements and rewards. Above all, we have attempted to be honest, not merely about the realities of classrooms as we have experienced them, but also about our own confusions and inadequacies. While we can inevitably offer only fragments of classroom practice, we hope that readers will recognize these, and be able to relate them to their own everyday teaching experiences.

The following have at some stage been members of the group, or have contributed to its work: Vivienne Adams, David Buckingham, Phil Cohen, Jon Davison, Pete Fraser, Andy Freedman, Nick Furlonger, Marie Gillespie, Jenny Grahame, John Hardcastle, Sylvia Hines, Sam Kingsley, Bethan Marshall, Richard Marshall, Roger Martin, Netia Mayman, Jo McClatchey, Lucy Moy-Thomas, Lydia Plowman, Chris Richards, Jocelyn Robson, Julian Sefton-Green, Jonathan Simmons, Martin Sohn-Rethel, Roy Stafford, Sian Statters, Alan Tobe.

In addition, the editor would particularly like to thank Celia Greenwood for her helpful and supportive comments on the manuscript.

David Buckingham
January 1990

List of Abbreviations

AIDS	Acquired Immune Deficiency Syndrome
BBC	British Broadcasting Corporation
BFI	British Film Institute
BTEC	Business and Technician Education Council
CDT	Craft, Design and Technology
CEE	Certificate in Extended Education
CGLI	City and Guilds of London Institute
CPVE	Certificate in Pre-Vocational Education
CSE	Certificate in Secondary Education
DES	Department of Education and Science
FEU	Further Education Unit
GCSE	General Certificate in Secondary Education
HIV	Human Immunodeficiency Virus
HMI	Her Majesty's Inspectorate
IBA	Independent Broadcasting Authority
ILEA	Inner London Education Authority
INSET	In-service Training
LEAG	London and East Anglian Group (Examination Board)
MSC	Manpower Services Commission
NCVQ	National Council for Vocational Qualifications
NEA	Northern Examining Association
RSA	Royal Society of Arts
SEG	Southern Examining Group
SLR	Single Lens Reflex
STAS	Science, Technology and Society
TVEI	Technical and Vocational Education Initiative
VCR	Video Cassette Recorder
WJEC	Welsh Joint Examinations Council

Introduction

Chapter 1

Media Education: From Pedagogy to Practice

David Buckingham

This book is concerned with classroom practice in media education. In this respect, it is unique. While media education in Britain has a long history, stretching back over fifty years, and while it is currently expanding at a remarkable rate, there have been very few attempts to describe or analyze what it looks like in practice.

Most books and courses on media education tend to start from the opposite position, and to move from 'theory' to 'practice'. The aim is generally to make accessible a body of academic knowledge about the media, and then to suggest how this might be translated into practical teaching strategies.[1] Yet there is a strange sense of unreality about much of this work. 'Ideas for teaching' — many of which would undoubtedly be most effective in an undergraduate seminar — are simply conjured out of thin air, or tacked on as an afterthought. Rarely is there any detailed consideration of what actually happens in classrooms when these ideas are put into practice.

As a result, many fundamental questions tend to be neglected. What do our students already know about the media? How does the knowledge we attempt to provide connect with this? How do students learn about the media, and what are the most effective teaching strategies? To what extent is the body of academic knowledge we offer either useful or meaningful to students? These are the kinds of questions which are inevitably raised by classroom practice: yet they are precisely the questions which have been marginalized and ignored by previous writers on media education.

This introductory chapter attempts to explain the reasons for this neglect of classroom practice, and to identify some of its consequences. In doing so, if offers a sketch of the recent history of media education, and of the dominant assumptions which inform it. In beginning to investigate our own practice, it is these taken-for-granted assumptions which we have largely sought to question.

*   *   *   *   *

The development of media education since the 1970s has been heavily overshadowed by academic media theory. To a certain extent, this privileging of higher education has been a strategic choice. In the early 1970s, it was argued that change would flow downwards through the education system, and that the establishment of film studies in universities and polytechnics would provide a secure basis for later developments in schools — a view which even at the time was probably anachronistic. Yet in practice, media education in schools has remained very much the poor relation: while academics have theorized away, practising teachers have effectively been excluded from the debate. By implication, it is academics who are seen to produce the knowledge, while the teacher's job is simply to transmit it to students.

In order to understand how this unsatisfactory relationship between theory and practice has arisen, we need to consider the nature of the theory itself. The contemporary version of media theory we are concerned with here began to emerge in the early 1970s, primarily in the journals *Screen* and *Screen Education*, published by the Society for Education in Film and Television (SEFT). The often uneasy combination of Althusserian Marxism, structuralism, semiotics and psychoanalytic theory effectively displaced earlier approaches based on Leavisite literary criticism.[2] During the 1970s, the influence of what came to be known as '*Screen* theory' spread way beyond the relatively small area of film studies, and contributed to a far-reaching transformation of academic disciplines as diverse as English, art history and social theory.

While the development of '*Screen* theory' in the 1970s was largely the province of academics, it also had significant *educational* implications. Perhaps the most fundamental of these was simply the privileging of theory itself. Following Althusser, a central emphasis was placed on the political role of theory: the only truly scientific knowledge was to be gained through the development of a theory of 'ideology-in-general' — any study of specific ideologies, histories, or social formations was rejected as mere empiricism. While there was certainly detailed empirical work on film texts published in *Screen* during this period, it is nevertheless remarkable how little there was, and how much of it was confined to a limited canon of 'approved' texts. There was very little work on television, or on media industries, and almost none on audiences. Empirical work of this kind was forced to take a back seat in favour of extremely generalized theories of film as an ideological or psychic 'apparatus'.

Beyond this, it is important to note the fundamental political pessimism of the theories which were advanced. At a time when major political battles were being fought between the labour movement and the state, *Screen* was busily developing a theory which proclaimed the almost total power of state apparatuses to determine consciousness and social action. The version of psychoanalytic theory appropriated by *Screen* in the mid-1970s simply compounded this: the individual subject was seen as hopelessly bound into a monolithic patriarchal 'symbolic order', from which there was little hope of escape. The media — particularly through the operation of such generalized categories as 'narrative' and 'realism' — were seen as the primary agent in securing this subjection. There appeared to be little point in distinguishing between different forms of realism or narrative — all were equally tainted with the 'dominant ideology'.

The only possibility of opposition lay in outright rejection, through anti-narrative and anti-realism, of the illusory pleasures of dominant forms. This privileging of the avant-garde, and the canonization of figures like Godard, was based on the assumption that texts could be judged as politically 'progressive' according to their own inherent characteristics, irrespective of the contexts in which they were read, or the audiences who read them.

'*Screen* theory' thus inevitably embodied a pedagogy — a set of implied relationships between teachers and learners. The journal's own pedagogy was relentlessly authoritarian: critics within its pages who questioned its increasingly inaccessible prose style and its political obscurantism were sternly reprimanded for their lack of theoretical rigour.[3] Certainly in the 1970s, *Screen*'s policing of the 'correct' theoretical line was marked by a degree of arrogance worthy of the sectarian Left at its most doctrinaire.

* * * * *

Despite — or perhaps because of — its failure to acknowledge its own pedagogy, '*Screen* theory' implicitly prescribed a pedagogy for teachers which was highly elitist. Media audiences were predominantly seen as duped and manipulated, often at a sub-rational level: for teachers in schools, the only hope was to expose the operations of the 'dominant ideology' by directly attacking the pleasures and preferences of students. Teachers were implicitly defined as members of a theoretical vanguard, charged with a missionary responsibility to alert the masses to the deceptions which were being practised upon them. At least in terms of its pedagogy, there was a fundamental continuity between '*Screen* theory' and the Leavisite approach it claimed to have abandoned.

The task of identifying a pedagogy for media education in schools fell to *Screen*'s sister journal *Screen Education*, and it was here that the contradictions were most acutely felt. One major problem here was that the monolithic analysis of the ideological role of the media also had to be applied to education. Indeed for Althusser, the education system was regarded as the major ideological state apparatus, whose function was essentially that of ideological reproduction.[4] Exactly how the functionaries of one ideological state apparatus were to generate critical teaching about another state apparatus was not made clear. The contradiction was simply effaced by a high degree of vanguardist rhetoric. Teachers were regularly described in *Screen Education* as 'socialist intellectuals' who could 'short-circuit the ideology of the state'. Teachers were urged to 'work on the contradictions which arise in the culture at the educational level', and to 'engage directly in cultural struggle in a manner which directly confronts social-democratic consciousness'.[5]

Precisely how this ideological short-circuiting and cultural struggle were to be achieved could not be spelt out. The privileging of theory led to a situation in which writing about classroom practice was not merely hopelessly unglamorous, it was also tantamount to bourgeois empiricism. The number of detailed accounts of classroom practice published in *Screen Education* in the 1970s could probably be counted on the fingers of one hand. As Judith Williamson remarked, teaching in *Screen Education* was rather like sex: you knew other people did it, but you never knew exactly what they did or how they did it.[6]

Despite its neglect of classroom practice, there was a clear position on pedagogy in *Screen Education*, which was fundamentally opposed to what it chose to define as 'liberal' or 'progressive' teaching strategies. In retrospect, it seems remarkable that at a time of major shifts to the Right in educational politics — for example, in the form of the Black Papers and the so-called 'Great Debate' — much of the rhetoric of *Screen Education* was directed not against the Right, but against the liberal Left, and in particular against the 'delusions' of the 1960s. Child-centred education was relentlessly caricatured, in a manner not far removed from that of Conservative leaders today: 'experience' and 'creativity' became the new swear-words.

Although *Screen Education*'s position was not necessarily consistent or unchallenged, it was certainly dominated by a denunciation of 'liberal' strategies like class discussion and practical work. Instead, what was needed was 'confrontation and analysis', a 'dismembering' of the 'dominant ideology', which would lead inevitably to radical political action. Teachers were urged to engage in 'direct teaching' (which presumably meant lecturing), as the only means of transmitting the knowledge which would prepare working-class students to take control of the means of production.[7]

* * * * *

In many ways, the legacy of '*Screen* theory' continues to inform media education in the 1980s. While the utopian rhetoric now seems merely absurd, the uneven relationship between academic theory and educational practice established at that time remains influential. This has resulted in some highly contradictory prescriptions for classroom practice.

As I have noted, most contemporary books on media teaching are fundamentally concerned with offering potted summaries of academic research. Of course, it is vitally important that teachers are familiar with this work, and that students are given access to it. Yet there is little recognition here of what students already know, or how this might relate to what they are expected to learn. The implicit assumption would seem to be that students' existing knowledge is essentially 'ideological', and thus invalid, and that the teacher's role is to replace this with valid, 'objective' academic knowledge.

At the same time, there is a clear acknowledgment — at least in some cases — that teaching involves more than simply dumping information on students. Students, it is argued, need to be active participants, rather than empty vessels. They will 'learn by doing' — although precisely *how* they learn is rarely addressed.[8]

Much of the practice recommended in these books, and adopted in teaching materials, in fact derives from 'progressive' English teaching. There is an emphasis on small-group work, on students making their own meanings and engaging in discussion and debate — in fact precisely those methods which were so strongly condemned in the 1970s.

Yet there remains an uneasy contradiction between the emphasis on a received body of academic knowledge, and the adoption of 'progressive' teaching methods. The work of Len Masterman, easily the most influential advocate of media education, clearly illustrates this.[9] While there are many contradictions in his account, Masterman's most consistent view of the media is as agents of a 'dominant ideology' which is imposed on passive audiences. The media 'engineer consent' to an unjust social order, although they do so in ways which are largely invisible to those who 'consume' them.

Thus, on the one hand, Masterman argues for media education as a form of 'demystification': through the development of analytical skills, and through the provision of 'radical information' about media institutions, teachers will 'liberate' their students from mystification and false consciousness. Masterman's approach is heavily oriented towards non-fictional forms, such as news and documentary, where it is assumed that the teacher can replace 'mystification' by objective truth. Genres to which this approach does not so easily apply — and in particular the fictional forms which are most popular with young people themselves — are largely ignored.

Yet on the other hand, Masterman also advocates 'non-hierarchical', 'democratic' teaching methods, which are based on 'dialogue' and 'a genuine sharing of power' in the classroom. In this scenario, the teacher is merely a 'senior colleague', rather than an 'expert' whose perspective is automatically privileged.

Clearly, this places the teacher in a highly contradictory position: on the one hand, s/he is seen to be in possession of a 'truth' which is not available to his/her students, while on the other, s/he is urged to engage students in an equal dialogue, and to avoid transmission teaching. The lack of any detailed description of real classroom practice makes it impossible to see how this might be achieved. It seems to be assumed, not merely that students are suffering from 'mystification', but that they will somehow recognize the error of their ways once ideology is made visible and the 'truth' is revealed. The possibility that the ideology of a text might be perceived in different ways by different readers, or that there might be a negotiation or struggle over meaning in the classroom, is effectively ignored. It is assumed that students will simply consent to the reading which a supposedly 'objective' analysis reveals. If only it were so easy!

This kind of contradiction also characterizes many teaching materials in media education. On the one hand, there is a commitment to 'learning by discovery', and to an equal and open dialogue. Students are urged to 'say what they think', and assured that 'there are no right answers'. Yet in many cases, there clearly *are* right answers, and the material has been selected and constructed in such a way that students will almost inevitably produce them.

This is perhaps particularly the case in teaching about media representations of areas such as 'race' and gender. Here, texts are often selected precisely because of the objectionable ideologies they are seen to contain. The texts are presumed to be self-evidently sexist or racist or otherwise 'biased', and the aim of 'analysis' is to enable students to detect this, and then to condemn it. While students are typically encouraged to reach their own conclusions, in practice there is often little space for them to generate their own readings, or to explore the contradictory pleasures which such texts may offer. It is as if potentially subversive or dangerous meanings must be policed out of existence by rigorous, rational analysis.

This strategy is particularly problematic when the texts chosen are those most popular with students themselves. Teaching about teenage magazines, for example, has rarely advanced beyond the routine condemnation of 'sexism' to investigate the complex and contradictory ways in which they are actually read, particularly by girls. The possibility that the magazines may serve positive functions for girls, or that they might already be read in a relatively distanced or critical way, is effectively discounted. Underlying the seemingly open invitation to analyze and discuss is the implicit assumption that the magazines are responsible for imposing false ideologies on their readers, and that readers simply swallow them whole. Despite the apparently progressive approach, the role which is assigned to the teacher here is in fact highly traditional: the teacher remains the moral and political guardian, responsible for leading students on to 'better things'.[10]

*   *   *   *   *

To be sure, there has been an on-going debate about 'pedagogy' in media education — although, as the use of that term itself would suggest, this too has been conducted at a highly theoretical level, largely among teachers in higher education.[11] As a result, it has been a strangely abstract debate, in which there is a good deal of heated confrontation between one 'position' and another, yet little concrete reference to specific instances of teaching and learning. While it is somehow acceptable to theorize about other people's pedagogy, it remains very difficult to describe what actually takes place in real classrooms.

Nevertheless, there has been a growing recognition in these debates that the realities of teaching and learning are more complex than some academic theorists would lead us to suppose. The aggressively libertarian notions of media teaching which were advocated in the 1960s and 1970s have increasingly been questioned. The idea that teachers could simply provide students with a body of knowledge which would open their eyes to a previously hidden reality has come to seem like so much wishful thinking. Teachers may attempt to 'tell it like it is', but students aren't necessarily going to believe them.

Judith Williamson's article 'How does girl number twenty understand ideology?', briefly alluded to above, was the first notable attempt to question this vanguardist approach towards media teaching.[12] As Williamson points out, however 'radical' the knowledge teachers offer, students can easily learn to play the teacher's game. Boys can learn to say the right anti-sexist things about images of women in the media, but this can end up simply reinforcing their belief that girls must be stupid to enjoy those images in the first place.

As Williamson argues, 'analysis' alone will not necessarily change students' attitudes. Unless the discussion of ideology in the media is related to students' own experience, to their sense of their own identity, it will remain a purely academic exercise: students will 'do' images of women in the same way that they 'do' medieval poetry or the history of the Tudors. As she suggests, there is a risk that ideology will be seen as 'what *other* people think, and the only possible explanation for why they believe such ''lies'' or ''propaganda'' is because they are stupid' — a risk which media teaching, perhaps particularly in higher education, has not always managed to avoid.

Although Williamson's article did represent a decisive — if very belated — acknowledgment of the complexities of classroom practice, there is a sense in which it remains tied to vanguardist notions of teaching. Williamson continues to assume that her students are victims of a monolithic 'dominant ideology', promoted by an omnipotent media, and that their only escape will be through a process of instantaneous conversion, provoked by their confrontation with the teacher — a kind of 'road to Damascus' version of media education.

Given the broader context of debate at this time, Williamson's article was clearly raising some uncomfortable questions, and it would perhaps be unrealistic to expect her to have answered these as well. Yet they are questions which have recurred in subsequent debate. For example, my own contribution to this debate[13] derives from a similar sense of the contradictions of classroom practice, and an acknowledgment that students will not automatically assent to the positions laid out by 'radical' teachers. While it is certainly possible that students will learn to play the teacher's game (as Williamson's students do), it is equally possible that they may resist it, not necessarily for profound ideological reasons, but simply because they enjoy challenging the teacher's power. Working-class students in particular are likely to resist the attempts of middle-class teachers to impose their own political beliefs, however surreptitiously this is done. 'Radical' teachers cannot easily step outside the institutionalized power relationships of the educational system, and the claim that they are acting on the students' behalf will not necessarily be accepted by the students themselves.[14]

There is, then, a growing recognition in these debates that many of the prescriptions for media teaching developed in the 1970s do not actually work in practice — and that the social dynamics of classrooms, and the learning process itself, are much more complex and contradictory than has previously been assumed. Yet, as I have indicated, the debates themselves remain highly abstract. The accounts of classroom practice are limited and anecdotal, mere ammunition for broader theoretical arguments. Here too, theory has been privileged over practice.

*   *   *   *   *

The developments described above have been accompanied and supported by other movements. Academic work on the media has increasingly moved away from the

monolithic approach embodied in '*Screen* theory'. The notion of the media as pur-
veyors of a single, all-powerful 'dominant ideology' has been displaced in favour of a
much more optimistic emphasis on diversity and contradiction. Largely in response to
feminism, there has been a growing engagement with the potentially subversive
pleasures of popular media texts, and a reaction against the puritanical and elitist ten-
dencies of earlier approaches. Media industries are increasingly regarded, not so much
as agents of the ruling classes, but as institutions whose power is highly precarious, and
crucially dependent on the consent of audiences.[15]

In particular, the 1980s have seen a renewed emphasis on the active role of media
audiences. While in certain cases, this has been motivated by a form of populism — a
desire to defend the preferences of 'ordinary viewers' at all costs — it has led to a widespread recognition of the diverse ways in which media texts may be used and understood.[16] Meaning is no longer regarded as something inherent in texts, but as a product
of the negotiation between texts and readers.

Particularly important for media education has been the development of qualitative research on children and television, which has sought to move beyond the notion
of children as passive victims or ideological 'dupes' of the medium.[17] What emerges
from this research is a clear acknowledgment that children are already sophisticated,
discriminating, and often critical viewers — an argument which advocates of media
education have often made, but whose implications have rarely been fully recognized.

Popular debate about the media has seen similar shifts. On the Left, there has been
a general move away from the commonsense conspiracy theory which was widespread
in the 1960s and 1970s. The assertion that the media are merely vehicles for ruling-class
propaganda is now about as fashionable as flared trousers and platform shoes. It is now
socially acceptable for liberal-minded middle-class people to watch and discuss popular
soap operas — although the same could not yet be said of game shows or the tabloid
press. While there is certainly an element of 'designer socialism' here, there is a sense in
which this more open attitude towards the media has been part of a broader reassess-
ment of the pedagogy of Left politics — an attempt, however limited, to engage more
positively with the 'progressive' aspects of popular culture.

However, it would be misleading to suggest that developments in the academic
world have simply filtered down to teachers, and that their practice has changed
merely in response to this. As I have implied, many teachers have learnt from
experience that attempting to propagandize students, or to impose their own readings
of media texts upon them, can prove highly counter-productive. While there remain
those who regard media education as a kind of crusade to save the working class from
ideological manipulation, there are many teachers who have been seeking to develop a
more productive approach.

*   *   *   *   *

In addition to these shifts in academic and popular debate, there have been changes in
the location of media education in schools and in further education. Conservative

policies on education have had ambiguous consequences for media teachers: while the education system as a whole has been under considerable pressure, media education has continued to expand throughout the past decade.

In the primary sector, notably through the research and development work sponsored by the British Film Institute,[18] there has been a growing interest in the possibilities of media education, particularly in the language curriculum. The development of GCSE has given a considerable boost to Media Studies courses in secondary schools, with many now offering the subject for the first time. More recently, there have been a number of new 'A' level courses introduced, with 'A/S' levels in the pipeline. The growth of vocational and pre-vocational education, initially under the auspices of the Manpower Services Commission, has opened up new spaces for media teaching in both secondary and further education: early fears that TVEI or BTEC courses would be confined to providing technical training have proved unfounded in many instances. The National Curriculum, initially regarded with considerable suspicion by media teachers, is turning out to be something of a mixed blessing: the substantial inclusion of media education within the core subject of English and its role as a cross-curricular dimension, while not without their limitations, will undoubtedly lead to a considerable increase in the amount of media teaching taking place in schools.

Of course, there is a good deal yet to be achieved. While there has been a considerable demand for in-service training in media education, the opportunities here remain very limited. In particular, there is an urgent need for longer, more in-depth courses — although it is precisely these kinds of courses which have been undermined by recent changes in in-service provision. As a new subject area, media education lacks a 'career structure', and thus suffers from a lack of continuity: media courses are often introduced by enthusiastic young teachers who tend to move on, leaving them in the hands of non-specialists.

Nevertheless, this expansion of media education has also seen a change in its character. The embattled vanguard of media teachers envisaged by *Screen Education* in the 1970s is no more — if indeed it ever existed in any substantial form. As a much broader range of teachers has been drawn into the area, so the aims and objectives of media teaching have become more diverse — and perhaps more confused. While the version of media education enshrined in Media Studies courses at GCSE and 'A' level is still recognizably derived from academic media theory, the approach to media education in primary schools or in TVEI schemes is much less reliant on an established body of academic knowledge. Practical media production by students — a strategy widely condemned in the 1970s, and still very much neglected by advocates of media education[19] — now plays a much more central role. In so far as one can generalize, classroom practice in media teaching is much less reliant on the kind of transmission teaching advocated in the 1970s, and much closer to the notion of active, student-centred learning which is promoted by TVEI, and is part of common practice in primary schools.

While these developments are broadly positive, it remains the case that there has been very little analysis or evaluation of what is taking place in practice. As media education expands, it is vitally important that there is a continuing debate about its aims and purposes, and that this debate is informed by a detailed consideration of classroom practice. This book is intended, then, not as a definitive statement, but as an initial contribution to this debate.

* * * * *

In this introductory chapter, I have attempted to offer a broad (and admittedly polemical) outline of the recent history of media education, in order to provide a context for the contributions that follow. Inevitably, my account has been very general: the relationship between the academic debates I have described and the actual day-to-day practice of teaching is bound to be tenuous and contradictory. Teaching involves negotiation and compromise: abstract notions of 'pedagogy' are not necessarily the most useful way of understanding the contingent realities of classrooms.

To a greater or lesser extent, all the contributors to this book share the common history I have described — although they would obviously interpret that history in different ways! As a result, while the contributions do address different aspects of media education, there is a shared agenda of questions which recurs throughout.

The first section of the book, 'School Knowledge, Commonsense Knowledge', considers the relationship between children's existing knowledge of the media and the knowledge they acquire in school. Both contributions here argue that children may be much more sophisticated users of the media than is generally assumed. However, they also point to the need for a cautious approach to interpreting data: talk about television, it is argued, needs to be analyzed in relation to the social and interpersonal contexts in which it is produced, and should not be taken at face value.

In Chapter 2, we describe and analyze a sequence of lessons on television advertising, and offer a critical account of a number of common pedagogic strategies in media teaching. As we argue, many of these strategies are based on somewhat questionable assumptions about students' existing knowledge of the media, and about how they learn. Through a detailed consideration of classroom discussion, we seek to question the notion of 'objective analysis' which is often given a central place in media education, and argue for the importance of locating learning within the specific social relations of classrooms.

In his contribution, Pete Fraser considers the popular discourses about television which are used by students and teachers in more open-ended discussion. He suggests that these discourses may significantly inflect our perceptions of television and of media education itself, in ways which are not always constructive. Using 'anti-television' discourses may serve as a guarantee of the speaker's 'adulthood' and 'responsibility', yet they also tend to conceive of children as ignorant, and may actively prevent a more considered exploration of the experience of popular television.

In Part Two, 'Theory and Practice', Roy Stafford and Jenny Grahame offer contrasting accounts of practical media productions undertaken by further education and school students respectively. As both authors suggest, the relationship between theoretical and practical work has always been one of the most problematic areas of media education. All too often, practical work has been reduced to a mere illustration of theory, in which the possibilities for students' learning are severely restricted.

Roy Stafford's account of his students' video production projects indicates the broad range of learning outcomes which can potentially arise from practical work. As he argues, practical work can provide a valuable means for students to give voice to their own cultural concerns, and to negotiate a rather different relationship with the educational institutions in which they are placed. In these respects, media education may make a unique contribution to the expanded notion of 'creativity' which is currently emerging in pre-vocational education.

By contrast, Jenny Grahame's contribution examines a much less open-ended approach to practical work, namely the use of simulation as a means of teaching about media institutions. While she acknowledges the considerable benefits of this approach in providing students with a concrete, 'hands-on' experience of processes which might otherwise remain distant and abstract, she also argues that it may be unnecessarily constricting. As she indicates, students' self-evaluation is a vital aspect of practical work, yet the methods which are currently used may be less than effective.

Part Three, 'Reading Representations', focuses on another central aspect of media education, namely teaching about representation. Both contributions here take account of the complex ways in which students make sense of media texts, and the ways in which the pleasures they derive from the media are part of their broader social lives. In rejecting the view of students as mere victims of media manipulation, they also seek to move beyond the propagandist approach to media teaching described above.

Julian Sefton-Green provides an account of his students' responses to a popular television series about a black family, *The Cosby Show*, and goes on to consider his experience of teaching about it. His students' judgments about the 'realism' of the programme reveal diverse and sophisticated understandings of the ways in which television represents the social world. Yet in teaching about the programme, and in debating the representation of black people in lessons, the power relationships of the classroom also determine students' responses, if not always in predictable ways.

Similarly, in Chris Richards' contribution, teaching about gender representation and sexuality in the media is seen to unsettle traditional teacher–student relationships. While media education is centrally concerned to develop a 'politics of subjectivity', to explore the relationship between social representations and 'personal' identity, male and female students may respond in very different ways to this challenge. As Richards argues, if we are to account fully for the complex role of the media in students' lives, we need to prevent media education becoming a merely instrumental process.

In the final section, 'Media Education and the Curriculum', we consider the relationship between media education and other curriculum areas — an issue which has become much more significant in the light of the National Curriculum proposals. The central issue here is the extent to which the conceptual and theoretical concerns specific to media education connect with those of other subjects with which it might seek to collaborate. Perhaps unsurprisingly, these relationships are far from straightforward.

In their contribution, Jocelyn Robson, Jonathan Simmons and Martin Sohn-Rethel describe the experience of implementing a whole school policy on media education across the curriculum in one London school. They identify some of the institutional factors which determined collaboration between departments, and suggest some reasons why certain collaborations were more successful than others. As they argue, the presence of a media education specialist and a degree of support from school management is essential if such cross-curricular integration is to be effective.

Finally, Andy Freedman considers the relationship between media education and English, which is likely to be a central issue in the implementation of the National Curriculum. As he indicates, the two areas have overlapping histories, yet on a theoretical level there are often distinct differences between them. In practice, however, these differences may be less significant: his analysis of the ways in which one teacher approached work on media and literary texts suggests that both subjects may rely on notions of 'objective analysis' which tend to reduce the diversity of possible readings of a given text.

Underlying all the contributions, then, is a series of questions about teaching and learning in media education. What do our students already know about the media, and how do they know it? What are we hoping they will learn, and what difference do we think it will make? How can we identify what students know and learn, and enable them to identify this for themselves? Clearly, these are the kinds of questions which recur throughout classroom research, although they have rarely been asked in the case of media education. The central point, however, is that these questions cannot be answered in any meaningful way on a general level, or simply by recourse to theory. We need to look in detail, at specific instances of teaching and learning, in specific social and educational situations.

For a variety of reasons, then, these questions have been difficult to ask, and it would certainly be premature to expect total answers to them here. We have sought to describe and analyze our own practice as honestly as possible. This has meant recognizing failure as well as success, and acknowledging the difficulty and complexity of what we have been trying to achieve. If this encourages others to reflect on and thereby to improve their own practice, our major aim will have been realized.

Notes

1 For example, Masterman (1980, 1985), Hartley, Goulden and O'Sullivan (1985), Alvarado, Gutch and Wollen (1987), Clarke (1987).
2 Probably the definitive statement of '*Screen* theory' is contained in Coward and Ellis (1977).
3 See, for example, Buscombe *et al.* (1976) and the response by the Editorial Board of *Screen* (1976); and Exton *et al.* (1977), and the response by Drummond (1977).
4 Althusser (1971).
5 See, for example, Grealy (1975, 1977); Ferguson (1977, 1977/78); Alvarado (1977).
6 Williamson (1981/82).
7 For example, Alvarado (1981) and Ferguson (1981).
8 See Masterman (1980).
9 Masterman (1980, 1985): for critiques, see Alvarado (1981) and Buckingham (1986) respectively.
10 For examples, see Leggett and Hemming (n.d.) and the programme *Young Once* in the Thames TV series *Viewpoint Two* (1981).
11 See Alvarado (1981), Masterman (1981/2), Williamson (1981/2), Connell (1983), Williamson (1985), Lusted (1986), Buckingham (1986), Masterman (1986), Bazalgette (1986).
12 Williamson (1981/2).
13 Buckingham (1986).
14 For similar observations, see Cohen (1988) and Dewdney and Lister (1988).
15 Fiske (1987) is broadly representative here.
16 For example, Morley (1980, 1986), Hobson (1982), Ang (1985).
17 For example, Durkin (1985), Hodge and Tripp (1986), Buckingham (1987b).
18 See British Film Institute Working Party on Primary Media Education (1987, 1988), and Bazalgette (1989b).
19 For example, Masterman (1985).

Part One
School Knowledge,
Commonsense Knowledge

Chapter 2

Stepping into the Void:
Beginning Classroom Research in
Media Education

David Buckingham, Pete Fraser, Netia Mayman

This chapter describes a small-scale piece of classroom research undertaken by three members of the group in two London schools in the summer of 1987. For all of us, this was our first systematic attempt to record and analyze what went on in lessons.

On one level, this is an account of a group of naive enthusiasts busily reinventing the wheel. We had the glimmerings of Big Ideas, but very little in the way of basic equipment with which to realize them. The whole idea of 'doing research' sounded extremely grand and important, but also quite daunting, and none of us was really sure what it was supposed to involve.

Yet the problem was not ours alone. What we were trying to do had no precedents for media teachers generally: the kinds of questions we wanted to investigate had hardly been raised, and there was no tradition (at least in media education) of the kind of research we were trying to undertake. At the very least, we hope that teachers and future researchers in the area will be able to learn from some of the mistakes we made here.

The aim of the chapter, then, is not to present anything as definitive as a set of 'findings'. Indeed, perhaps the main thing we learnt from the experience was how difficult it is to find out anything — particularly when it comes to identifying what students have learnt. As a result, much of what is offered here is in the form of questions rather than answers — questions not merely about the process of 'doing research', but also about the aims and methods of media education. It is these latter questions which this research raised for us in a very clear and challenging manner.

*   *   *   *   *

In planning our strategy, we opted for an area of study which was both familiar and fairly easy to handle in terms of teaching — that of television advertising. We arrived at this choice quite quickly, perhaps partly because it was an area which we instinctively felt to be 'safe'. Like all good media teachers, we 'knew' that advertising was a Bad Thing, and that we should be encouraging kids to see through it: the point of what we were doing didn't need to be debated. At the same time, our choice might have reflected some anxiety about this — a sense, perhaps, that in trying to teach children about television advertising we had been teaching them things they already knew, or which simply didn't connect with their experience — and particularly their pleasure — as viewers.

The choice of television advertising as a focus — however arbitrary it may have seemed at the time — did therefore provide a useful means of investigating fundamental questions. Our central concern here was with the relationship between children's existing knowledge about the media and the academic knowledge we make available in schools — an issue we felt had been significantly neglected in the past. How accurate are the assumptions we implicitly make about children's relationship with the media? How effective are the strategies we use in intervening in that relationship? What new knowledge do we want them to acquire, and what difference do we think it will make? What implications does this have for the relationships between teachers and students?

Fundamental as these questions are, the research inevitably provoked even more basic epistemological dramas. As we discovered, we couldn't begin to answer the broad questions raised above until we knew what would count as evidence. How do we identify what children already know, or what and how they learn? Many of the answers to these questions offered by traditional research seemed simply inadequate. The 'knowledge' we were concerned with could not be defined merely as a set of testable facts which children either possessed or did not possess. While certain facts about advertising might be important, it was the significance, the interpretation of the facts which was crucial.

*   *   *   *   *

Advertising has typically been regarded by critics and researchers as a 'hidden persuader'.[1] It is seen as intrinsically deceptive and dishonest. It stimulates 'false needs', both for specific products — particularly those which are regarded as 'unnecessary' or harmful to health — and for consumer goods in general. It makes children 'materialistic' and 'consumerist', and reinforces dominant stereotypes of class, race and gender. Children are predominantly seen as passive victims of this powerful form of persuasion. Because of their limited knowledge of the world, and their lack of cognitive 'defences', they are presumed to be more at risk, and thus in need of adult protection. Younger children in particular are deemed to be confused or ignorant about the basic purposes of advertising and the relationships between commercials and reality.[2]

In several respects, the basic assumptions which have informed research and debate in this area are similar to those which inform arguments about children and television violence. The relationship between texts and audiences is regarded as a process of behavioural cause-and-effect, in which children are seen as highly vulnerable. This view has been aptly characterized by Brian Young[3] as 'child-as-innocent and advertiser-as-seducer'. It is a view which carries a considerable emotional charge, not least because it condenses many broader anxieties about the relationships between adults and children.

This 'commonsense' account of the relationship between children and advertising also coincides with dominant views in media education. Many influential advocates of media teaching implicitly regard children as passive victims of the ideological effects of the media. According to this account, the pleasures which children derive from the media are merely a form of delusion, a disguise for more covert ideological persuasion. By uncovering 'hidden' ideological meanings in media texts, it is argued that teachers may 'demystify' their students, and thereby 'liberate' them from their false beliefs.[4]

If we were faintly uneasy about many of these articles of faith to begin with, we were certainly much more so by the end of the research. The 11-year-olds and 12-year-olds we were teaching were clearly not deceived by advertising: while in certain cases they were fascinated by the adverts we discussed, in general they were cynical or indifferent about the claims they were making. Far from exerting a hypnotic power over their minds, advertising was a passing source of pleasure which they could take or leave. Enabling them to 'analyze' particular adverts may have sharpened their understanding of how they were constructed, but it didn't necessarily make them any more 'critical' than they were to begin with. While there were things they didn't know about advertising, most of what we implicitly saw as the important information was already familiar, even commonplace.

*   *   *   *   *

The research took place in two London schools, which with a complete lack of originality we shall call school A and school B. School A is a large inner London comprehensive, with an extremely diverse intake, both in terms of class and ethnic background. School B is an outer London voluntary aided grammar school: although selective, it also has a diverse intake, with substantial proportions of Afro-Caribbean, Asian, Cypriot and other ethnic groups. Both schools are mixed.

Both of the classes were in the final term of their first year at secondary school. In the case of school A, neither of us had taught the class before: in the case of school B, the class was taught by their regular history teacher. Neither of the classes had, at least to our knowledge, experienced any formal media education before.

Our teaching was in four main stages. The aim of stage one, which lasted for the first one-hour lesson, was to get some sense of what the children already knew about television advertising. We began the lesson by screening a short videotape of around twenty adverts, and then split the classes into smaller groups for discussion. The groups had been given a brief agenda of questions, and we also moved between groups, contributing where we felt it was necessary.

Stage two, which lasted for the next two lessons, focused on three adverts which had been included in the initial tape: 'Fiat Croma', 'Smiths Bacon Fries' and 'KP

Nuts'. We had selected these particular ones partly because they offered a range of different types of advertising: while the Fiat Croma advert was primarily aimed at an adult market, the other two were aimed at younger viewers, and were much less 'serious' in their approach. At the same time, we particularly wanted to focus attention on gender representation, and the three adverts suggested some interesting questions here.

Our aim, therefore, was to enable the students to engage in some close analysis, and to raise some more general questions about gender representation in particular. Each group in the class concentrated on one of the adverts, and a set of worksheets was provided, asking the students to look at different aspects of the advert ('objects', music, 'style', actions and words) in terms of what each of these 'said' about the men and women shown. The general conclusions of each group were fed back to the class in the last half of the second lesson.

In stage three, the focus narrowed even further. We had taken another of the adverts from the initial tape, for 'Impulse' body mousse, and produced a set of slides of each shot within it. The teacher led the class through a frame-by-frame analysis of the advert, while the students completed an outline storyboard, indicating camera positions and angles, commentary, music and so on. A certain amount of 'technical' information was provided here, while questions were also raised about the 'content' of the advert, again particularly focusing on gender representation: an outline plan for these had been agreed in advance. This stage lasted for two lessons.

Stage four lasted significantly longer than the previous stages, or than any of us had anticipated. The students were asked to produce an advert in tape/slide form, again working in small groups. The brief for their advert was in the form of a simulated 'memo' from the director of an advertising agency, and asked them to produce a one-minute advert for a new range of hair care products for boys. By choosing a product traditionally associated with girls, it was hoped that the exercise would again raise questions, not merely about advertising in general, but also about gender representation in particular. At this stage, it was vital to be able to call on additional teacher support, and to spread out into other classrooms or offices (or, in one instance, a cupboard!). This stage lasted for around eight lessons, and concluded with a group presentation of the finished adverts.

At each stage, we attempted to record what took place, using audio tape, the students' writing and our own field notes. Although this became much more difficult in the final stage of work — as we became much more preoccupied with the logistics of the situation — we nevertheless ended up with a vast body of data. At the end of the whole project, we asked the students themselves to evaluate what had happened in the form of a short audio tape, in order that we could compare our perceptions with theirs.

* * * * *

As this brief account suggests, each stage of the work involved a different pedagogic approach. Stage one was, if anything, closer to audience research than teaching — although, as we shall see, some of our interventions in the discussions were distinctly 'teacherly' in style, and made them much less open-ended than we initially intended. Stage two was a more familiar media studies activity, involving systematic analysis, guided by a framework of questions provided by the teacher. Stage three took the form of front-of-class teaching, and involved a certain amount of straightforward imparting of information. Stage four was significantly more open-ended: while there were certain constraints on the activity (for example, concerning the subject and the target market of the advert), there was a considerable amount of room for students to come up with their own ideas, and to see them through to the finished product.

This diversity of pedagogic strategies is probably typical of most media teaching, despite the extraordinary degree of polarization which has characterized debates in the area.[5] Perhaps more significantly, the *sequence* of activities is one which most media teachers would recognise as good practice: 'analytical' work precedes 'practical' work, rather than vice versa. The implicit assumption (or hope) is that the 'theoretical' insights gained through analysis will inform the students' production work — although precisely how this 'transfer' takes place has rarely been addressed.

The differences between these pedagogic approaches were apparent in a number of fairly obvious ways, as the following account will indicate. There was much more teacher talk in stage three than in any other stage, for example. While we were fairly clear about the likely outcomes of stages two and three, we were much less clear in the case of stage four. Perhaps most significantly, the kinds of questions we were asking in stages one and four were much more genuinely open than in other stages. Nevertheless, it would be easy to exaggerate these differences. Even with the more open-ended activities, we found it difficult to restrain ourselves from adopting a traditional, directive teacher role.

The fact that we were 'doing research' may have made us much more aware of this than we might otherwise have been. In effect, we were caught up in a set of conflicting roles and motivations: we wanted to observe 'what would have happened anyway', but we also wanted the students to get on and do some work — partly because this is what school is supposed to be all about, but also because we wanted to find out Something Significant, which we implicitly felt was unlikely if we just left them to 'mess around'. The schizophrenic stance which is embodied in the notion of 'participant observation' is particularly fraught where the researcher is also the most powerful person in the situation, who is primarily responsible for the 'success' of the activities which are taking place.

*   *   *   *   *

This conflict manifested itself in a basic uncertainty about the kinds of questions we should be asking, and the extent to which we should be directing the activities. At least for one of us, this uncertainty appeared to precipitate an attack of teacher-researcher neurosis in the very first discussion.

As noted above, the aim of this discussion was to probe what the students already knew about television advertising. We began with a set of questions which we hoped would serve as a stimulus to open discussion, rather than a set of instructions to be worked through. We hoped that the students would set their own agenda once things were under way, and leave our questions behind.

In practice, these good intentions were not always carried through. Indeed, if we look at the questions we asked, it is clear that a hidden agenda was already in operation:

1   What are your favourite adverts?
2   Why do you enjoy watching them?
3   Are there any adverts you don't like? Try to explain why.
4   What do you think adverts are for? Who are they made for? Whom do they benefit?
5   Have you been influenced to do anything as a result of a TV advert?

The first three questions appear relatively neutral, yet even here there are implicit assumptions being made about children's relationship with advertising. We assumed that children would have 'favourite' advertisements in the same way as they have 'favourite' pop groups or football teams — in other words, that the pleasures afforded by advertising possessed a certain importance in their lives, and that their relationship with it was to some degree 'self-conscious'. In practice, many of them were unable to think of particular adverts, and many were prompted by the selection we had just screened.

The requirement to explain 'why' they liked or disliked particular adverts is even more problematic: in effect, it is asking children to account for their pleasure in rational terms — a difficult activity, even for adults. Perhaps unsurprisingly, many of the responses to these questions were of the monosyllabic 'it's obvious' variety, 'it's just funny' and 'I like the music' being two common observations.

The unfamiliarity of the task and (in school A) of the teachers involved probably led the students to be more reticent than they might otherwise have been, and to treat the activity more as a 'test' than an invitation to open discussion. We tended to assume that the students were more familiar with being tape-recorded than they probably were; and, at least to start with, this led to a certain amount of 'tape-recorder shyness'.[6]

The remaining questions are much more leading, however. They implicitly invoke a discourse about advertising which the students were likely to have encountered before, whether in adult discussion or in school itself. This is the 'critical' discourse we have already identified, in which advertising is seen as deceptive and dishonest, and as having dangerous effects on those who are impressionable — notably children. As we shall see, the students did make use of this discourse — although much more confidently in school B than in school A. Nevertheless, it is notable that they did not generally regard themselves as impressionable, and tended to displace the influence of advertising onto 'other people'.

On another level, these questions were implicitly designed to test the students' knowledge of specific facts about the advertising industry — 'whom do they benefit?' being the most notable example. In school A, these questions met with rather bored, even faintly irritated responses:

DB: Why d'you think they show adverts, then?

Alvin: I don't know ...

Francis: You've got to advertise things ... you can't just get a car ... a brand new car, you want to show it to people, you don't just chuck it in the showroom, where people don't even know. You see it on telly.
          [Pause]

Alvin: It makes the day longer for television, adverts.

DB: So if they didn't have adverts ...

Alvin: The day'd be shorter, the television.

DB: ... So why do they show them, then?

Francis: Advertise something.

Andreas: Products.

Alvin: To show the new things out.

DB: ... So why do they have adverts on ITV and Channel Four, and not on BBC?

Mark: They don't want to ...
          [...]

DB   [returning to the question sheet]: What about this question: who are adverts for?

Alvin: They're made for the public.

DB: And who do they benefit?

Alvin: The world, I suppose.
          [Pause]

Mark: The shop owners. 'Cause they advertise food, and you go and buy food in the shop.

The teacher is clearly probing here, both for specific information and for indications of a 'critical' discourse, yet is meeting with little success. Like other students in the class, they appeared to be somewhat vague about what for us was a highly salient fact — that independent broadcasting is funded by advertising revenue. Again, only the more middle-class children seemed able to use the 'critical' discourse, and even here their facility with it was limited. Andreas' use of the term 'products' here is significant, and recurred later in the discussion:

> Mungo: Maybe they need adverts 'cause they can't get to sell the product.
>
> Andreas: They want to sell their products.

Andreas echoes Mungo's use of the term supportively, but their intonation is quite hesitant, suggesting an unfamiliarity with the term and the discourse from which it derives.

In the case of this discussion, the teacher explicitly pursued these issues with a series of highly directive questions:

> DB: So what happens? If you were a company and you wanted to get an advert put on TV, what would you do?
>
> Francis: Save up enough money.
>
> DB: OK, what would you need money for?
>
> Francis: For the advert, for paying the people.
>
> DB: And what would you do then?
>
> Francis: I'd see what I should put in the advert. I might be selling about five different products. Which one isn't selling very well? Right, I'll put it in the advert.

The discussion continued in this vein, with the teacher desperately 'fishing' for a particular piece of information. The students' reaction when it was ultimately revealed was significant:

> DB: What kinds of things might we do with our advert?
>
> Andreas: Go to the company that's filming the programme that you're going to interrupt.
>
> Mungo: You have to ask if they want to interrupt it.
>
> DB: And then?
>
> Andreas: They're going to have to watch it to see if it's good enough.
>
> DB: And then?
>
> Andreas: Then the company has to pay the ITV or Channel Four to put it on.
>
> DB: Aha! Did other people realize that?
>
> Francis: It's obvious, isn't it? You can't just put on an advert which they don't know about. You've got to pay the people who are doing that.
>
> DB: Is that obvious?
>
> Mark and others: Yes!

What is particularly interesting about this little game of 'guess what's in my mind' — apart from its shameless abandonment of the non-directive researcher role — is the difference between the teacher's and the students' judgments about what constitutes important information. While the students do 'know' that it costs money to put adverts on television, as well as to make them — or at least claim they do — this information is not particularly salient for them, as it clearly is for the teacher. The teacher interprets the students' failure to volunteer this information as ignorance — a view which the final exchange clearly reveals to be merely patronizing.

In general, responses to these questions about the functions of advertising in school A were largely on the level of Francis' final comment — 'It's obvious, isn't it?' Some responses were extremely disarming —

> NM: Why do ITV show ads, do you think?
> Alison: To have breaks in between, maybe. To run the tape . . .

— while others seemed designed to stop the teachers in their tracks —

> NM: How do adverts get on TV?
> Barry: It's obvious. By the aerial.

As these responses suggest, the important issues for these children were not the macro-economic questions about capitalism and mass persuasion, or even those of consumer rights: they were much more concerned with their own immediate experience as *viewers*, rather than as consumers of products and services. Pleasure, or the lack of it, was the paramount consideration.

Predictably, they liked adverts which they found amusing, which had good songs in them, or interesting special effects, and they clearly enjoyed imitating key lines or slogans. While some adverts appealed to specific groups — some of the boys partic-ularly liked the male-oriented 'Castlemaine XXXX' adverts, for example — most had more general appeal. There were many imitations of the cool dude who orders a Babycham with the immortal words, 'Hey, I'd love a Babycham'. Nevertheless, it is significant that in both cases these were 'grown-up' products which children themselves were unlikely to have purchased.[7] The only instance in which loyalty to the product may have guided their judgment was that of 'Adidas', a currently popular designer 'label'. In some cases, however, children were unable to recall the names of products, even where they were able to recount the advert in some detail.

In terms of dislikes, adverts which were more straightforwardly 'serious' in their approach — often those aimed at an adult market, such as the 'Fiat Uno' advert we looked at in more detail in stage two — were widely considered 'boring'. The 'Bounty' 'desert island' advert was similarly dismissed:

> Touriya: I hate the Bounty adverts, 'cause it's boring. What's the point of going
> to all that trouble for a chocolate when you can just say it?

Some expressed annoyance at adverts which were too elliptical — 'I hate some short adverts with no words in. You don't even understand what it was about.'

The main problem with advertisements, though, was that they interrupted programmes, particularly films: 'like when a film's coming to a really exciting bit, and there's a break, it really annoys you.' Advertisements were judged negatively to the extent that they disturbed the children's pleasure as viewers, and only rarely in terms of the claims they made about products.

Ultimately, few of the children were inclined to regard advertising as a capitalist conspiracy, or even as potentially misleading. Alison, for example, saw the whole process as mutually beneficial:

> Alison: They're made for the public. Well, not really the public . . . but the shop-keepers have to sell them. So we all benefit really: they get the money and we get the goods.

While few other children offered such apologies for capitalism, only one group saw the issue in terms of 'consumer protection':

> Wayne (reading question): Who are they made for? Who do they benefit?
> Barry: Well, they benefit the people who make them.
> Curtis: They benefit the people in the business.
> Barry: They're, like, to sell things and make money.
> Others [confusion of voices]: . . . yeah, and you get so much money out of them . . . yeah and those little kids . . .
> Wayne: Yeah, Mum, I want one of those . . .
> Curtis: Yeah, the batteries never work . . .

Even here, though, the group strongly disclaimed the possibility that they themselves were vulnerable to the influence of advertising: only one boy admitted to have 'copied a bit of karate' from an advert, but that was 'a long time ago'.

In other groups, opinion was divided on the question of whether advertising had ever influenced them: a couple of children could think of examples where they had tried products they had seen advertised on TV, but in general advertising appeared to play a fairly small part in guiding their choice of purchases — or at least as far as they were aware or willing to admit. While there were occasional instances of outright hostility to advertising — 'all I can say is, adverts are rubbish' — the issue generally appeared to evoke few strong feelings either way.

* * * * *

As we have indicated, our aim in setting up this discussion was to gain some insight into what the children already knew about television advertising. Yet it would clearly be mistaken to regard these responses as a simple reflection of their individual or even collective perceptions. As Hodge and Tripp[8] have argued, what children say in such contexts cannot be taken as a straightforward representation of what they 'really think'. What children say does not necessarily tell us what they know. Indeed, as the extended example quoted above clearly indicates, *how* they know may be as important as *what* they know.

On one level, therefore, the central question here is how we evaluate the status of these responses — how we read children's readings. We might attempt, for example, to distinguish between what they 'think' and what they feel they ought to say. Yet even this runs the risk of over-simplification, since there are so many potentially contradictory factors which may be brought to bear. For example, we might hypothesize that children's comments are determined by their perceptions of the task at hand, their inferences about the teachers' motivations, and by what they know of the views of other members of the group. But separating all these different factors, and accounting for their significance, is unlikely to be an easy task. How do we decide which statements to treat as evidence of what children 'really think'? How do we know that we are taking all the relevant factors into consideration? Ultimately, it may be misguided — or at least impossible — to somehow 'subtract' the context from the text of what children say, and thereby arrive at the 'truth' of what is in their heads.[9]

*   *   *   *   *

Before exploring this issue further, it is worth contrasting the responses already outlined with those of the students in school B, which are significantly different in a number of respects. Perhaps the most notable difference here is the greater degree of cynicism towards advertising displayed by students in school B. While their discussions of specific adverts, and their reasons for liking or disliking them, were very similar to those of the students in school A, their responses to the questions about the purposes of advertising were significantly longer and more 'critical'. The 'who benefits?' question in particular produced almost universal agreement that it was only 'the companies' who did.

Concerns about 'consumer protection' and about the potentially misleading effects of advertising were also a major focus of discussion:

Martin: Some of the products on the adverts . . . you think it must be brilliant, fantastic, one of the best things you've ever seen . . . so you go to the shop and buy it and when you take it home it's completely different.
George: You go to the advertising . . .
Chris: If that happens, all you do is go to the consumer advice people.

(Compare this with the rather hesitant grasp of the consumer rights discourse shown in school A.)

The students offered several examples of this kind of discrepancy between the products and the claims made about them in advertisements, which were only briefly mentioned by one group in school A:

Shadi: I think it's adverts like the one for Sindy doll and things . . . they show it all complete with everything . . .
[Girls agree, boys start interrupting.]
George: One thousand pounds for a Sindy doll!
Chris: At the bottom, it says everything's sold separately.
Others: It's such small print, you have to need a magnifying glass.

> Ilia: On the Matthews turkey roast one, it really gets on my nerves. I hate that, it puts you off the product when it goes: 'It's bootiful'.
>
> Others: Yeah.
>
> Ilia: It shows perfect breasts, but when you get it . . .
>
> [General laughter]

As in the brief discussion of these issues in school A, however, it is notable that the students do not regard themselves as primarily 'at risk': on the contrary, their concern was generally displaced onto younger children, for example in the case of cartoons which feature heavily advertised toys such as Transformers. Just as adults displace their anxiety about the effects of television onto children, so children displace it onto those younger than themselves: it is always 'other people' who are most at risk.[10]

In the case of one advert in the compilation the students were shown, we were given what at least a couple of us perceived as a *parody* of this kind of warning to the impressionable viewer. A man is shown cooking his 'Danepak' bacon while a fire engulfs the building: eventually the man escapes at the last minute, taking care to drop his meal into the fire brigade safety net before he jumps himself. The following caption appears at the end of the advert: 'In a real fire, get out first, then call the fire brigade'. Gillian expressed considerable concern about this, although here again it was displaced onto 'other people'.

> Gillian: I don't like that advert . . . that we just saw about the fire . . . because I know this may sound stupid but some people might be encouraged to think that saving, like, chocolate cake in the oven is more important than saving themselves.
>
> Mary: It says 'in a real fire, get out and call the fire brigade' . . . but the first time I didn't even see it.

The intriguing point here is that Gillian and Mary appear to take the advertisement literally — that is, they ignore the possibility that the warning, like so much of the advert itself, may not be intended 'seriously'.

Yet again, however, this response can be interpreted in a number of ways. It may be that their judgment about the advertisement's modality[11] is different from ours: they are judging it to be 'realistic' and 'serious' (that is, as possessing high modality) whereas to us it seems deliberately 'unrealistic' and 'humorous' (and hence low modality). It is significant that for the children in school B the adverts which were judged most negatively were those which were perceived as aspiring to realism, and somehow failing. Thus 'documentary-style' adverts, such as those for pet food or soap powder, and in particular the 'Matthews Turkey Roast' advert, were generally mocked. Significantly, the ending of the 'Impulse' advert — which was considered in much more detail in stage three — was also judged to be 'unrealistic': it was felt that the ending broke with the 'realistic' tone of the rest of the advert, and was thus merely absurd. This issue of modality judgments is a complex one, particularly given the level of self-parody which is increasingly to be found in advertising: we shall return to it in our discussion of the second stage of the project.

At the same time, Gillian's and Mary's judgment of the advert could derive from what they perceive to be the implicit demands of the context, and in particular from their desire to appear 'grown-up': by finding issues to worry about, they can adopt the terms of an adult 'critical' discourse about advertising, and thereby appear adult themselves. In other words, what they say is important about the advertisement may reflect what they think adults would find important, rather than what they 'really think'.

The importance of acknowledging the context of children's responses was particularly apparent in school B. The reactions of the children while watching advertisements as a whole class were often very different from the points they made in subsequent small-group discussion, and these were different again from their contributions to the 'plenary' in front of the whole class. On the most obvious level, the presence or absence of the teacher and the size of the group clearly determine what children are prepared to 'own up' to. Thus while some were prepared to admit in the small-group discussions that they had been influenced to buy products as a result of watching adverts, in the whole class discussion this was often displaced onto others — 'younger kids' or, in a number of instances, 'my mum's friend'(!). On another level, the context of viewing in a large group also favours certain kinds of interaction — particularly singing or talking along with the advert — which are as much to do with a kind of collective 'play' with the text as with the text itself. In the case of the dreaded 'Matthews Turkey Roast' advert, for example, the class derived considerable enjoyment from good-humoured mockery and reciting the advert as it was played, yet proclaimed intense dislike of it in discussion.

* * * * *

If we take the responses of children in school B at face value, then, it certainly appears that they were much more 'critical' of advertising generally. Indeed, their criticisms extended beyond the more obvious concern about the misleading claims of advertisements towards the more ideological issues we wished to raise in stage two:

Gillian: I hate sexist ads where you get things like Flora . . . all the ladies are in there making sandwiches and the men are outside having fun playing cricket.

Lucy: There's one advert where mum is making the tea and dad's playing football.

This is, of course, exactly the kind of thing most media teachers would want to hear — although it does raise the more awkward possibility that the children already 'know' most of the things we might want to teach them. In general, most of the children in school B gave voice to a considerable degree of cynicism about advertising

— which would suggest that notions of media education as a form of inoculation against capitalism would be at least inappropriate.

By contrast, most of the children in school A would appear to be precisely in need of this: while some of them were able to state the economic functions of advertising fairly clearly, and were occasionally critical of the claims which advertisements make, many of them appeared implicitly to regard it as merely a form of 'information' about products.

However, this is a rather superficial reading. As we have shown, the children's responses are far from consistent, and are highly dependent on the context in which they are uttered. We cannot assume any simple relationship between what children say and what they think or know or do.

Thus, in the case of school B, it may well be that the children have simply learned the responses which they feel are expected of them. Other children in the school in fact told the teacher that they had 'done' advertising in primary school, and had been 'warned' about it there: and one fourth year group groaned at the suggestion that they should look at advertisements in a lesson 'because we've just been writing letters of complaint to the ASA in English'. These children clearly displayed a facility with the 'critical' discourse about advertising — for example in their use of words like 'product' and 'consumer' — whereas only the more middle-class children in school A were familiar with this, and even they were uncertain. Yet we can assume that children's ability to produce this discourse is necessarily a reliable indication of the degree to which they are 'critical'?

In the case of school A, and particularly in the discussion quoted at length above, it emerges that the children 'know' at least some salient media studies information, but do not produce it to order — perhaps because it is taken for granted, or else not as important to them as it is to the teacher. The unfamiliarity of the situation means that they simply don't yet know the 'rules' which would tell them what they are expected to say.

This line of argument could lead to a radical scepticism about the whole enterprise of media education. Schooling in general clearly does represent a form of socialization into a body of discourses, a set of rule-governed ways of generating acceptable statements. The crux, however, is that this is the case both for 'traditional' and 'progressive' forms of teaching — yet it is advocates of the latter who typically refuse to acknowledge this. For example, as Gemma Moss[12] has shown, while much of the rhetoric of contemporary English teaching is premised on notions of 'self-expression', the specific forms of expression which are cultivated in classrooms are highly circumscribed, even though the 'rules' themselves are rarely overtly stated. Likewise, the rhetoric of 'liberation' which Valerie Walkerdine has traced in British primary education[13] is manifested in a set of practices which are in fact highly normative. As we have indicated, this notion of 'liberation' is one which has also been employed by media educators — yet the power to liberate, and the definition of what constitutes a liberated consciousness, typically remain the preserve of the teacher.

Thus, the fact that the children in school B are able to produce an 'adult' and possibly more 'middle-class' discourse about advertising does not necessarily mean that they are less vulnerable to its influence than those who cannot. Just as boys can learn to produce the required anti-sexist responses for their feminist teachers without having to question their own basic assumptions,[14] so students can learn that a certain kind of 'critical' discourse will win them approval from the teacher, and they will come to be able to produce it on demand. All that may be happening in such encounters is that students are replicating the analysis the teacher has provided.

*   *   *   *   *

If anything, these issues were raised even more acutely by the later stages of the work. Yet if the methods we employed in the first stage were hardly adequate as a means of gaining access to the children's existing knowledge, the extent to which our teaching strategies provided the children with any meaningful new knowledge remains extremely difficult to define.

Our approach in stages two and three was a familiar one for us and, we would suspect, for media teachers generally. While there were differences between the two stages, particularly in terms of the degree of overt teacher control, the kinds of questions we were asking, and the kinds of answers we were looking for, were quite similar.

If the 'hidden agenda' was at least partly implicit in stage one, it was much more explicit in stage two — from the heading of the worksheet, 'How are men and women shown in TV advertisements?' onwards. While the opening question on the worksheet was relatively open — 'was there anything very unusual or surprising about the advert?' — those which followed were much more specific and tightly focused. Question two asked each member of the group to offer one word describing each of the main male and female characters in the advert. For question three, the students were asked to analyze the advert more systematically, using a set of categories we had provided — namely objects, music, style, actions and words (a brief explanation of the latter three was provided). In each case, the task was to write down what each of these things 'say' about the men and women in the advert. Using this analysis, students were then invited in question four to 'put together a longer description of the way men and women are shown in the advert'. Question five invited them to compare this advert with other examples, and was designed to provide a point of comparison with the first question: 'Are men or women often shown this way in ads? Was there anything noticeably different about the way they were shown in this ad? Give examples to back your ideas up.' Finally, we asked the group to note down any points of disagreement which had arisen in their discussion.

In media studies terms, this is probably a fairly typical set of 'analytical' questions.

It attempts to move the students through an ordered sequence of activities, which might be broken down as follows:

1   Stating first reactions (question one).
2   Describing, in an increasingly detailed and systematic manner, the different elements of which the text is comprised (questions two and three).
3   Identifying associations or meanings for each of these elements (question three).
4   Adding these associations or meanings together to produce a summary of the overall ideological meaning of the text (question four).
5   Comparing this meaning with other instances of the same category of text, and thereby reaching conclusions about their overall ideological function (question five).

The core of this process, and the part which outwardly appears least speculative, is in stages two, three and four: in working through these stages, we presume that students will be able to move beyond their initial subjective responses and arrive at a closer, more objective understanding of the ideological meaning of the text.

While we did not use the terms 'denotation', 'connotation' and 'ideology', it was certainly this model of a three-stage analytical procedure — originally drawn from the early work of Roland Barthes — which informed our approach. Len Masterman describes the model as follows:

> The teacher's first task is to encourage his [sic] pupils to generate from images *descriptions* of what they see at a *denotative* level . . . Secondly he may encourage pupil *interpretation* by drawing attention to the *connotative* levels of meaning in cultural images and objects. What does each denotative quality *suggest*? What associations do that colour, that shape, that size, that material have? Discussion, at first free-flowing and open-ended, will gradually become less so as definitive patterns and clusters of associations become evident and the group move into interpretation at the *third* level, that of *ideology*, 'the final connotation of the totality of connotations of the sign', as Umberto Eco has described it. What does this programme *say* through its complex of signs and symbols? What values are embodied here, and what does it tell us of the society in which it finds a place? Who is producing this programme, for what audience and with what purpose?[15]

This model is so familiar to media teachers that it almost amounts to a kind of 'commonsense': yet its implications in terms of students' learning have rarely been addressed. On closer inspection, the model appears to be based on a number of questionable assumptions about the relationships between readers and texts, and about the ways in which children learn.

Firstly, the model implicitly presumes that meanings somehow reside in texts, rather than being produced by readers. The text is seen as the sum of a series of discrete elements, which can be separated out and laid on the operating table for dissection. Although some meanings may be 'hidden', they can be recovered if we use the correct analytical tools: the superficial outer layers can be peeled away to reveal the kernel of ideology which lies at the core.

In a sense, this approach defines the 'meaning' of a text in terms of what it 'says' — as we did ourselves in question three. What it effectively ignores is how texts 'work' — that is, the processes which readers are invited to engage in as they read. For example, it cannot account for the whole dimension of narrative — the ways in which texts mobilize expectations, and then confirm or subvert them as we read, the sequence and manner in which information is revealed, and so on. Likewise, it is difficult for this kind of analysis to account for differences of modality — the fact that a given item in one text may appear highly 'realistic', while in another it may appear much less so. Humour — which was a particularly important element in the children's discussions of advertising — is a significant indicator of modality, since it can enable a text to 'say' one thing and 'mean' quite another.

Secondly, the model breaks down the process of 'making meaning' into what are assumed to be its constituent parts. Yet there is an increasing body of theory and research which suggests that the process does not work in this way. The division between denotation (description) and connotation (identifying associations or meanings) is essentially an analytical one: there is no such thing as 'pure' denotation, since the description (or indeed the initial perception) of an image inevitably involves assumptions and hypotheses about its meaning.[16] 'Reading images', like reading written texts, does not proceed in an orderly fashion from the basic 'decoding' of its smallest elements to an overall identification of its meaning.

Finally, in terms of teaching, the model clearly presumes that analysis will result in a single conclusion about the meaning of the text. While 'connotations' will initially be diverse, 'definite patterns and clusters' will emerge, leading towards a general consensus about what the text 'says'. Yet what if such a consensus cannot be reached? What criteria can be used to distinguish 'valid' from 'invalid' readings? Are teachers simply to impose a definitive reading?

What this model effectively ignores is the inevitable diversity of readings of any given text. The implication of Masterman's account is that while 'connotations' may be multifarious and possibly subjective, 'ideology' enjoys an objective existence, and can be 'revealed' through the application of a set of neutral analytical tools. Once ideology is exposed or named, its effects are reduced — the reader is 'liberated' from the oppressive power of the text.[17]

In practice, 'critical analysis' is thus far from being an open-ended procedure. Many of the 'analytical' questions media teachers ask are 'closed' questions: they are effectively requiring students to identify aspects of the text which teachers themselves have previously defined as important, and thereby to lead to certain predetermined conclusions. 'Analysis' can often degenerate into an exercise in replicating the teachers' reading: alternative readings can be dismissed as subjective or merely 'uncritical'.

* * * * *

To some extent, our choice of adverts for analysis in stage two represented an attempt to move beyond the limitations of this model. We deliberately chose adverts we at least saw as relatively complex, and open to diverse interpretations: if they were 'sexist', it would be difficult to regard them as overtly offensive, and to this extent a 'correct' or 'critical' reading would not be immediately obvious.

In the 'Fiat Croma' advert, a woman appeared only fleetingly at the very start of the advert: the main narrative concerned the man driving half way across Europe to meet her at the opera house in Vienna. To employ 1970s *Screen* jargon, the woman functioned here as a 'structuring absence', motivating the narrative yet not contained within it. By contrast, the 'Smiths Bacon Fries' advert appeared to play with established stereotypes and expectations. The only female character here was the apparently innocent Little Red Riding Hood: yet she responded to the Big Bad Wolf's request for crisps by delivering a swift karate chop and then tossing him over her shoulder. 'KP Nuts' offered an instance of role reversal. It followed a woman's demonic search for peanuts, in which she was transformed (via animation) into a wild bull and a huge American footballer. Her all-consuming lust for peanuts led to a complete lack of interest in the rather wimpish man who appeared to be pursuing her.

In the event, the groups working on 'Fiat Croma' ran into considerable difficulties. Perhaps the main reason for this was that for most of the advert the woman was simply absent. While we had seen the implicit narrative here as one of romance — rugged man drives car through dangerous landscape to meet woman — the students simply ignored the woman's role altogether. In this instance, we had perhaps gone overboard in our desire to avoid the obvious: the students were either unable — perhaps because of their unfamiliarity with such 'elliptical' narratives — or simply unwilling to read the advert in this way.

At the same time, their refusal to consider the advert in any detail may also have been determined by their dislike of it, a dislike which took many forms. The classical music used in the advert 'went with the car,' but was generally agreed by the students in school A to be 'boring' and 'rubbish'. They were clearly aware that the advert was not for them: it was for 'richies' (i.e. rich people), for the 'trendies' and 'older people' who watched Channel Four. Students in school B were scathing about its lack of 'realism': how had the car managed to get across Europe so quickly, and where did the man change his clothes for the opera?

When pressed in subsequent discussion, the students were clearly aware of the implicit claims the advert was making about the car. The scenes showing the car driving through snow had been included 'to show how good grip it was', and the journey as a whole was suggesting 'the car can go long distances . . . can cope with all types of conditions'. Nevertheless, the appeal to wealth and sophistication was widely resented: while the car was clearly a 'good car' and not a 'rubbish car', only 'richies' would be able to afford it.

The other two adverts were more generally liked, and perhaps for this reason provoked some more detailed analysis. The following discussion of 'Smiths Bacon Fries', taken from school B, illustrates a number of important points:

Lucy [chairing the group, and acting as 'scribe']: Right. Look at the left-hand column. What do these things say about men and women in the advert?

George: Objects. We don't understand objects . . . music.

Robert: What's objects got to do with the men and women in the advert?

Lucy: I suppose if it was objects . . . if you saw a sink and you saw a woman at it, you'd say the sink was to do with the woman and the advert was saying . . .

Kaz [referring to the beginning of the advert, showing the wolf blowing down the pigs' houses]: Oh yeah! So the man would be the houses being blown down.

Mary: Yeah, because the men build bad houses.
[laughter]

George: It says men build bad houses.

Robert: Pigs build bad houses.

George: Male pigs build bad houses.

Mary: They all are.
[laughter]

Lucy: Male pigs build bad houses.

Mary: Not just male pigs . . . all males.

George: Oh shut up.

Lucy: Don't Mary . . . this is the advert . . . [writing] male pigs build bad houses.

This discussion is interesting for two reasons. Firstly it suggests that 'analysis' is not a neutral procedure, but inevitably involves a degree of negotiation: the advert itself is a kind of pretext for a display of good-humoured hostility between the boys and the girls in the group, a kind of game around the issue of sexism. Mary begins the game, seizing the opportunity to irritate the boys in the group by pointing to the incompetence of the male characters in the advert. While George is prepared to admit that the advert is showing men in a bad light, Robert is much less prepared to do this, and makes George revise his comment: it isn't all men who build bad houses, just male pigs. Mary returns to the attack: her second comment — 'they all are' — could be seen as ambiguous, suggesting either that all of the houses are 'bad' or that all men are pigs. While Lucy is prepared to accept George's compromise formulation — she repeats 'male pigs build bad houses' — Mary pursues the broader anti-male point, successfully earning a display of irritation from George. Finally, Lucy intervenes in her role as chair, returning the group to the discussion of the advert: 'this is the advert', not the real world, they are talking about.

Secondly, this exchange clearly demonstrates that the anti-sexist agenda which was implicit in our line of questioning was already apparent and familiar to the group. Lucy's second comment, about the woman and the sink, indicates that she is already aware of the kinds of associations which the group is supposed to be looking for. Indeed, the game itself suggests that the agenda is not merely familiar, it can also be actively *used* by the girls to score points off the boys.

This group went on to consider the music in the advert:

Gillian:	For the woman, when Red Riding Hood comes along, it shows her skipping . . .
Kaz:	Daintily . . . and the music changes, sort of soft.
Lucy:	So would you say, when you see another part of the glen with flowers in . . .
Mary:	. . . leafy . . .
Kaz:	It's a fairy tale . . . it's like once upon a time and they all lived happily ever after.
[?]:	That was at the end though. At the beginning when the pigs were there, it was more sort of . . .
Robert:	No, the music was the same all . . .
Samantha:	No it wasn't . . . it changed when the woman came in.
Lucy:	So first of all the music for them was sort of . . .
George:	. . . muscular . . .
Kaz:	. . . strong . . .
Robert:	Yeah.
George:	Stronger rhythms.
Lucy:	So we'll say the music has stronger rhythms for pigs and wolf.
Robert:	Quite jolly music.
Samantha:	It's not MacDonalds.
Lucy:	[reading from worksheet] What do style, the way the advert was shot, its general look, tell us?
George:	What?
Samantha:	It was very colourful.
George:	What was what?
Gillian:	It is as if it is in a show.
Lucy:	Yeah . . . in a theatre . . . you can tell from the background it's a set.
Robert:	Yeah, the trees look like bits of paper.
George:	The set was so fake.
Robert:	That doesn't ruin the advert.

Kaz: The set was badly done.
          [. . .]
Gillian: I think the story is taking the mickey out of the actual fairy tale.
Robert: Yeah, it's changing the whole thing around, from Little Red Riding
          Hood being a nice jolly person . . . and the pigs being little and weak.
George: It's the same ending though . . . all the pigs survive, so does Little
          Red Riding Hood.

This extract again illustrates some more general points about the students' discussion of the adverts. Clearly, the exercise produced some valuable small-group talk. The students are working hard to find words to do justice to the complexity of their perceptions, progressively refining and qualifying their observations as the discussion proceeds. The role of more 'technical' terms is interesting here: the words 'rhythm' and 'set' are repeated, and appear to offer a kind of definitive status to the children's comments. Significantly, it is these words which find their way onto the worksheet which Lucy is completing. Their talk is also highly collaborative, at least for the most part: while there is room for dispute, it is also possible for individuals to advance quite tentative ideas without seeming to be intimidated. While Lucy occupies a more directive role as chair — she initiates new topics, asks questions of the group and summarizes what others have said — everybody contributes to the discussion.

What is also notable here is the fact that the students are simply extremely perceptive. Here, as in many of the other groups in both schools, we were struck by the precision with which highly specific details were recalled, often on the basis of a couple of viewings. Points which were disputed were sometimes resolved by replaying the videotape, but nevertheless a number of specific details were noted which we ourselves had failed to register.

Yet this was more than simply a matter of perception: the recollection of specific details was guided by their sense of the overall meaning of the advert. For example, the students discussing this advert in school A noted the class difference between the wolf and the pigs which was shown by their clothing: the wolf is 'posh' and wears a top hat and a monocle, while the pigs are 'working men' who wear dungarees and lumberjack shirts. As in the above discussion, the advert was compared with the fairy tales (or nursery rhymes) on which it is based:

Mark: It was surprising, because normally in the nursery rhyme the wolf is
      bigger than the pigs, but here he isn't.

This group also noted the artificial lighting and the caption at the start of the advert ('In a leafy glade (somewhere off the A25)') as contributing to its deliberate lack of realism.

At the same time, it is far from clear whether our questions and interventions in discussion played a constructive role in this process. In the case of the discussion in school B, the categories we provided do appear to enable the group to work through the advert in a relatively systematic way, and to 'formalize' their observations. While the categories themselves were relatively abstract, only George appears initially to adopt a principled refusal to understand the more 'technical' terms, such as 'objects' ('we don't understand objects') and 'style'. The question about 'style' in particular enables them to come up with evidence to support their sense of the deliberate artificiality of the advert, and its play with fairy-tale conventions. The set is 'fake' and 'badly done', but this doesn't 'ruin the advert' because it is part of its attempt to 'take the mickey out of the actual fairy tale'. This complex understanding of the modality of the advert contrasts with the discussion of the Fiat Croma advert, where the group found it difficult to move beyond the relatively simplistic judgment that it wasn't 'realistic'.

We might also wish to claim that the questions 'slowed them down' and encouraged them to look for evidence to support their readings, and thus perhaps to be explicit about details they would otherwise have ignored. To some extent, of course, this is impossible to ascertain. Would this group have noticed the change in the music when Red Riding Hood enters if they had not been asked to look for differences between male and female characters?

On the other hand, the worksheet also appears to 'police' their discussion in ways which may be less constructive. Lucy leads the group through the questions quite rigorously: once she has found an acceptable answer, she then ignores further contributions and moves on to the next topic. Thus, for example, the idea that the music for the male characters has a 'stronger rhythm' appears acceptable to her, perhaps partly because it uses a suitably technical term ('rhythm') but also because it conforms to the anti-sexist 'hidden agenda', with which — as we have shown above — she is already familiar. Other potentially interesting observations get lost in her rush to the next question: Robert and Samantha's comments, for example, could have led to a consideration of the generic source of the music, and the way in which it supports the advert's ironic stance towards the fairy tale.

In terms of our interventions in discussion, it was again clear that we were unable to avoid being directive, to a degree which in retrospect seems quite unnecessary. As in the earlier discussions, the fact that we were 'doing research' made us aware of inconsistencies — even a kind of hypocrisy — in our teaching. Our repeated assurances that there wasn't any 'right answers' here were patently hollow. Many of our interventions took the form of getting students to note elements which we had previously identified as important: what we were essentially asking for was that students should replicate our own analysis, and reach similar conclusions to ours, particularly on the questions about gender representation. It is significant that when students noted aspects which we ourselves had not, our response was more one of surprise and hesitancy than instant acceptance. Responses which fitted, or could be made to fit, our overall interpretation became admissible, while those which did not had to be carefully scrutinized or negotiated away.

More broadly, there is the question of whether the children actually learnt anything new from the exercise. Studying a single advert in a great deal of detail was almost certainly an unfamiliar activity for them, and we might at least have expected them to become more 'observant' as a result — although it is also the case that since adverts are generally shown many times, 'close viewing' may be easier in this case than it is with other types of television. At the same time, they were much more prepared to engage in this kind of activity with adverts they enjoyed than with those they clearly regarded as 'not for them'.

Beyond this, we can only hypothesize about the extent to which the exercise advanced their understanding of our underlying questions about gender representation. As we have shown, the basic agenda here was familiar to them, and they were also clearly aware that at least the latter two adverts were untypical to some degree. Thus, in the case of 'KP Nuts', one group in school B wrote succinctly in response to questions four and five:

4   The men are supposed to be interested in nothing except the woman. The woman is wild and sexy and couldn't care less about the men. She just wants the peanuts.
5   Sometimes it is the other way round: the men are brilliant and the women are not. Whenever the two are together they always fall in love.

What emerges fairly clearly from reviewing the children's discussions and the completed worksheets is that the exercise itself was actually rather easy for them. While the students in school A had more difficulty with writing, their discussion revealed a very clear and incisive analysis. Particularly in the case of school B, where the students were generally more able to verbalize their understanding, one is tempted to conclude that the activity provided little in the way of new knowledge or understanding. What are we to make, for example, of the responses to the KP advert on this worksheet (from school B):

Glasses symbolise being ugly and corny ... American football player symbolises tough ... Peanut symbolises she has no control over her desire [sic!] ... Bull shows she is tough and determined ... Music shows that the woman is wild ... Style shows that the advert is quite ridiculous and zappy ... Woman was supposed to be sexy and irresistible to men ...

These 12-year-olds have clearly already mastered the skills we were attempting to teach. Short of taking them through Barthes in the original French, it is difficult to see what one might do next.

*   *   *   *   *

Stage three involved more traditional front-of-class teaching, and was much more explicitly directed towards establishing right answers. We had chosen one advert from our original sequence — for 'Impulse' body mousse — as a focus for some very detailed analysis. The advert itself followed the familiar narrative established by countless 'Impulse' adverts. A woman wearing Impulse body mousse is seen boarding a train; she accidentally collides with a man, who smells the perfume, and then pursues her; the man is then seen ordering flowers from the waiter on the train, which he sends to the woman with a note; the advert ends with a close-up of the woman's knowing smile as she receives the flowers. This narrative is intercut with shots of the woman applying the body mousse, presumably earlier in the day. The voice-over extols the virtues of the product, ending with the inevitable slogan, 'Impulse . . . Men just can't help acting on it'.

While this choice obviously related to our interest in gender representation, our main concern here was to enable the students to appreciate the complexity of the production process, and the detailed decisions which are involved in making even a comparatively straightforward advert. This meant providing a certain amount of information about the industry — for example about how advertisers decide on a particular 'product image', how adverts are shot and edited, how long they take to produce, how many people are involved, and so on.

Our motivation here was twofold. Firstly, we wanted to prepare the students for the practical work which was to follow, and to enable them to make informed and conscious decisions about their own production work. For example, we hoped they would become aware of the different types of shots they could use, and acquire a vocabulary for describing them, which would make their own choices less arbitrary. Clearly, we were assuming that certain of the 'skills' necessary for practical work could be acquired through analytical activities, and that it would be possible for students to transfer understandings from one type of work to another.

Secondly, in common with most media teachers, we implicitly hoped that informing students about the production process would somehow 'demystify' the medium, and thereby lessen its influence. Here again, we were making a number of assumptions about the students' existing understanding, and about the ways in which this might be developed or changed. Very much against the evidence of the previous two stages, we presumed that students needed to be informed — or at least reminded — of the fact that advertisements are deliberately constructed, in case they should fall prey to a kind of naive realism. Likewise, we implicitly presumed that the information we were providing was new, that the students would recognize its importance, and that it would fundamentally alter their reading of advertisements in general.

We worked through the 'Impulse' advert one shot at a time using slides, while the students made notes on a storyboard we had prepared. This made for fairly laborious teaching, and took much longer than was really appropriate for this age group. Yet while the two classes were generally united in their dislike of the advert, their responses to the teaching style were quite different. Although they eventually became restless, the students in school A clearly enjoyed this activity more than the previous work. In particular, the task of classifying the shots by camera angles and positions and completing the outline storyboard was one they took to with a vengeance — possibly because here at last was an activity with straightforward right answers. The students in school B were similarly restless, and somewhat less responsive, although as we shall see their subsequent written observations on the lesson revealed a degree of active engagement that had not been apparent at the time.

There were two different types of questions being asked here, which we might term 'analytical' and 'technical'. 'Analytical' questions focused on the content and style of the advert, along the lines of those asked on the worksheet in stage two. 'Technical' questions were concerned with camera angles and positions, with lighting and editing, and to a lesser extent with the basic logistics of filming the advert. Clearly, analytical questions were significantly more 'open', in the sense that they invited speculation and even disagreement: technical questions generally had single right answers.

In practice, however, this distinction was not quite as absolute. In the case of the technical questions, we were inclined to behave as though absolute answers existed, when in fact there remained at least a margin for speculation. While the difference between a low-angle and a high-angle shot, for example, is fairly clear, the difference between a medium shot and a medium close-up is rather more open to interpretation. Nevertheless, the students seemed quite willing to accept our authoritative (if occasionally arbitrary) judgments.

In asking analytical questions we were clearly looking for certain kinds of answers, and tended to cast around until we got them. As in the two previous stages, there was a considerable amount of 'guessing what's in teachers's mind' here. The following extracts (taken from school A) illustrate this process fairly clearly:

NM: Now, that's the first shot. What can you tell about the place that we're in?

Student: France.

NM: What makes you think that?

S: Flag, flag [on the front of the train]

NM: What, er . . . Is it France now?

S: It could have been.

S: No.

S: It could have left . . .

DB: What d'you mean?

S: It could be at a different place. It could have travelled from France to somewhere else . . .

S: It's an old train, but . . .

S:	Look at all that luggage there, guy . . .
NM:	Why have they got the old train?
	[pause]
NM:	There's something special about this train, is there? Do they always have trains like that in France?
S:	. . . no . . . no . . .
NM:	So there's something special about this train. OK. [changes slide]

Despite some probing, the students are not yet attuned here to the kind of answers which are being sought. Their misinterpretation of the teacher's third question ('is it France now?') leads them slightly away from the point the teacher is pursuing — which is effectively that the steam train plus the French setting creates a kind of nostalgic glamour or romance. In fact, it is only later in the discussion, when the parameters of the activity are more clearly established, that this 'required' response is produced. By contrast, their responses here are disappointingly 'literal', and the teacher quickly moves the discussion to the next shot.

NM:	Now, have a look at this woman.
Boys:	Hunky! Hunkee! Look at her nose man!
NM:	Can you not all shout out at once, otherwise we'll have to have to say hands up only, which gets a real drag.
Boy:	Miss, she's got a boy's haircut . . .
NM:	Hold on. Listen to the question before you start answering. What age is this woman?
S [various]:	Twenty-two . . . twenty-five . . . twenty-five . . .
NM:	Anybody disagree with any of that?
S:	She's about thirty . . .
S:	No . . .
S:	Fifty-eight!
S:	She looks about thirty . . .
NM:	Between twenty-five and thirty.
S:	Twenty to twenty-five, maybe.
NM:	What could you say about her background?
S:	Happy . . .
NM:	What sort of school would you think somebody like that went to?
Jacob:	All-girls school . . .
S:	. . . posh . . .
S:	Posh, yeah.
NM:	Posh all-girls school. Private school?
S:	Yeah . . .
S:	School!?
NM:	What tells you that?

Jacob: The way she dresses . . . like her clothes, they're not like . . . they look rich.

NM: Her clothes . . . that's very interesting, you can tell that from so little of her clothes.

Jacob: Look at that jumper, it looks rich.

NM: Interesting . . .

S: She's rich!

NM: D'you think she's got a job?

S: Yeah . . .

Jacob: No, she doesn't need a job.

NM: If she does a job just for fun, what do you think it is?

S: Works in a bank . . .

S: Train driver . . .

NM: Works in a bank. Train driver?
    [laughter]

S: . . . I think she works in a bank . . . secretary . . .

S: She works at Ali's caff!

By now, the group is beginning to come to grips with the activity, and to produce more required responses. As in the previous extract, the teacher's questions work in two stages. She encourages the students to speculate about information which the text does not reveal, or about the world beyond the text itself — for example, about how old the woman is, about her background or her job, and so on. She then follows up with questions which ask for evidence from the text to support these ideas — 'what tells you that?' or 'why do you think that?' In effect, this is taking the denotation-connotation process, used in the previous stage, in reverse: hypotheses about the meanings or associations of the images are allowed to precede the observation of details.

While the initial questions are apparently open invitations to speculate, it is clear that the teacher works hard to move the discussion in a particular direction. Aside from her disciplinary response to the boys' sexist comments at the start of this extract, her main strategy is one of positively reinforcing 'correct' answers, often by simply repeating them. In other cases, the correct response can be deduced from intonation (as in 'Private school?' or 'Train driver?'). Jacob in particular is rapidly learning the rules of the game: he is able to construct what is effectively the required stereotype on the basis of minimal information, not because of any extraordinary analytical powers, but simply because he is better at guessing what the teacher wants to hear — which is essentially that the woman is one of the idle rich.

The other students also begin to recognize this game, and participate with some enthusiasm. At times — for example here in the discussion of the woman's age — the discussion resembles a kind of auction, with the students making a series of 'bids' at the correct answer. Alongside this, there are those who are more interested in subverting the game through displays of wit. The suggestion that the woman might be 58, or that she works as a train driver or in 'Ali's caff' (in *EastEnders* — the first of a number of intertextual references to other TV programmes in this discussion), are perceived as funny largely because they are so obviously at odds with the required answer.

Here, and elsewhere in the discussion, the students responded enthusiastically to the invitation to build up narratives about the characters' lives beyond the text, although these were often inflected with considerable cynicism. Curtis, one of the prime movers here, went on to speculate that the woman needed the body mousse because she has been 'working in the mines', and that the man, far from having a highly paid job, in fact had a paper round! Intertextual references also proved important here: it was suggested that the woman 'thinks she's Maddy Hayes' (from the US series *Moonlighting*) and that she needed the mousse because 'she does the washing up in Fairy Liquid'.

> NM: [Changing slide] Does this picture give you any other information about her?
>
> S: It looks like she's running.
>
> Jacob: She's going to see somebody.
>
> NM: What makes you think she's going to see somebody?
>
> Jacob: Maybe her rich parents.
>
> NM: What does the bag tell you?
>
> Curtis: Going to see her grandma to take her some groceries.
>
> NM: Is she going away for a long time?
>
> S: No . . .
>
> S: She's just going somewhere . . .
>
> S: It's Saturday shopping.
>
> [. . .]
>
> NM: So she's sort of going out for fun, is she?
>
> S: Yeah . . .
>
> S: No!
>
> S: Miss, she's going shopping.
>
> S: To get her mum some . . .
>
> NM: So you think she's going to go down Tescos and do all that sort of . . .
>
> S: [unclear]
>
> NM: Or is she going round Next, and clothes shops and things? Or whatever it is in France?
>
> Jacob: Things like Monsoon, stuff like that. [Laughs] Richy shops. Harrods . . .
>
> NM: Right . . . Now . . . [moves on to next slide]

As the discussion proceeds, it increasingly takes on a dynamic of its own which is much more concerned with the struggle for control and for space, and much less with the analysis of the advert itself. This is not to say that it becomes confrontational: in effect what we are witnessing is fairly good-humoured banter, a display of verbal energy and occasional wit, rather than a passionate debate. While the teacher retains control — she is the only person with the right to ask questions, for example, and she guides their progress through the slides — she also provides a kind of arena in which the students can compete over the right to speak and define meaning. Her own status as final arbiter of the meaning of the advert is not seriously questioned — unless we count the subversive humour of Curtis and others — although in a sense it ceases to matter what the meaning is.

It is certainly significant here that while the girls generally contributed well in small-group work, they tended to leave the more competitive arena of whole-class discussion to the boys. Although there were only a few girls in the class, only one of them spoke to any significant extent, and she was able to do so more through the force of her personality than the relevance of her contributions. The boys' sexist abuse of the woman in the advert — which recurs later in the discussion — is also important here: it effectively represents a claim to control the arena, and to exclude the girls' perspective — significantly, the girls do attempt to dispute the boys' claim that the woman is 'ugly', but they are shouted down. Perhaps the most galling aspect of this for us as teachers was the fact that the boys had the nerve to complain about the girls' failure to participate:

Curtis: Miss, they haven't answered none of the questions.
Jacob: Know what I mean?
Curtis: Just sitting there.
NM: Maybe if you didn't interrupt so much they'd get more of a chance.
Andreas: We have to interrupt because they don't say nothing. [etc]

The situation described here is not, we would argue, particularly unusual: nor can it simply be dismissed as an instance of a 'difficult class' — indeed, we have all taught classes that make this one seem positively angelic. We would accept that this kind of whole-class discussion is not an easy activity to attempt with younger students, and we persevered with it longer than was tolerable. Nevertheless, the extracts here are taken from very early in the lesson, before the group became really restless.

The crucial point here is simply the difference between what is actually happening and idealized descriptions of what *should* happen — for example, Masterman's account of class discussion quoted above. The problem with such accounts is that they effectively ignore the power relationships which characterize all classroom interaction — both between teacher and students and between the students themselves.[18] 'Analysis' in this context cannot be merely neutral or scientific procedure: it is essentially a struggle over meaning and power, which cannot be seen apart from broader social relationships.

*   *   *   *   *

Of course, this is not to say that this discussion did not reveal some sophisticated responses to the advert. Quite fine details, such as backgrounds and gestures, were identified as contributing to the overall image of the product. Nevertheless, the general response was one of cynicism:

> Curtis: None of it's true. They just say that to make you buy it. Like those stupid toys. They say it does this and it does that . . .

One factor which was important here — as in the earlier example of the 'Fiat Croma' advert — was the children's resentment of the advert's appeal to middle-class notions of glamour and taste. The characters were repeatedly described, with some contempt, as 'rich', 'trendy' and 'posh'. The students' attempts to 'debunk' the advert were often expressed in terms of the mundane nature of their own lives — 'she's going to see her grandma to take her some groceries', 'he does a paper round', 'he's a dustman', 'she's not allowed to wear make-up or anything'. Here again, the students clearly felt that the advert was 'not for them' and that its attempts at glamour were merely corny.

The students in school B were equally in little doubt about the advert's lack of realism, but appeared more willing to enter into the fantasy, albeit with a certain degree of distanced amusement. In their written accounts, the girls in particular were keen to speculate about what the man and woman were thinking and the content of the letter the man sent with the flowers, although they did so with a marked degree of irony:

> Everything looked neat and tidy and the carriage was at least first class! This added to the image of the advert.

> I think the man thought when he saw the girl (even though he seemed to fancy the waiter more by the way he was looking at him!): 'She looks beautiful and smells absolutely gorgeous'.

> In his note he probably said: 'I love you and your smell. I am sending you these flowers as a token of my love.'

> When the man first saw the woman, I think he thought 'God, she's gorgeous'. And when the lady receives the flowers, it's more 'Money, he's got it . . . I need a new shirt!'

By contrast, the boys were concerned to identify the functions the advert might have for a male audience. Speculation about the potential target audience was a major focus of class discussion, as Darren's subsequent report on the lesson indicates:

> I do not believe that the Impulse advertisements are aimed as much at women as they are at men, funnily enough. This is of course because of the shots of the women putting the spray onto themselves. There was a

suggestion that the women are shown as such to show other women how to apply the spray. Arguments against this were:

1 Wouldn't there be application instructions on the bottle?

2 The voice in the advertisement explains that it is an 'all-over body spray'.

I believe that apart from making a woman (supposedly) smell nicer, Impulse is also seen as a way to improve sexuality. For example, let us take the ordinary husband and wife. The husband sees the advertisement. He therefore urges his wife to buy the 'Impulse' so that he can see more of what is shown in the advert at home.

Darren's account is obviously extremely sophisticated, and would not seem out of place in a GCSE coursework folder. Nevertheless, the kind of critical distance which is displayed here was certainly implicit in the contributions of the other students. The overall response to the advert might reasonably be described as a mixture of indifference and irony, occasionally spilling over into cynicism and even resentment. While some of the students took pleasure in the romantic fantasy which was offered, they clearly recognized it as such: much more pleasure was obtained from a kind of subversive play with the meanings which were produced, for which the advert itself was merely a pretext.

Ultimately, this raises crucial questions about the purpose and the effectiveness of this kind of 'analytical' approach. The idea that analysis will somehow 'demystify' the text, or 'liberate' the students from its power, clearly presumes that students are 'mystified' and somehow enslaved by it. At least in this instance, this certainly appeared not to be the case. The students were not 'duped' or 'taken in' by the advertisement: it was quite obvious to them that it was a deliberate fabrication, which was designed to market a product, rather than a piece of neutral information or a simple reflection of the real world. As a result, they found the exercise itself relatively easy: while they did not always produce the precise form of words we were looking for, they had little difficulty in identifying the important components of the product image, and speculating about the connotations these were intended to evoke.

On the other hand, this kind of critical, even cynical response was precisely what was demanded by the situation. Here again, the students could simply have been telling us what they thought we wanted to hear. One could argue that we were using 'analysis' as a means of socializing students into making 'ideologically correct' media-studies-type responses. Were we not simply encouraging them to replicate our 'critical' reading in response to some fairly overt cues which we provided?

Whether we regard the exercise as 'successful' thus depends upon how we interpret the students' responses — and indeed upon what we see as the point of the exercise in the first place. There would seem to be at least three possibilities here. One could argue that the exercise provided the students with analytical tools and critical approaches which they did not already possess — although the fact that they found it relatively easy would tend to contradict this. More cynically, one could regard it as an exercise in stating the obvious, and thus perhaps as merely redundant: although equally one could argue that stating the obvious is an essential first step along the way to examining it and moving beyond it. Finally, and even more cynically, one could regard it simply as a form of training in saying the 'right' things: although one might argue that all education is ultimately about learning to say the right things in the right situations — or, more grandly, about giving students access to privileged forms of discourse.

However one resolves these questions, it is important to acknowledge that students will be asking them as well: how do they perceive the purpose of the activity, and what do they think they are learning? One of the questions which students often ask at the end of a piece of analytical work of this nature is 'so what?' While we may have high-level theoretical answers to this question — 'so we can understand the processes by which meanings are produced' — or indeed low-level utilitarian ones — 'so you can pass your Media Studies exam' — neither may be satisfactory from the students' point of view. If we are to forestall the 'so what?' response, it is vital that students themselves should be aware that they are learning, and able to see the tangible consequences of their work.

* * * * *

These broad questions — about how we as teachers interpret what is happening and how students themselves understand the purposes of their work — were also raised, in a somewhat different form, by the final stage of the project. Here again, there appears to have been a significant mismatch between our initial aims and what actually took place, which caused us to question many of our fundamental assumptions.

The activity here was significantly more open-ended than the previous ones. We provided the students with a brief to produce their own advertisement, written in the form of a memo from the accounts director of an advertising agency to the 'creative team':

From: Accounts Director
To: Creative Team
Client: Head Start Ltd

Head Start Ltd make a wide range of hair care products, including shampoo, conditioner, colour and hair gel. Most of their advertising in the past has been aimed at girls and young women, although market research shows that boys and young men are now becoming more and more concerned about looking after their hair.

Head Start Ltd. now want to reach this new market, and are about to launch a new range of products specifically aimed at boys aged between 12 and 17. They have asked us to come up with a *name* and a *slogan* for the new range: and they also want us to prepare a *one-minute TV advert*, with *between ten and fifteen shots*. They want us to create a modern, stylish image for their products, which will appeal to many different kinds of people. It's very important that the Head Start image is new and different from other adverts.

Could you design a *storyboard* for the advert, including some ideas on the commentary and the music you would like to use?

This brief was designed with a number of considerations in mind. We chose a product which the students themselves would be likely to buy, or at least be interested in. At the same time, we wanted to raise questions about how advertisers target specific audiences, and about gender representation, and for this reason we chose a product traditionally associated with (and marketed to) girls which was now to be sold to boys. In logistical terms, we also had to design the brief in order that the students themselves could be 'actors' and the advert itself shot in and around the school. We asked the students to present their advert in the form of a tape/slide sequence, largely because this would be technically more straightforward and more controllable than video.

The approach we adopted here is, again, a fairly familiar one in media teaching.[19] Essentially, the students are being required to simulate 'dominant' professional practice, rather than to create 'alternative' or 'oppositional' forms. Nevertheless, it is far from being simply an invitation to imitate: the exercise is designed so that students have to think through problems for themselves, for which there are not necessarily ready-made solutions. The exercise provides an opportunity to explore, in a concrete manner, more general 'theoretical' issues which the students had already addressed in their analytical work. In this respect, the process, and reflection on the process, is significantly more important than the finished product.

The effectiveness of this approach clearly depends upon a number of factors which may be extremely difficult to achieve. It presumes that students will be able to accomplish this 'transfer' from analytical to practical work, or at least that they will be able to perceive the underlying connections between them. It also presumes that students will share — or can be made to share — the teacher's perception of the importance of process, as opposed to product, and that they will be able to make explicit the assumptions and understandings which have informed their work. At the very least, the effectiveness of the approach relies on a self-reflexive style of thinking which may be very demanding, particularly for younger students.

As might be expected, this stage of the work was logistically much more complex than the preceding stages, and correspondingly more difficult to monitor. Many of the groups divided their work into smaller tasks, and much of the time was spent outside the classroom 'on location', which made audio recording impossible. In addition, we were concerned that the activity should not drag on unnecessarily, and that each group should have a finished product they could be reasonably satisfied with. As a result, we felt our own role became quite directive — although it is notable that in their evaluations, the students did not agree that this was the case.

Once the brief had been introduced, our interventions took two main forms. Firstly, we had to introduce the students to the equipment — cameras and tape recorders — and make sure they were able to use it successfully. We had chosen to use SLR cameras rather than automatic cameras: although SLRs are more complex to use, past experience had shown that even quite young students were able to pick up the basic principles fairly quickly, and tended to achieve better results than with automatics. At least to begin with, we controlled their use of the cameras, checking the light readings and setting the focus, although they were soon able to use them themselves. We also required each group to produce a detailed storyboard before going out with the camera, which meant that questions about camera angles and composition could be discussed beforehand.

Secondly, we were concerned to enable the students to work effectively in their groups, to prevent disputes and to ensure that everyone was able to participate. One additional reason for choosing a product aimed at boys was that boys were likely to be featured fairly heavily as 'actors', which in turn meant that the girls might stand more chance of getting to use the equipment than might otherwise have been the case — although a certain amount of intervention was still necessary in order to ensure that this happened.

While we did intervene in determining the 'content' of the advertisements themselves, our concern here was as much to do with logistics — with what would be feasible given the time and resources available — as with any 'theoretical' issues. While we did occasionally attempt to draw students back to the brief, and to place the underlying questions about audience and representation back on their agenda, there was certainly a sense in which we all tended to lose sight of these once the activity was under way. This was partly a result of the fact that the logistical concerns became more urgent, but it was also because we were not entirely sure what we were looking for. If we were hoping that students would 'transfer' insights from their analytical work into their practical production, what kind of evidence of this were we seeking?

One particular problem here concerns how we 'read' the adverts which the students ultimately produced. On one level, they could be read — and summarily dismissed — as merely imitative. While many of them were highly inventive, few of them departed from the established forms of advertising or indeed from traditional gender stereotypes. There seemed to be a kind of mismatch between their general cynicism about advertising, expressed in previous stages, and their apparent willingness to follow patterns which were much cruder than those of the adverts they appeared to enjoy most. Thus, a number of the adverts adopted a 'before and after' narrative, in which the product was strongly associated with notions of masculine power. For example: a boy with unruly hair is mocked by his friends, tries the new hair gel and is transformed into a macho guy surrounded by admiring girls. Or: a boy/tramp is attacked by a gang of thugs, takes out and applies the hair gel, and defeats the thugs with the aid of martial arts and the gel container itself.

Yet even from these brief accounts, it is apparent that there is a danger of taking the students' work at face value — or of assuming that the students themselves were doing so. At the very least, it would be possible to read the adverts not as evidence of deep-seated sexism and subordination to mass culture, but on the contrary as parodies of those things.

This issue of humour and parody is a complex one, because it inevitably rests on an uncertain contract between the writer and the reader: what is intended as parody may not be read as such, and there is always the possibility of inferring parodic intentions where none exist. Indeed, the notion of 'parodic intention' is also problematic: one can say things in jest, but simultaneously mean them — in which case one is using parody as a means of disclaiming responsibility. These observations are particularly pertinent to advertising. One might well argue that in the wake of successful campaigns like those for Benson and Hedges cigarettes or Heineken lager, parody and self-reflexivity have become the dominant modes of modern advertising. In order to avoid the potentially alienating effects of 'hard-sell' techniques, advertisers have increasingly adopted a tongue-in-cheek approach which enables them to make claims about products which are both serious and humorous at the same time — 'I bet he drinks Carling Black Label'.

In this case, one of the fundamental problems — not only in retrospect, but also at the time — was in determining whether the students were 'taking it seriously'. The very crudity and absurdity of the adverts, and the amusement which they provoked, would tend to lead to the conclusion that they were not; although the relish with which they were acted out might suggest that they were. This led to a kind of anxiety on our part, which surfaced in various ways. In the case of the 'martial arts' advert, for example, one of us asked the group whether they thought the violence might not disturb their potential audience, only to be told 'they'll know we don't mean it'. In other instances, we intervened in discussion in an attempt to accentuate the parodic or satirical elements in the adverts, and thereby to undermine what seemed at least at face value to be a glamourization of macho behaviour — for example, by having a shot of the girls secretly laughing at the 'cool' boys admiring themselves.

In a sense, these attempts to make things explicit — and perhaps a little more ideologically sound at the same time — were simply missing the point. In some ways, the crucial factor in the activity was that things didn't have to be made explicit for the benefit of the teacher or anybody else. Like all simulations, it had a kind of ambiguity written into it: it was possible to take it seriously and not take it seriously at the same time. Clearly, we were not asking the students to 'express themselves' for the benefit of a real audience, but on the contrary to produce a hypothetical text for a hypothetical audience. In a sense, we were offering them an opportunity to try something on for size without having to make any commitment to buy it.

The students' use of parody reinforced this sense of disengagement. Particularly where one is addressing issues such as sexuality, parody can be used as a means of avoiding a potentially painful or embarrassing form of self-exposure. In our experience, this strategy is often adopted by adults engaged in exercises of this nature, and it may well have served a similar function here.

In expecting a transfer of the conceptual learning which we had hoped would ensue from our analytical work to this more open-ended practical activity, we were clearly assuming that the two would fit together in a particular way — that the students would be able to 'apply' conceptual knowledge gained in analyzing advertisements to the quite different activity of producing their own. Yet the relationship between reader and text is clearly very different from that between writer and text: both involve the active construction of meaning, yet the space for negotiation is quite different in each case.

Furthermore, the kind of analysis we had attempted to encourage was highly *rationalistic*: it was implicitly premissed on the view that breaking a text down into its component parts will somehow give us rational control of it, and perhaps thereby free us from its influence. Analysis seeks to intellectualize, and thereby to regulate pleasure — and perhaps, for certain analysts at least, to supplant dominant pleasures with alternative or oppositional ones. Practical work, by contrast, allows much more room for *play* with 'media language', with the symbolic resources which are to hand: it can engage much more easily with pleasure and fantasy, with the sensuous, non-rational aspects of the process.

Nevertheless, there are certainly dangers in posing this distinction in such absolute terms. As we have indicated, the 'analytical' discussions recorded above are not without their pleasures, and they do allow considerable space — albeit 'in the margins' — for play with language and with meaning, for example in the ways in which the students elaborate or move beyond the text, or in the jokes which seek to subvert it. Likewise, the constraints built into the practical simulation, particularly those concerned with the target audience, set limits on the extent to which the students can indulge in the 'free play' of fantasy (even assuming this were possible in the classroom context) — although it is notable that these often tended to drop out of sight as the work progressed, and had to be constantly reintroduced by the teachers.

* * * * *

The elements of parody described above could be taken as evidence of a transfer between the analytical and the practical elements of the work, although as we have suggested, they are at least ambiguous. Certainly in the students' evaluations of the exercise, there were few explicit indications that this aim had been achieved, or indeed that it had even been perceived in the first place. Nevertheless, this does not necessarily mean that it did not happen: what the evaluations demonstrate is simply that the students' perceptions of the outcomes of the exercise were quite different from our own.

In terms of what the students felt they had learnt, it was the social or inter-personal skills which they saw as most important. Many said they felt the experience had helped them to learn how to work with each other as a group, and that this had been possible because they had been left alone for much of the time without teacher intervention:

Stewart (School B): It involved many people's efforts. It is nice to think that everyone made some contribution to the final outcome . . . it was made good by the fact that no one was in charge. Thus everyone had an equal say in what was going on. In fact it turned out that some of the people who didn't say as much made some of the best suggestions.

Nina (School B): It showed us we all had to pull together and cooperate to produce something.

In the case of one group in school A, who conducted their evaluation on tape, there were some quite frank accounts of the relationships within the group, as the following extracts indicate:

Mungo: It was quite a fun group to work with, I'd like to work with them again. I enjoy [this kind of work] more than doing written work . . . we could do a lot more things . . . it's much more fun for all of us, teachers and pupils . . . I could've worked harder but I think I worked quite hard.

Touriya: Mungo was a bit selfish 'cause when he was doing the slides he never let anyone else have a go. Alison, she was acting like a posho really . . . but she was quite fun really.

Jacob: I tried to take over at times and I did succeed, 'cause I always succeed.

Touriya: When you work with Jacob he says 'I am the master'. Who is the master? He says 'me!' Sometimes he tries to take over, but it's only for a time . . . sometimes he makes us crack up.

Despite occasional personality clashes, all of the groups were united in their enthusiasm for this kind of small-group work — an approach which for both classes was relatively unusual. One aspect which many of the students remarked upon was the opportunity to get out of the classroom, and to use the space and resources of the school in different ways.

Jacob [acting as 'interviewer']: What about going on location, did you like that?

Touriya: Yeah, it was wicked . . . more enjoyable than doing writing or reading or something like that.

Jacob: What about the work would you like to do again?

Touriya: Yeah, I'd *love* to do it again.

In addition to these broadly 'social' benefits, a number of the students also commented on what they had learnt about advertising, although this seemed confined largely to 'technical' aspects, such as understanding more about how adverts are made, and learning to use cameras and tape/slide equipment themselves:

Jacob (School A):   Yeah, I'd like to do it again . . . specially going on location, 'cause you're not in a stuffy classroom all the time, getting out and about taking pictures, having fun, and while you're doing that you're learning, 'cause it's teaching you how to use the camera and putting the slides together and putting the beeps [synchronising pulses] on, stuff like that.

Farhana (School B): It definitely taught us more about adverts. We now know how sketches are drawn first and also slides can be made . . . the teachers just gave us helpful tips but did not tell us what to do and what not to do . . . the project also helped us to see how much work it takes just to make one shot, one advert, and just think — we see about 1,000 shots per day, which takes hours to perfect.

Despite this latter comment, it is notable that few of the students explicitly compared their adverts with 'the real thing': while they occasionally acknowledged that they were lacking professional production values, in general they seemed pleased with what they had achieved — in our view at least, quite justifiably. Using tape/slide may have been a positive virtue here, in that it is so obviously unlike broadcast television that at least some of the grounds for comparison do not apply.

This, at least, was the situation for the groups themselves. In the case of school B, however, the adverts were shown to an audience consisting of other first-years, and met with a rather polite response, which was perceived as a disappointing end to the whole project. Clearly, making students' practical work available to a wider audience beyond the group itself can be a useful part of the process: the problem is that it may give an unnecessary prominence to the product itself, and leave it open to being judged purely by professional standards.

While they were often frank and even self-critical about relationships within their groups, none of the students in either school commented on the 'theoretical' issues — the 'Media Studies' questions about audience and representation — which we had hoped the activity would enable them to address. This could be taken simply as evidence of failure, although it may well be unrealistic with students of this age to expect them to make explicit connections of this kind. To ask somebody what they have learnt from a particular activity — as we were effectively doing here — is to ask a very difficult question indeed: and while it was certainly possible for them to be self-reflexive about their behaviour in the group, it may simply have been too difficult for them to sum up the more theoretical aspects of their learning.

Nevertheless, the students' responses here do clearly indicate that their priorities were quite different from ours. The exercise was enjoyable and fun in a way that most things they do in school are not — at least according to them. It also made for rather different relationships between teachers and students from those which normally obtain. In this respect, the students' responses to the exercise were largely determined by the broader context of school life. The most notable thing about this work for them was simply that it was adopting a different pedagogy from that which applied elsewhere: the content itself was merely secondary.

Ultimately, the central question which is raised here is that of evaluation. Clearly, the students may have quite different criteria for judging the success or failure of a piece of practical work from those which we as teachers feel to be important. In this instance, they may indeed have learnt what we hoped they would learn, but it was the other things they learnt which, from their point of view, were much more important.

*   *   *   *   *

The issues raised by this research were inevitably diverse, and took us well beyond our initial agenda. In writing this account, we could not hope to tell anything like the whole story: we have had to select fragments of data, which clearly cannot represent the full complexity of what took place. Contradictions and inconsistencies, events which we could not understand or explain, have inevitably been suppressed. A degree of coherence has emerged in the writing which was certainly not apparent at the time.

So what is the status of the data we have presented, and our reflections upon them? Our own observations are clearly heavily invested with our theoretical 'biases' and concerns. We were not mere bystanders, but active participants in the situations we have described, and had a considerable degree of power to determine what took place. As such, we can hardly be trusted. Yet at the same time, neither can the children's own responses and observations be seen as a simple reflection of the truth. As we have indicated, what children say does not give any straightforward indication of what they think or know or understand. We cannot 'get inside children's heads': all we have to work with is language, a medium which is notoriously unreliable and inconsistent.

Ultimately, therefore, the major epistemological questions remain unanswered. How do we find out what children know? How do we identify what and how they learn? The kind of research we have undertaken here could hardly claim to provide answers to these kinds of questions: indeed, it has significantly unsettled our own comfortable assumptions that answers *can* easily be found, either by researchers or by teachers.

These difficulties could sanction a retreat to 'safer' research methods — and in particular methods which seek to evacuate the researchers' presence from the research process. Indeed, a good deal of ethnographic classroom research seeks to achieve precisely this aim. The researcher becomes invisible, or at least 'a fly on the wall', whose account of the situation is uniquely privileged above those of the participants, the teachers and students who are merely 'objects of research'. In comparison, the approach we have adopted here is often denigrated as not 'true research', and is pejoratively termed 'inquiry'.

We would argue that this search for more objective, 'safer' methods is not merely illusory, but also runs counter to the needs and concerns of teachers themselves. As ethnographic researchers have increasingly acknowledged,[20] to attempt to write oneself out of the process is simply misguided. In producing this account, we have attempted to be self-reflexive about our own role, to acknowledge the difficulties of the process, and our own inconsistencies and inadequacies. At the very least, this has alerted us to some of the contradictions, even the hypocrisies, of our own practice: yet it has also contributed to a broader questioning of many of the basic assumptions of media education.

This self-reflexive stance thus has implications, not merely for research, but also for the teaching process itself. The kind of epistemological questions we have raised are not merely pedantic, 'academic' ones. On the contrary, they are the questions teachers have to face every day of their working lives. Teaching, in this sense, *is* a form of research, in which the relationship between theory and practice is dialectical. Teaching involves forming and testing hypotheses, collecting and evaluating data, in a continual process of action and reflection. The kind of research we have undertaken here is, in this sense, simply a more elaborate version of this everyday process — it has enabled us to engage in a more systematic, extended reflection on our own practice than is possible under the normal conditions of teaching. The data we have collected clearly do more than simply illustrate pre-formed theories: at a number of points, they have forced us to make explicit the theoretical assumptions, particularly about the nature of the learning process, which underlie our taken-for-granted practices. They have enabled us to rethink, not simply *how* we teach, but also *what* we teach.

One fact which emerges very clearly from this research — and it is one which we feel has often been neglected in media education — is that teaching and learning are inextricably embedded within broader social relations, which are inevitably relations of power. Books on media teaching are fond of offering prescriptions and recommendations for classroom practice, but most of them balk at describing the complexity and difficulty of what actually takes place. As a result, what we are offered are idealized accounts — accounts in which students passively absorb the 'radical' knowledge which teachers hand down[21] or in which teachers act merely as 'colleagues' on an equal footing with students.[22] In our view, such accounts do not even begin to acknowledge the realities of schools and classrooms, but rather seek to wish them away.

By contrast, our account has sought to identify the social relations of teaching and learning at a number of points. As we have argued, we cannot consider the activity of 'analysis' in isolation from the power relationships which obtain between teachers and students, and between different groups of students in the class. We cannot divorce what is taking place in practical work from the broader context of students' other experiences of schooling, and the power relationships they encounter beyond the lesson itself. Much of the learning which took place, both in the analytical and the practical work, was not primarily concerned with the media: on the contrary, it was precisely *about* social relations themselves. These are not, we would argue, factors which can somehow be 'filtered out' of the process, a kind of 'communication noise' which we can afford to ignore. Social relations are not a distraction from 'real learning', but an inherent part of it. To seek to reduce them to a set of statistical 'variables' which can be systematically isolated and 'accounted for' is to ignore the complexity of the situation. To suggest that they can simply be wished away is to place both teachers and students in positions which are ultimately untenable.

Notes

1 For the definitive early statement of this position, see Packard (1957).
2 See, for example, Palmer and Dorr (1980) and Adler *et al.* (1980).
3 Young (1986).
4 See Buckingham (1986).
5 See, for example, Alvarado (1981), Masterman (1981/82), Williamson (1981/82) etc.
6 See Barnes and Todd (1977) for a discussion of these issues.
7 See Cullingford (1984).
8 Hodge and Tripp (1986).
9 See Potter and Wetherell (1987).
10 See Cullingford (1984) and Buckingham (1987b), Chapter 4.
11 Hodge and Tripp (1986), Chapter 4.
12 Moss (1989).
13 For example, Walkerdine (1985).
14 See Williamson (1981/82).
15 Masterman (1980); Masterman's approach derives from the early work of Roland Barthes, for example Barthes (1977).
16 See Hall (1980) and Barthes (1977).
17 See Buckingham (1986).
18 See Alvarado (1981).
19 See Grahame (1990).
20 For example, Hammersley and Atkinson (1983) and Willis (1980).
21 Alvarado (1981).
22 Masterman (1980).

Chapter 3

How do Teachers and Students Talk about Television?

Pete Fraser

'At times it seems that the entire culture revolves around the images and sounds that emanate from the TV screen and that all talk is somehow television talk'.[1]

'They [Parents] think that television takes over people's lives.' (Elizabeth, aged 12).

A combination of these two comments seems to me to sum up the life of the Media Studies teacher. Casual talk about television programmes while they are on and after they have finished; more structured classroom talk in GCSE Media Studies and increasingly in lower school English lessons; academic talk in seminars and Teachers' Research Group meetings: talk about television certainly seems to dominate my life!

This chapter focuses on the ways in which teachers and students talk about television. It seeks to analyze the commonsense ideas about the medium and its relationship with its audiences that circulate in everyday discussion. These commonsense ideas about television are important for media teachers for a number of reasons. To a large extent, they define students' existing conceptions of the object of study, and their expectations of what media education might be about. They set limits to what might be said about television, both within the classroom and beyond it. And they also define our colleagues' expectations about the aims and methods of media education, in a way which has implications not merely for our own work, but for its place in the curriculum as a whole.

*   *   *   *   *

While television is certainly discussed in a wide variety of ways by different groups of people, one can point to the existence of a number of distinct, if overlapping, 'discourses' about it — sets of ideas and key terms which tend to recur, both in everyday conversation and in broader public debates. As I shall argue, these discourses about television have particular functions for their users: they define, not merely the object of discussion (television), but also the position of the speaker in relation to others. Discourse about television thus inevitably condenses many broader concerns and anxieties about the political or moral state of the world.

In this section, I shall identify a number of such discourses about television which appear to predominate in public debate — for example, in books, newspapers and television programmes aimed at a general audience. These discourses could obviously be a major topic of study in their own right. It would be impossible here to tease out the nuances and contradictions of each discourse, let alone identify their historical evolution. At the risk of over–simplification, then, I have confined myself to a brief sketch of five discourses, which were employed by the teachers and students whom I interviewed.

The first three are essentially *anti–television* discourses, although they derive from different political positions: I have labelled them 'Right', 'Liberal' and 'Left'. The remaining two tend to intersect these, although they are more concerned with making distinctions *within* television output, albeit from almost opposing positions: I have labelled these 'Quality' and 'Hedonistic'.

Right

This discourse is probably the most dominant in public debate, and can be traced particularly in the editorials of papers like *The Daily Mail* and in the pronouncements of its principal exponent, Mary Whitehouse. In this discourse, a number of concerns are brought together: a suspicion of new cultural forms and their assumed effects, often expressed in moral panics; fears about specific social and cultural groups, e.g. youth and blacks; a perceived decline in moral standards and organized Christianity; and the presence of sex, violence and 'bad' language on TV. Users of this discourse seek to construct a consensus of 'ordinary viewers', particularly parents, who are set against anonymous 'manipulators', 'sociologists' and other 'so-called experts'. There is frequently a nostalgic harking back to a 'golden age' before the advent of television.

Liberal

This discourse shares the concern voiced by many on the Right with the 'decline' of the family, and the need to preserve the 'innocence' of childhood. A variety of medical and cultural arguments are used here to prove that TV is both physically dangerous and intellectually inhibiting. The viewer is predominantly defined as a passive 'TV addict', helplessly enslaved by the mesmeric control exerted by the medium itself.[2] Much of the blame here is seen to lie with 'irresponsible' parents, who have merely abandoned their children to an 'electronic childminder'.

The most extensive argument from the Liberal position is that concerning the superiority of reading over television viewing.[3] Reading, it is argued, requires concentration and mental effort, unlike television. It helps to develop imagination and intellectual abilities, which television merely undermines. Television, it is asserted, is simply 'chewing–gum for the eyes'.

Left

This discourse tends to have less currency in popular debate — perhaps not surprisingly, given the political positions of the popular press. Nevertheless, there is certainly a commonsense view popular on the Left which rests on similar assumptions about the 'power' of television. Here again, the viewer is seen as a dupe, a passive victim of ideological manipulation.[4] 'Bias', on the part of those running the medium, is the most frequently used term in popular forms of this discourse, with the work of the Glasgow University Media Group[5] being perhaps the best known in this respect. It feeds into popular conceptions of 'representation', in which the falsehoods and stereotypes of TV are directly contrasted with 'reality'.

Another underlying feature of this discourse is a puritanical approach to pleasure. As Jane Root[6] has noted, many standard Left criticisms of popular TV are dependent upon quite reactionary definitions of 'good taste'. Yet while the Right tends to see television as endangering the status quo, the Left commonly argues the opposite — that it is largely responsible for preventing people, particularly the young, from questioning dominant values and beliefs.

In all three cases, television is clearly the focus for a much broader set of anxieties. As Ian Connell has argued, blaming television provides a simple explanation for much more complex phenomena, which people may be unwilling to face.[7] In each case, the audience for television is regarded as essentially passive: while children are seen as its most frequent victims, it is adults — parents and teachers in particular — who are defined as protectors.

Quality

While a good deal of public debate about television is concerned simply to condemn the medium and its harmful effects, there is often an attempt to exonerate 'quality' television from blame. While this notion of 'quality' is often used simply to distinguish between television itself and other art forms — as in the high culture/low culture debate — it is also used to distinguish between what is seen as 'good' and 'bad' television.

'Quality' tends to be defined here according to middle-class tastes, and using criteria derived from more traditional art forms. Because 'art' tends to be described in terms of individual creativity, TV is dismissed as a kind of false art, except in instances where a guiding creative force can be identified. Hence the value attached, particularly in British TV, to such writers as Dennis Potter, and the lack of it attached to the teams who write soaps, for example. Certain programmes, often by virtue of their genre, are perceived as 'quality', and praised by broadsheet and tabloid alike. The literary adaptation is seen as particularly praiseworthy, while the single play, the documentary and the (British) mini-series are also frequent recipients of praise.

Fears about 'quality' have dominated current debates about the future of broadcasting, with the same anti-Americanism emerging as it did in 1955 with the advent of ITV. Thus the discourse can be seen to have a strategic prominence at the moment, as a means of mobilizing support for terrestrial broadcasting, and particularly the traditional public service brief.

Hedonistic

This last discourse might well be seen as the inverse of the 'quality' discourse, since it is built around the kinds of programmes which are typically despised as 'trash'. This discourse is particularly apparent in the trivia columns of the tabloids, like *The Sun*'s 'Twenty Things You Didn't Know About . . . 'and radio programmes like that of Steve Wright. It implicitly claims to take programmes at face value: thus it would talk about a comedy only in terms of whether it is funny, not in terms of its moral or ideological position, or its artistic merit.[8]

Despite this overtly anti-intellectual celebration of television as 'harmless fun', it could be argued that there is still an assumption that the users of this discourse know 'real' quality when they see it, even if their principal object of discussion is 'trivia'. If the 'Quality' discourse defines its users as 'educated' and 'tasteful', using the 'Hedonistic' discourse can be a way of announcing one's own lack of pretentiousness, one's affinity with 'the people' and resistance to those who take things 'too seriously'.

* * * * *

A teachers' leader yesterday condemned the television soap opera, *EastEnders* as an evil influence and warned against the plays of Dennis Potter.

'The whole nation is totally drugged by *EastEnders*,' said Mr Peter Dawson, general secretary of the Professional Association of Teachers. 'The programme projects as normal highly deviant forms of behaviour'. Mr Dawson included homosexuality, swearing, crime, infidelity and drunkenness among his list of deviancies.

'*EastEnders* is a very good soap opera, brilliantly acted and superbly written,' he said. 'And that's the problem. It conveys the impression that that is what real life is like'. Mr Dawson urged parents and children to abandon sex, horror and *The Singing Detective* in favour of news, documentaries and science programmes. Parents' ability to make moral judgments was undermined by television, said Mr. Dawson. 'What are parents supposed to say to their children about sex before marriage? They watch television and see that this is the norm in our society'. Adults were hypocritical in demanding that teachers set standards which they themselves did not follow.[9]

It is now generally recognised that there is a sizeable gap between the life experience of many teachers and the everyday lives of most of their pupils.[10]

While the *Guardian* story above might represent the point of view of one teachers' association, is it any way representative of how teachers think? One of the aims of my research was to identify some of the discourses teachers commonly use in discussing television. I conducted a survey of the views and preferences of the teachers in my school, using a questionnaire, and then followed this up with some more in-depth discussions. In this section, I would like to consider a series of extracts from one of these discussions.

Those taking part were given the following questions to get their discussions started, though they were told they could deviate from them as much as they wished:

1   What do you like/dislike about television?
2   What would you/wouldn't you want children at this school/children generally to watch, and why?
3   What do you think children should be taught about television?
4   What do you imagine is taught in Media Studies?

The teachers were given a tape recorder and left to their own devices after an introductory screening of extracts from some popular TV to get them going.[11]

The extract I want to consider begins as follows:

Alan: I think the thing I disliked about nearly all of those clips . . . I know they were specially selected possibly to provoke this kind of response . . . was that they contained or they help create a sort of a hierarchy of values in which crass materialism reigns. The introduction to *Dynasty* with its Rolls Royces and its yachts and its expensive jewellery and all the rest of it. The absolute mindless responses in *The Price is Right* to winning these microwaves . . . and these sorts of things really is . . . you get a question like this 'what do you like/dislike about TV?' and it's so broad and there are different aspects to television and all of those there it seems to me emphasize one particular thing and that's the thing I find really offensive, this promotion of crass materialism.

Anne: I think, especially from America as well, children do have this image that in America everyone is rich and you know it's all wonderful. They really do have this image that is so far from the truth. I dislike that a lot.

Mark: And also that they should aspire to those kinds of values anyway.

Anne: That's it.

Alan: This is directly encouraging it . . . almost leaves no alternative.

The discussion is dominated for long periods by Alan,[12] who has a very 'deliberate' delivery, with long pauses where he is obviously not expecting to be interrupted — clearly a useful rhetorical device for the classroom! He makes clear attempts to shape the agenda within the questions set according to his own terms. His contributions are always the longest and in many ways the most generalized, with even his anecdotal points framed in terms which suggest that their status is beyond doubt.

Alan uses the 'Liberal', 'Right', and 'Quality' discourses extensively. His repetition of the construction 'crass materialism', with the addition of 'promotion' and 'offensive', in his first contribution, enables him to set out his position in such terms that it is difficult for anyone to respond in a contradictory fashion without losing face. Any pro-television arguments must now be in his terms, so that they must look for different kinds of TV if they are to find anything positive to say. Alan has thus set out the values he sees implied by much of the content of popular TV, has attacked the audience in Liberal-Right terms ('mindless'), and indicated in quite strong terms ('offensive') how the programmes appear to him.

Anne's response is to take up his point about the 'materialism' of *Dynasty* for her own more Left-Liberal concerns. She moves the discussion slightly from a first-person distaste for popular TV to fears about the ideological effects of such images on children, as well as a conventional Left position on the 'gap' between reality and representation.

The word 'do' is emphasized both in its repetition and in her tone of voice, which almost implies hopelessness, a characteristic (not surprisingly) of Left discourse in general! The assumption here is that children's image of America is determined by the viewing of a small set of programmes largely drawn from one genre, disregarding the image they might get from other genres, such as Crime. A further assumption is that such an image is of itself harmful, and that there is an objective truth about the USA which would be better for the children to know.

The most significant feature of this utterance, however, again seems to me to be on a local level, as Anne adopts the 'concerned parent' role in a situation where Alan has already set out his own agenda as dominant. Clearly, the group has already been constituted as 'teachers' for the purposes of my study. Yet there is, nonetheless, a sense

Pete Fraser

in which they are constructing themselves in that role as the discussion unfolds. It would, after all, be possible for someone to refuse to play the game on that level: for example, they could simply talk about their favourite programme and imitate characters from it or sing the theme tune, as the children did in their discussions. Yet it would be surprising if such a thing did occur, since above all teachers have to be seen as 'responsible adults', in front of both children and colleagues, and the public adoption of any other role could easily precipitate a crisis. This discussion must be seen as a public occasion, since those taking part are not a group of staffroom friends, used to discussing a range of topics informally together, but are in many cases colleagues already involved in power structures, who may never have spoken to each other before on anything other than administrative or subject-based matters. Thus the only roles they can adopt in such a setting are those appropriate to 'responsible' adults.

Alan's next lengthy contribution is very much within the Liberal discourse, with a puritanical notion of pleasure attached:

Alan: The other negative effect is this business of how television stops you from doing other things... that it's such an easy thing to do. You walk in, turn it on and you watch anything and it cuts down on how sociable people are, that they get out and do things in their community, that they get involved in all sorts of things outside the house. They don't now, and where people even used to go to the cinema, they now, 60 per cent of them compared to six years ago, or ten years ago, go to the local video shop and buy a video . . . I mean it's a very very antisocial thing or rather it can make people very antisocial.

The assumptions about television in this statement are considerable. Again the power of the bad object and the passivity of the viewer are taken for granted. Its 'easiness' is of itself seen as bad, suggesting that leisure time ought somehow to be work, while what people would be doing if they were not watching TV is stated quite baldly. Alan then makes an interesting and powerful discursive move by plucking spurious statistics from the air to validate the authority of his statement, before his final shot, describing TV once and for all as antisocial. Thus a TV-versus-community opposition is set up, as well as the more familiar, and recently disputed, opposition between TV or video and cinema.

Sally: I'm sorry, about [question] number one... we're just saying that all those things on there were pretty awful. I watched *Dallas* when it was on and it's similar, very similar to *Dynasty*. I don't watch *Dynasty* but watch *Dallas*. I used to love it when it was on, you could sit down once a week and watch and not have to think about anything else, I got very involved with it but I wasn't taken in by it, it was just real escapism.

Mary: I did with *EastEnders*, I used to watch that for nearly two years, but I had to stop doing it . . . it was . . . [unclear].

Sally: One programme doesn't matter though, if it was everything it would be different, but just one . . .

Sally's interjection here is an attempt to return to a previous question, which she had been unable to consider earlier. She refers back to the clips shown at the beginning of the discussion in an effort to defend her own taste. Her defence is somewhat apologetic, perhaps on the level of 'it might be a problem for others, but not for me'.

The distinction between fiction and reality is often seen by adults as a problem for children, and even by some critics as a problem for adults — particularly soap-viewing females. Here, Sally pre-empts the possibility that she will be so classified by saying that she 'wasn't taken in by it', a problem Anne had previously identified for children. Mary approaches her taste in a slightly different way, with another disclaimer, however, which makes the programme begin to sound like an unhealthy habit, which of course echoes the rhetoric of the Liberal discourse. Sally sees the problem existing only in terms of overdoing it — 'if it was everything' — but in both cases, they have been obliged to apologize for a personal preference.

Alan's next intervention ignores Sally's and Mary's contributions altogether, as with both body and verbal language, he excludes those present from the category of television viewers, almost forcing any contradiction thereafter to be aggressive:

Alan: Yeah [nodding sagely]. I think television is marvellous in places like old people's homes and mental institutions where people have got [laughter] . . . my brother who works for a halfway house for these sorts of people, he um... he said if you uninvented the television there'd be a tremendous explosion within society because at the moment so many people are pacified by it, particularly people who have been released from mental institutions or kicked out because of Government policies and now eighteen hours a day they sit mindlessly watching television and it does keep them passive even if it's not constructive, and they wouldn't have anything else to do otherwise, and in that sense I think it's a good thing... or for people stuck in hospital, but for the normal fit healthy young, I think it should play a relatively minor part.

There is a sense in which his comments could be seen as deliberate provocation — they certainly raise a laugh — but there is also a sense in which he sees himself making a serious point: certainly his last line seems to be. He also sets out a familiar opposition between 'passive' and 'constructive' and again uses the term 'mindlessly', here perhaps to refer to mentally ill or senile people, although this is nonetheless a familiar term to describe *all* TV viewers in the Liberal and Right discourses.

John now enters the discussion with an obvious power play, initially contradicting Alan to defend certain types of television, then shifting the agenda entirely onto *Blind Date*.

John: I think whether you watch it mindlessly or not depends on whether or not you've got a mind in the first place . . . I think you get out of it what you're prepared to put in.

Mary: Yeah, but you have to have that wider sort of experience in the first place to be able to discriminate about what people are watching.

John: Having said that, who watches *Blind Date*?

Mark: I watch it.

Anne: I've seen it from time to time.

John: Does it embarrass you?

Anne: Yes it does.

Mary: I find it awful.

Mark: Yeah, I mean it does have a certain fatal fascination like *The Price is Right*, for me it's just like...

Sally: It's so unreal though, isn't it, *Blind Date*?

John: It's strange isn't it? Because everybody, well most people I know watch *Blind Date* but they're all very ashamed of watching it.

Anne: And yet you want to see it to the end to see who they go with, it is compulsive.

Mary: I think that before, they make it up, I don't believe those people are bona fide lonely hearts.

Mark: Oh I think they are.

Mary: I really do, I've read something like that somewhere I think.

Alan: It's so heavily scripted, isn't it?

Mary: It's so pre-planned, exactly, and the whole thing, at the end, they nearly always slag each other off.

Mark: It doesn't really matter whether it's false or not, it's still false even if it's not set up, it's still an amazingly false situation, but there's still something interesting about it, this sort of talking round a screen and what will appeal to people.

Sally: Yes, the other thing is if you give the same one as they are given, pick the same one as they are going to pick . . .

John's first contribution posits, for the first time, the notion of the active viewer, a position refined by an intervention from Mary using the 'Quality' discourse, with the word 'discriminate'. In a sense, John seems to imply that they will all recognize the mention of *Blind Date* as referring to a familiar line on mindless viewing, since *Blind Date* is one of those programmes frequently cited as being in poor taste and appealing to the 'lowest common denominator' in the 'Quality' discourse.

Alan is strangely(!) quiet during the exchange on *Blind Date*, his one intervention nonetheless suggesting that like everyone else in the group, he does watch it. In attempting to deal with a text which they all know to be the object of derision, particularly within the 'Quality' discourse which all have implicitly accepted from the start of the discussion, the teachers appear to negotiate an ideological dilemma. They do watch the programme and yet must maintain face in front of fellow professionals. John addresses this point explicitly, after several others have shamefacedly admitted watching it.

This seems to allow space for the others to say what they like about it, or at least to negotiate the contradiction, with John himself avoiding losing face by adopting a chairing/teacherly role in framing the discussion more in the form of a question, albeit an implicit one: why are people embarrassed to admit that they watch *Blind Date*? Significantly, however, they move from making modality and quality judgments to describing the programme as acting upon the viewer. In this way, they are able to avoid admitting to an active preference for the programme, and instead confess to being 'under its power': in effect, they manage to displace the 'blame' from themselves to the programme.

Similarly, by constantly referring to the 'false' nature of the programme, they implicitly attempt to demonstrate their distance from — and in effect superiority to — the mass of viewers who presumably do not realize this. Yet the pleasure of the programme remains a problem for them. Mark tries to explain this in terms of a 'fatal fascination', again suggesting the programme has a 'pull' on the viewer, while Sally, at the end, seems to acknowledge the source of pleasure as being joining in a game, a sort of identification, for the duration of the programme, as it was for her with *Dallas*.

Perhaps unsurprisingly in the light of this discussion, most of the teachers here defined the aims of media education in terms of protecting children against a potentially harmful influence: whether as 'responsible adults' or 'concerned parents', they saw their role as being to wean children off television, and to encourage them to recognize that 'there are other things in life'. Children were seen here as victims of a form of 'manipulation' which was 'much too subtle' for them to detect: there was a 'huge uncritical acceptance of what television has to offer.' At best, media education might encourage children to use television as a 'resource', primarily for its factual programmes.

* * * * *

Hodge and Tripp offer an intriguing suggestion about the reason for adult dismissal of popular television:

> In terms of power and control in the classroom, teachers maintain discipline
> by establishing respect, by knowing more than their pupils do about what is
> considered important. If teachers know less about the more popular shows,
> they have an obvious interest in claims that these shows are unimportant,
> or, better still, positively harmful.[13]

Ultimately, they suggest that it is the instability of adult power that is at stake in these competing definitions of TV. The Right discourse regards TV as a dangerous force, poisoning the young mind; similarly, the Liberal discourse sees it as destroying children's innocence. The Left discourse posits TV as doing ideological damage, and the 'Quality' discourse sees it as a threat to particular class-bound cultural forms. It is not surprising that is is these four discourses that adults are most inclined to mobilize in an educational settng and in any situations where the tenuous nature of their power over children needs to be reasserted. The use of such discourses enables the adult to promote a 'good teacher' or 'good parent' image, while other discourses are repressed, surfacing only briefly and uncomfortably.

> I'm sure most teachers probably watch *Neighbours* but they're probably into programmes like *Blockbusters*...they watch things like wildlife programmes or something like that so they can come to school next day and talk about it. (Pauline, aged 13).

*   *   *   *   *

The second set of extracts I would like to consider is taken from a discussion with a group of third-year students.[14] They were left alone with a tape recorder and the following questions:

1   What are your favourite TV programmes?
2   What do you like/dislike about TV?
3   Which TV programmes do you think adults would dislike you watching?
4   What TV programmes do you think teachers watch?
5   What TV programmes do your parents watch?
6   Why do you think this research is being done?

The discussion begins as follows:

Richard: Jonathan, what are your favourite programmes?
Jonathan: My favourite programmes are...*Neighbours* [sings] [laughter].
Premila: I like *The Cosby Show*, it's very good. [inaudible, several speak at once].
Jonathan: I like *Black Adder* and *Fawlty Towers*, I think they're very good too, personally.
Premila: *Fawlty Towers* is a bit old.
Jonathan: No, but it's...I love the bit at the top where it goes 'farty owls'. [laughter]
Anna: It says 'fatty owls'.
Jonathan: Farty owls! [laughing].
Anna: I liked it when they found the rat in the kitchen.

The discussion begins with the use of what I have called the 'Hedonistic' discourse, as the students play with the theme tunes and with being left alone with a tape recorder. Silly voices are used to mock other discourses, there is a lot of laughter and everyone speaks at once. The main points of the discussion to begin with are concerned with the bits of *Fawlty Towers* that they like. When one compares this with adult discourse on tape or in the survey, it is intersting to find that the adults never talked about specific bits of the programmes and only rarely mention actual programm titles.

Jonathan: What do you dislike about television?

Premila: I dislike . . . I dislike sexism.

Anna: Premila's talking about how she's watched all the baby programmes.

Premila: I do! [indistinct: *Sooty Show*?]

[series of 'shh . . . one at a time'. Anna continues making jokey point, Premila tries to continue]

Premila: I dislike sexism on TV, all the time they have to just degrade women on TV, they always do that. [Richard interrupts, supportive but indistinct] Any big film with sex in it, they're just degrading women all the time.

Richard: Especially those comedians that come on *New Faces*.

Anna: Oh, I hate that programme.

Jonathan: And Now . . . [spoken in style of programme]

Premila: Sometimes people try to make jokes out of it, out of being prejudiced.

Jonathan: Yeah, and racist.

Anna: I think it's really stupid, on *New Faces*.

Premila: There was this black comedian and he was putting down his own race, going like 'swinging on the jungle trees' and things like that, putting down his own race. [pause]

Here Premila begins to inject a note of 'seriousness', while the original conversation continues. Clearly hers is a Left discourse, but in this context it is resisted by Anna who continues a separate point involving some teasing about watching 'baby programmes'. Despite this attempt to resist seriousness, Premila continues and succeeds in overriding Anna. The boys seem to be supporting this attempt to make a serious point, but once she has made it, Jonathan returns to the 'Hedonistic' discourse. He is able to slip easily between the two, as his next utterance is a supportive one, about racism on TV being a bad thing too. Anna steadfastly ignores this however, as she determinedly carries on in Hedonistic terms, her comment on *New Faces* being a qualitative rather than a ideological judgment.

Premila's next contribution takes her agenda further from sexism to racism, after which there is a pause followed by a return to the question about favourite programmes. It is not without significance that Premila is Asian and the other three members of the group all white. Significantly, the others do not disagree with her —

indeed the boys are quite supportive — but none of them seem to see any point in taking the discussion any further. In subsequent discussions with the group, sexism and racism were raised only rarely.

My assumption from this is that the children tend to have limited access to this particular discourse — something which Media Studies will offer them — and thus it does not figure in casual conversation about TV as highly as some others. For Premila, it would perhaps be logical to assume that the issue of 'race' in particular has a higher priority, but it might equally be possible that her contributions here are intended to mark herself out as the 'serious' member of the group, addressing the teacher with what she thinks he would want to hear. Although the children have been left alone, the tape itself is clearly addressed to me: indeed, there are a number of points on the tape which seem to be more specifically directed to me personally, including several where I am addressed by name. While this kind of direct address is sometimes used for 'serious' answers which they assume will please teacher, at other points it is clearly used to send me up.

> Jonathan: What do you think teachers would dislike you watching?
> Premila: Do you think teachers dislike the fact that we watch TV?
> Jonathan: No. If we don't do our homework, yeah ... Do you think they'd dislike it if we watched programmes like all those films on Channel Four about sex on TV?
> Premila: I don't think they would, most young teachers. You get the older teachers like ... who'd be angry, but people like Mr Fraser, they don't give a toss. [Much raucous laughter and repetition of last line].
> Anna: I don't like how a lot of American programmes call themselves shows.
> Jonathan: When I went to France the TV over there is really shit compared to what we have here and all the ... [interruptions, shouting of 'sh-ugar'] and all their TV programmes, they're all dubbed and I'd seen about half of them [...] They're all dubbed and I saw about four films and I don't think I actually saw anything French apart from the Lotto.
> Premila: There's this really rubbish film on Sundays on Channel Four and all the dubbing is rubbish ... *Empress Wu*. [Impressions of bad dubbing follow].
> Jonathan: What do your parents watch?
> Anna: My Dad likes watching stupid arty programmes.
> Jonathan: Art programmes? Why do you think they're stupid though?
> Anna: Because I'm stupid and I'm not a cultured person.

The 'Quality' discourse is invoked at several points here, with Jonathan's anecdote about French TV and particularly with Anna's description of what her Dad watches. Her tone of voice and her subsequent remark about not being 'cultured' seem to me to be ironic. By 'stupid' it could be that she means the same as teenagers mean by 'boring' — i.e. that these are programmes which do not seek to address a teenage audience and thus can only be explained in such terms.

The discussion of what teachers wouldn't want them to watch is as much about how children perceive adults as it is about television programmes. Their assumptions are based on a notion that teachers' primary aim is for them to get their work done and secondly on a particular conception of older teachers not wanting them to have access to certain forms of knowledge — in this instance, about sex. Again, though, they are able to slip between a relatively serious discussion and raucous 'play'.

Premila: My Dad watches things like *The Two Ronnies* and *Fawlty Towers*.

Anna: Oh, my Dad is always saying 'have you seen the one with the rat in the biscuit tin yet, or the one with the dead body yet?'

Premila: My Dad watches *Dogtanian and the Three Muskehounds*! [chaos erupts, resulting in the singing of the theme tune and 'shush' from Richard] [. . .]

Premila: What do you think teachers watch and why?

Jonathan: Um . . . not a lot [. . .]

Premila: I think teachers watch *Jackanory* and *Gardener's World* and you know . . .

Jonathan: Oh Premila, don't be so stupid.

Anna: No, they don't . . . Mr Fraser watches anything!

Premila: I think most teachers probably don't watch that much TV.

Jonathan: My Dad's a teacher and he watches all the [?] programmes, but he has a lot of marking to do.

Premila: My Dad doesn't watch normally the amount of TV I do, he's not an addict like most of the youngsters . . . he just watches it now and then.

Anna's remark about her father's way of watching *Fawlty Towers* could be interpreted as an expression of either pleasure at the game they play or annoyance at his interference with her viewing. Premila's revelation about her father watching children's programmes continues a form of play at the expense of adults, who have been ridiculed at several points. Here parents have been gently mocked, older teachers scoffed at, and there are several jokes at my expense too, about what I'm assumed to watch. Part of the function of the discussion for the group as a whole is clearly to ridicule adult attitudes to TV: in effect, they are 'getting their own back' for all the judgments adults pass on their viewing tastes. Here again, it is not without significance that the performance is partly directed towards me.

Later on in the discussion, there is a marked settling down as they appear to have decided that there are only a few minutes of the lunch break left and they ought to put down some 'serious' opinions. In a calmer atmosphere, they address my final question about why the research might be being done:

Richard: Why do you think this research is being done?

Anna: I'd have said this research is being done to help him get his degree.

Jonathan: No, but why do you think we're doing it anyway?

Premila: Because people are blaming TV for a lot of things like because sex and violence and the effects like the Hungerford massacre and this and that, they're blaming TV and people want to do research . . .

Jonathan: [incredulous] How can they blame TV?

Premila: They've been saying, you know, too much sex and violence on the TV and *Rambo* and this and that, so people are trying to work out the effects of TV and work out people's watching habits.

Anna: My sister didn't watch *Rambo* but she's still very violent.

Premila: That's why people are trying to work out whether it's got anything to do with TV.

Richard: It could have something to do with cartoons. I mean that's possible.

Jonathan: Oh yeah, *Tom and Jerry* . . . bloody heck!

Anna: It's very violent.

Richard: It seems very funny . . . but even so.

Jonathan: I mean that's all they do, just hit each other.

Richard: And they use knives in it as well, guns and things.

Anna gives a 'commonsense' answer, but Jonathan insists on delving deeper. Premila's response is a range of examples quoted from the Right discourse, from which she distances herself, and towards which Jonathan exhibits incredulity. The arguments are rehearsed further with most of the key words and phrases of the Right discourse recurring: 'Rambo . . . sex and violence . . . effects . . . Hungerford massacre'. Anna deflates such a litany, however, and deliberately reverses the Right model of effects with the reference to her sister's behaviour. Richard seems to have some familiarity with the discourse as he introduces the possibility of cartoons encouraging violence. There is mild agreement on this, probably since cartoons are no longer particularly their own favoured viewing, and perhaps because such 'displacement' arguments offer an explanation of the violent behaviour of Anna's younger sister!

* * * * *

These students joined with several others for some further taped discussions chaired by me, looking at some of the issues raised in the original tape. Three topics which recur in popular discourses about television had particular prominence: the opposition between television and reading, the contrast between the past and the present, and the question of the 'effects' of television.

On the opposition between television and reading, an obsession of the Liberal discourse, it would appear that parental fears[15] about children not reading enough are justified, as the students seem to dismiss reading as an activity.

Carolyn: I prefer to read a magazine to a book as there's a lot more going on in a magazine.

Premila: It's just that because there's TV, if there wasn't TV, and I was bored, all through my childhood I'd have probably been turning to books rather than TV . . . I just find it so tedious, I can't sit and make myself read a book, I just fall asleep half way through anyway.

Anna: If you want to read a book, you've got to go to the library and select one, you can't really tell what it's going to be like till you've read it and you've got to find the book first amongst all these shelves of books and you just see the cover, but if you're watching television you turn it on and if there's something on, you just sit there and watch it, you don't have to go and choose it.

However, I would not want to take these points at face value. For a start, there is again a sense in which the students are playing a 'serious' role, particularly when I am present, distancing themselves from the 'child-self' by adopting an 'adult-self', dismissing certain programmes as 'childish', and adopting adult discourses. In this case, as in the teachers' discussion of *Blind Date*, they effectively displace the 'blame' for this state of affairs, arguing that they don't read enough because of the nature of television compared to books, not because of any active choice on their own part.

There is also a sense in which a particular definition of 'reading' operates in this discourse, in which reading is defined as fiction, and in particular 'Good Literature' — a definition straight from the 'Quality' discourse. Certainly when the parents interviewed talked about reading they seemed to mean fiction, and both parents and children referred to comparisons between books and their TV serializations. By this criterion, probably the children don't read much, although this excludes the substantial amount they do read from non-fiction sources, such as newspapers, magazines, school books and so on.

Some of the students also focused upon a romantic image of the past:

Sam: Figures in shops, they used to have these old tin soldiers and things, but now they've got all these plastic images of all cartoon characters — 'Real Ghostbusters', 'He Man', 'Transformers'. There isn't anything that's originated elsewhere really.

Anna: Not like in them Olde Days, they'd sell a toy train or something and you'd have to make up a character, nowadays they give them personalities so children don't have to use their imagination anymore.

This argument of course echoes a Liberal position, although they clearly distance themselves from 'other' children, and send up a rose-tinted image of the past — for example in Anna's reference to 'them Olde Days'. Natasha scoffs at this whole obsession with the past:

> Parents don't want their kids going out and buying a Rambo figure or some monster . . . parents remember . . . parents live in the past! Let's face it they want everything how it used to be — they think, oh wow! the good old days.

This seems to me to represent a deconstruction of adult discourses, which Elena takes further into 'Right' effects territory:

> Next thing you know, children are going to be walking up to house plants and going: 'hello little weed'.

As with Anna's point about her sister being violent without watching *Rambo*, this turns the 'effects' model around, so that the kind of viewing adults recommend to children (in this case, *Watch With Mother*) becomes the object of anxiety.

Apart from discussion of the influence of TV on children's reading, the students discussed the other 'effects' which TV is often assumed to have:

> Premila: People blame things on TV . . . because a child is lazy, they blame TV . . . TV is the cause of all this.

Her use of 'people' and 'they' indicates her own distance from such a statement. Other children had heard of copycat incidents which they assumed to be the result of TV, probably because that was how they were reported in the press:

> Richard: In *EastEnders*, when Angie tried to commit suicide, this girl actually did, she saw Angie do it and she did.
> Elena: This boy went out with his friend, said 'alright, Robin Hood did this', and hanged himself on the assumption that he would rise up as Robin did.
> Devi: Michael Ryan, they said after that he was watching all these violent movies and it was because of what they did in the movies that he went out and shot people.

While all three of these stories have reached the status of myth, there is in fact no evidence that any of them is true. Natasha's response suggests that they have not necessarily swallowed the assumptions underlying these myths wholesale, though she still takes the story to be true:

> I'd agree that people are influenced by TV but . . . I think that girl who committed suicide after seeing Angie . . . must have been depressed in the first place . . . she wouldn't have done it for the fun of it.

Thus, while the students are clearly familiar with many of the popular anti-television discourses I have indentified, they are also careful to distance themselves from them. In many cases, they explicitly reject the more nonsensical assumptions of these discourses, although they are also able to use them as a means of appearing more adult than their peers, and in order to please teacher.

While many of the anti-television discourses identify children in particular as their major focus of concern, these children at least appear much more autonomous in their relationship with television. Compared with the teachers, they are much more willing to acknowledge and celebrate their own pleasure in the medium, without feeling this is something they have to 'own up to' — although this is notably less the case when there is a teacher present. Implicitly, they recognize that adults' concern about the influence of television is as much a reflection of adults' own anxieties — and in particular, the instability of their power over children — as a genuine response to the way in which they themselves use the medium.

*   *   *   *   *

This research has a number of implications for media teachers. To begin with, it shows that any discussion of television between teachers and students needs to be understood in the context of the power relationships that exist between them. Teachers may have a good deal invested in presenting themselves as people who are not 'taken in' by television, and who are seeking to 'protect' children from the trivial or even dangerous pleasures it provides. Students may adopt adult discourses simply in order to please teachers, or alternatively may use their judgments about television as a way of mocking or 'getting one back' at them. In this respect, discourse about television can never been seen as merely neutral.

At the same time, it is clear that many popular discourses about television explicitly conceive of children as unsophisticated and even ignorant. Furthermore, they often seek to undermine and invalidate the pleasures children derive from the medium: pleasure can only be spoken of within the ultimately very limited terms of the 'Hedonistic' discourse. Yet students are likely to 'read' the intentions of media teachers through the prism of these commonsense discourses. Unless we explicitly demonstrate otherwise, they will perceive our aims as being to wean them off television, or to protect them from it.

On a general level, this means acknowledging the fact that our students are already sophisticated and 'critical' viewers. We need to ensure that their pleasures in the medium can be accepted and investigated, rather than simply condemned. We need to abandon the view that children are inevitably 'at risk' from television, and that our aim is to rescue them from it.

At the same time, students should be enabled to identify and to question the underlying and often unstated assumptions which inform their own judgments about television, and indeed those of their teachers. One potential way of doing this would be to make these discourses themselves an object of study in media education. Perhaps at the beginning of a Media Studies course, students might be encouraged to collect and analyze a range of 'secondary' material about television, or about the media more generally, taken from newspapers or from television itself. They might conduct 'research' of the kind recorded here into the attitudes of their parents and teachers, and discuss the reasons why particular discourses are so dominant. To begin in this way would encourage students to adopt a much more questioning and self-reflexive approach to studying the media themselves.

One further implication of this research concerns our colleagues' perceptions of media education, and its place within the curriculum as a whole. The school in which I work has a long tradition of media education, yet for a variety of reasons it has tended to remain somewhat of a separate 'enclave'. The responses of the teachers recorded here indicate a need to think through the ways in which we present what we teach to colleagues, and also to parents, particularly if we hope to integrate media education with other curriculum areas. It is necessary to acknowledge the enormous amount which many adults have invested in an antagonistic relationship to TV, and that this will not necessarily be easy to challenge. To what extent should we use the anti-television discourses I have identified to make the case for media education? How can we avoid our work being perceived on this way? And how can we encourage colleagues to adopt a more constructive approach to teaching about the media?

Notes

1 Allen (1987), p.1.
2 See, for example, Winn (1977).
3 Large (1980), Trelease (1984) and Postman (1983) all develop this argument.
4 For a critique of this position, see Connell (1984).
5 For example, Glasgow University Media Group (1982).
6 Root (1986) p.65.
7 Connell (1984).
8 Taylor and Mullan (1986) provide an 'academic' counterpart to this approach.
9 D. Ward *The Guardian*, 2 August 1989.
10 Murdock and Phelps (1973), p.3.
11 The extracts used included *The Price is Right*, *Dynasty* and *Howard's Way*.
12 All teachers' names have been changed.
13 Hodge and Tripp (1986) p.178.
14 Grateful acknowledgments to all those who took part in this research, particularly the third-years who gave up a lot of lunchtimes for lively discussions: Jonathan Armstrong, Devi Beekarry, Elena Christou, Natasha Goburdhun, Richard Meek, Anna Rubins, Premila Sivanesan, Carolyn Solomon and Sam Townend.
15 These concerns were certainly voiced by some of the parents I interviewed as part of this research. Typical comments included: 'Perhaps you could encourage them to read the book about it afterwards' and 'It breaks my heart, because every other member of my family reads and Richard has virtually given up reading.'

Part Two
Theory and Practice

Chapter 4

Redefining Creativity: Extended Project Work in GCSE Media Studies

Roy Stafford

Introduction

Practical work has had a long and difficult history as part of media education. Media theorists have always treated 'hands-on' experience with suspicion, fearing a fall into what Len Masterman once called 'the technicist trap',[1] the promotion of product and technology over process and ideology. The great risk with practical work, it is argued, is that students will simply learn to ape the professionals, and that a critical, analytical perspective will be lost. Conversely, some progressive educationists have adhered to notions of creativity, in which the purity of the experience of practical work has appeared to be unsullied by the dirty work of critical reflection.

A compromise appeared to have been reached in the early 1980s whereby media educationists agreed that practice and theory must be synthesized, that one should not be discussed without the other. In effect, however, this often meant that practical work was reduced to a practical *exercise* — a means of 'proving' media theory, often through 'code-breaking'. What was lacking from this analysis and its attendant pedagogy was any theoretical understanding of practice itself. Care was taken to delineate the different concepts which made up the core of media theory but similar care was not lavished on practice.

This consensus has been broken because of three separate but interlinked developments which have taken place in the last few years:

1   Curriculum development has gradually moved in favour of student-centred, resource-based, activity learning. There has been a shift away from traditional academic exercises requiring close teacher control towards more open-ended projects and case studies. Students may be expected to work in groups without supervision and may be involved in simulated and actual work experience.

2   The 14–19 Curriculum has been pressurized to become more 'vocational' and this has meant an increasing interest in the vocational and practical aspects of media education. New 'A' level and GCSE courses in

Communications and Media Studies have brought practical work components into traditional Humanities syllabuses, while new courses under the aegis of CPVE, CGLI and BTEC[2] have seen the development of media education within pre-vocational and vocational courses aimed at employment in media industries.

3   Developments in electronics technology have made available high-spec but low-cost equipment in audio, video, photographic and computing applications. The constraints on student work are lessening and the argument about not aping professional practice is becoming more difficult to pursue. Previously, the institutional constraints of the classroom added to the limitations of equipment meant that only part of the production process could be undertaken realistically. It is now possible to organize student 'commissions' for real clients which can be undertaken within open-ended project time. In video production there are now a number of schools and colleges which can engage in sophisticated production and post-production work and the 'non-professional' quality of the finished product is a function only of the tape format and not the production methods.

Practical work has also been formally recognized in the most significant curriculum development in media education during the last few years, namely GCSE Media Studies. Here, practical work occupies between one-third and half of the overall assessment. In 1988, 10,000 candidates were assessed on practical work, and numbers are likely to increase at least in the short term. Clearly, any confusion over the role of practical work makes even more difficult the knotty problem of devising assignments and appropriate assessment methods. The earlier notions of practical work are no longer tenable. What must replace them?

This paper puts forward a tentative proposal for a new view of practical work and in particular video production. It argues that practical media work requires a range of skills and understandings which may be unique to the field. In particular, the necessity for group work in most forms of media production and the development of creative skills in a particular institutional/industrial context requires media teachers to recognize a set of skills and understandings which have previously been ignored. This paper is therefore concerned to excavate in order to produce the buried outlines of a pedagogy for practical work.

Critical Perspectives on Practical Video Work

The first portable video equipment became available to schools and colleges around 1974–75. Relatively difficult to operate and offering a monochrome image, the new medium did not find immediate favour with teachers who had previously sought to develop a good standard of work on Super 8 cine film. However, it did attract those who appreciated the facility to obtain images without the time-lag of film-processing and also the relative cheapness of longer shooting with reusable tapes. Much of the classroom work which utilized the new video technology was undertaken with the pupils who represented a major problem for schools in the mid-1970s, namely the 'low-achieving' 15-year-olds 'caught' by the raising of the school leaving age to 16. In further education a similar group of students on basic skills courses was often offered practical video work as a 'non-academic' activity. Much of the work was poorly organized, under-resourced and lacking any form of assessment. Some work had real educational value but too often it was seen in a rather patronizing way as a means of keeping 'difficult' students occupied. In the 'failure' of the productions themselves it also reinforced the lack of achievement for these students.

Writers promoting a critical form of media education were understandably dismissive of work which they saw as ignoring analytical skills. Bob Ferguson details this early history in an influential article, published in 1981.[3] The flavour of his polemic can be tasted in the following extract describing typical practice:

> ... the camera was often 'squirted' at its subject and the dizzy, boring and incoherent results thus obtained could be justified as experimentation. When plots were attempted they were puerile .... The results, if seen by the unconverted, seldom convinced them of the desirability and effectivity of practical work in film and video.

Ferguson identifies two possible justifications for this kind of work. Firstly, some teachers imported the notion of 'creativity' from English teaching (cf. 'creative writing') in order to fill the intellectual gap in practical work. Secondly and very differently, some teachers saw practical work as a means of emulating professional practice and 'learning through doing' that film and television production is a complex business. Ferguson compares these approaches unfavourably with a third approach, namely 'deconstruction' or 'rule-breaking exercises'. This is an analytical activity, which involves students manipulating meaning rather than creating it. Ferguson sees it as open-ended in the sense that it 'does not have to embrace a single mode of televisual, filmic or dramatic construction as *correct.*' It is a means of interrogating media conventions which allows students to refuse dominant, transparent production styles and messages. This view of practical work as rule-breaking — for example, in the form of interview exercises or audio-dubbing of re-edited footage — became the orthodoxy for many media educationists in the early 1980s.

Ferguson himself had been a successful proponent of practical film work at Hornsey College of Art in the late 1960s.[4] Yet in 1981 he argued that 'For the students involved [this work was] more of a social than an educational undertaking'. He appears to be rejecting his previous work as based on experiential rather than cognitive learning, and as symptomatic of the weaknesses of a 'liberal studies' approach. Many media teachers in the early 1980s turned against both the 'progressive' pedagogy of liberal studies and the skills-based, 'active' learning approach characterized by the various schemes promoted by the Manpower Services Commission.

Len Masterman's influential book *Teaching About Television*[5], published in 1980, shares Ferguson's misgivings about many of the justifications previously offered for practical video work. He also recognizes the poor quality of most attempts to emulate professional production. However, he sees the importance of establishing a pedagogy for practical work which recognizes the potential of video as an expressive medium, but one which must be used in relation to students' own language and culture and which 'harnesses group resources'. He suggests a whole range of potential activities, which includes both code-breaking exercises *and* more extended projects and simulations.

In 1980, Masterman devotes seven pages to practical television work and, despite his misgivings, looks forward to video as 'an integral part of a more total liberating education'. Yet in 1985, in his equally influential book, *Teaching the Media*,[6] practical work is allowed just over a page. Practical work is now 'not an end in itself, but a necessary means to developing an autonomous critical understanding of the media'. Extensive and time-consuming projects are far less significant than code-breaking and (closed) simulations. It is perhaps unfair to characterize a significant change in Masterman's position with just a few quotes, but the tone of his writing suggests a conversion to the orthodoxy, in which deconstruction exercises became the *only* acceptable form of practical work.

Ferguson and Masterman have spread this approach to practical work through their writings and teacher education programmes and to a certain extent they have been supported by the British Film Institute Education Department in its reluctance to engage with practical work beyond the closed exercise. However, it would be wrong to give the impression that the orthodoxy has remained unchallenged.[7] Jim Hornsby, writing a BFI Advisory Document in 1984,[8] recasts some of the earlier arguments. He identifies the 'creativity' approach and renames it 'aestheticist'. The fears of technical instruction which developed in media educationists as they gazed in horror at those institutions which invested heavily in sophisticated video technology under the aegis of the MSC (especially from 1984 with its Technical and Vocational Education Initiative) are neatly summed up in the disparaging term 'technicist'. Against these despised forms, Hornsby identifies two 'oppositional' or 'alternative' media education approaches, deconstruction and 'progressive content'.

Hornsby sees two weaknesses in deconstruction. Firstly, such exercises can be reduced to simply proving a theoretical point and in doing so students may be involved in producing a meaningless statement. He argues that learning to use conventional codes and understanding why they produce meaning can be more productive. Secondly, he turns the professional emulation argument around by pointing out that:

> . . . deconstruction exercises also risk ignoring the fact that practical media

work in an educational context is always, obviously, distinct from professional practice. In my view, exercises should therefore be structured in terms of the real reasons for this difference rather than from a perceived need to deconstruct professional conventions.

This seems to me an argument for addressing the institutional constraints of the school/college and the perceived position of the students.

This argument also carries through to the other form of 'oppositional practice', the attempt to develop student projects concerned with issues which are seen to be handled unsatisfactorily by broadcast television. There is almost an inverse form of theoreticism here. Formal considerations are virtually ignored, to be replaced by concerns over representation. Students are encouraged to tackle 'images of women' or 'youth culture' without any consideration of the forms used by broadcast media or the institutional practices which inform them: it is assumed that students will somehow naturally contest the meanings of the professionals.

Hornsby's argument is aimed at rescuing practical work from the reductivism that sees it only as a single practice, and as an adjunct to theory. While the value of deconstruction exercises is not in doubt, some of the assumptions about creativity and simulated professional production which have recurred in this debate are in need of reappraisal. This view is supported by some recent writing which explicitly refers to GCSE projects. Jane Arthurs, writing in 1987,[9] offers a very clear reading of Hornsby and an illuminating personal experience:

> ... I never really understood what was meant by continuity editing and why it is a deeply ideological process until I tried to replicate it myself ....
> [T]heory does not in itself generate practice ... practice derives from relations with the real world and from this actively constructs meaning.
> The implications for devising student projects are that productions should arise out of the immediate context of students' lives.

This less reductive view of the relationship between theory and practical work is one I hope to develop in this chapter.

Context of the Research

The research discussed in this chapter is based on close observation (as tutor in charge) of a group of students at a Further Education college in London during the academic session 1988–89. The students were aged 16–19 and undertaking a one-year GCSE Media Studies course. Students were observed during 'academic/theoretical' classes and those periods labelled 'practical'. Study material included the theoretical assignments, finished video products, production logs and interviews conducted as a form of debriefing practical work.

The College

The college is situated in an inner London borough with many indicators of social deprivation. The borough has a history of very high youth unemployment and one of the lowest take-up rates for post-16 education. Afro-Caribbean students suffer disproportionately from unemployment and tend to leave school at 16 and apply for college places in inner London. In the college, they form the majority of students on GCSE courses.

The college began its life as a centre for technical education, especially in relation to telecommunications, electronics and sciences. It concentrated on 'high-level' work (i.e. post-'O' Level) and attracted overseas and home students from a wide geographical area for its relatively specialized courses — both full-time and day-release. General education was confined to 'A' Level.

During the 1980s a number of factors brought about a dramatic change in the college's recruitment and curriculum offer. Changes in recruitment policies by major employers saw a fall in demand for day-release courses, while the development of Equal Opportunity Policies within the ILEA saw pressure mount on college managements to make provision for the local community. Recognition of the eventual impact of the declining birth rate also acted as pressure on management to seek new sources of students. The college responded to these external changes by offering new 'low-level' access courses: this led to a student body which was younger, less academic and less 'disciplined' by the work environment.

While these changes met with some resistance among traditional vocational staff, they were generally welcomed by the 'academic' department of the college, charged with providing general education. While media education continued to be part of the department's offer of 'academic' courses, mostly at GCSE level, and played a part in 'servicing' vocational courses, it also offered the department a chance to develop its own vocational courses. With the gradual 'vocationalization' of the 14–19 curriculum it was recognized that a department seen as purely academic might be in a weak political position within the college, especially when bidding for scarce resources.

In this context, media education provided a model for 'mix 'n' match' course provision, bringing together academic and vocational work. This in turn allowed for relatively generous resourcing in terms of staff time, accommodation and equipment budgets, in contrast to traditional academic Humanities subjects. As a new form of provision, media education courses were not constrained by established conventions for course organization, or by teaching strategies which might be found elsewhere in the college on purely academic or vocational courses. It was also hoped that media education would attract 'new' student groupings, primarily groups who might share an aspiration to work in the media industries, but who might bring to the courses a wide range of interests, abilities and ideas. In practice, the courses did attract an interesting mix of school-leavers and adults.

The Students

There are two groups of media students in the college, defined by their motivation. One group has aspirations towards a career in some part of the media industries, while the other has less clear aspirations and chooses media courses for less instrumental reasons. The former group is much larger and forms the basis for the sample of students observed in this research.

The particular GCSE class contained several students aged 16 on entry, several of whom were attending on a link arrangement from a local school which was unable to make a wide sixth-form curriculum offer. A large group of students was aged 17–18, having already attempted CPVE or GCSE in college or school sixth form. Finally there was a small group of older students taking the subject on a part-time day basis. Unfortunately, most of these students were unable to complete the course for a variety of reasons and are not included in the sample.

Five of the students had previously completed a CPVE Media Industries course and had some inkling of what was to come. Six of the group were also taking GCSE Photography and GCSE Critical Studies in Art and Design, which gave them greater support in terms of both theory and practical work. Generally, the more able students were not taking other subjects with obvious links to Media Studies.

The Course

The Southern Examining Group (SEG) Media Studies syllabus followed in the college requires candidates to demonstrate an understanding of the 'core concepts' of Media Studies and also to 'construct their own representations of their ideas and experiences using one or more media'. The Assessment schedule prescribes six coursework assignments, which may relate to one or more concepts and which may contain practical elements, representing two-thirds of the total marks; and a practical project representing one-third of the total marks.

The practical project may be undertaken as group or individual work, and can employ a range of media. It is intended to act as an opportunity for candidates to demonstrate practical skills in the interpretation of a theme in a chosen medium. Candidates must maintain a production log which is assessed alongside the project. Marks are awarded equally across four assessment categories: degree of finish, content, appropriateness (for intended audience and of medium to content) and student self-evaluation.

The main scheme of work was organized around the 'core concepts', each of which related to a coursework assignment. An attempt was made to involve students in a range of learning situations and to require assessed work to be presented in other forms apart from written essays. These assignments were as follows:

1 Audience: survey and analysis of the magazine market (including production of a magazine cover).
2 Narrative: analysis of *mise-en-scène* and narrative structure in a thriller and a melodrama. Video production exercise on narrative sequencing.
3 Institution: visit to Museum of the Moving Image plus short questions.
4 Industry: film industry production simulation.
5 Representation: analysis and research into the presentation of sports personalities.
6 Genre: analysis of generic conventions and presentation of ideas for genre production.

Where these assignments required some form of practical work, this was primarily seen as an *exercise* whose principal objective was to develop understanding of the core concepts. Consequently, careful direction was given and students were not assessed on acquisition of technical skills. The most significant piece of practical work was contained in the narrative assignment, and consisted of a video exercise in creating a suspense narrative based on *The Visit*.[10] Students first constructed a storyboard from the photographs in *The Visit* pack. Working in groups of four or five they then wrote a shooting script for a short narrative and, after a brief introduction to portable video equipment, shot the necessary scenes around the college. The shots were logged and, using the storyboard as a guide, the tape was edited by the teaching staff under instruction from the groups.[11] Each group also created titles and chose a music soundtrack. Some students already had experience of using video, but in most cases this was a learning experience where the 'given' shots taken from *The Visit* allowed them to concentrate on organizing their production and using the camera without having to worry about developing a *mise-en-scène*. The exercise concluded with a student evaluation of how the group had attempted to create suspense in their narrative.

This exercise provided the necessary introduction to the more extended practical project in a number of respects. It gave students experience of working in a group, and demonstrated the importance of planning and preparation. It also provided some insight into the potential of video production, and gave them some experience in evaluating their own work.

At the end of the Autumn term, after this exercise had been completed, the students were asked to undertake a mid-course review. They were placed in small groups and given a list of open questions about the term's work and an audio cassette recorder. It was hoped that this might provide some indication of how well the students had understood the core concepts of audience and narrative. In practice, most students felt self-conscious about presenting their ideas for the recorder. The comments they made were brief and cautious. There was little evidence of deep understanding and the ability to apply conceptual knowledge. However, there was evidence of enjoyment in the course and an appreciation of the teaching approach. It is also likely that the experience of a formal 'review' helped some students to understand what was required in the self-evaluation of the subsequent practical project.

The Practical Project

The Practical Project was introduced early in the Spring term. The pattern of teaching changed so that work on 'core concepts' continued in one period, while the other period (on a Friday afternoon — such is the timetabling fate of new subjects) became an open workshop reserved for the practical project. The project was quickly identified as an 'open' commission and easily distinguished from the 'closed' exercises associated with the coursework assignments.

The GCSE syllabus requires that students work individually or collectively on a theme and that the assessment schedule must clearly show where they have received assistance. I provided thematic titles which I thought might allow students to choose something that they felt able to make a statement about: 'London 1990', 'Springtime', 'Holidays', 'In Vogue' and 'On the Street'. Most opted for one of the last two. I left them to form their own groups and to formulate their ideas. They did not have to attend each class but I did require them to come and discuss their project as soon as they had a working title. From then on I expected them to come to me for advice on how to use technology or to book equipment or facilities.

In practice, some students were always there, while others I hardly saw. I did monitor the progress of each project as carefully as I could (partly by fishing for information on the college grapevine, partly by quizzing the regular attenders). As the deadline approached I tried to restrain my teacherly instincts to rush in and make things happen. I attempted as surreptitiously as possible to make helpful suggestions, to demonstrate techniques, to discuss with groups what they had planned. I was determined that the groups would work on their own ideas, but I was also determined that no group should fail for lack of support. In the event, I didn't have to 'rescue' any group. I spent most time with a group who were quite competent at organizing themselves, but rather lacking in ideas, and who produced the most conventional videotape. Despite the help I gave, the finished products were seen very much as the 'property' of the groups and not an exercise they had performed for me: this is certainly clear from the account of two groups' work which follows.

Group A

This group comprised three students, Sandra, Colette and Alan.[12] Their initial idea was to make an audio tape on the theme of 'Springtime'. This was prompted by the recent arrival in the college of an 8-track mixer and a desire to use music and sounds in an original way. The three students were among the more able in the class and wanted to be 'different'. However, they were not a natural 'group' and they tended to work independently, looking for material and developing ideas. For a couple of weeks they made little progress in attempting to find appropriate sounds to evoke ideas of 'romance, rebirth, freshness and vitality'. Eventually, the two young women decided to record the sounds of a tennis match. Because the college lacked good quality portable audio recorders, they were advised to take a camcorder, with at least a reasonable audio facility, to the local tennis club. Inevitably perhaps, their exploits attracted the attention of other students, who recorded them playing tennis. Viewing the rushes, they began to think about the possibilities of a videotape production.

Meanwhile, Alan, who had been absent for a couple of weeks, returned with a 'rap' which he had written on the Springtime theme. The next week, Sandra and Alan found an empty classroom and set up the camcorder with a view to recording Alan performing the rap to a backing track which he had chosen from his own collection. Once again, the recording was interrupted by the influx of many other students (no teachers were present). This time, however, Sandra retained control of the camcorder and was able to develop her ideas about how to record what was now quite a lively event. Colette was absent through illness and I was concerned that the group would not complete. I urged Sandra and Alan to make a firm decision about whether or not the project was now a videotape production. They were excited by the rushes and decided to go ahead. I explained the basic idea of pop video production, i.e. laying an audio track on videotape and then inserting appropriate images. I pointed out that they already had some images, and suggested they prepare a shooting script for the rest: they agreed.

There were now only three sessions left. In the first, the audio track was mixed on the 8-track with Alan and Sandra (who was also a drama student and proved to have an excellent voice) both laying a vocal track on top of the backing track, which Alan tweaked to his own satisfaction. The recording was rushed and not aided by my own lack of experience with this new equipment but at least it was done and preparations for the following week were undertaken with enthusiasm. Sandra's considerable organizational skills came to the fore and she recruited the best dancers she could find and scoured the college for appropriate locations and props. It is worth noting that one location she chose was a part of the college which, while it offered dramatic possibilities, also housed the most conservative vocational department. The invasion of this holy space by a group of rapping, dancing students, unsupervised and not cowed by authority, did not go unnoticed by staff or students, and Sandra and her dancers were not unaware of the challenge they represented in an institution not renowned for its positive response to rap culture. The other major location for the dance (and Alan's performance of the rap) was the Students' Union area — a dark and dreary location which posed considerable lighting problems but which remains central to the 'culture' of the college.

In the last week Sandra appeared with ideas on how to edit her forty minutes of video material down to the four-and-a-half minutes of the recorded rap. I edited this to her instructions (and, I have to confess, a few added ideas of my own). She expressed her satisfaction and the project was complete. But this was not the end of the story. Everyone who had taken part and all their friends had to see the final product. Several screenings were organized and copies were made. The video was an undoubted success with its audience. The technical quality was not good but the 'creativity' in the writing of the rap and the performance skills in song and dance were evident to any audience. More importantly perhaps, the tape represented a true celebration of the black culture in the college and as such was something that 'belonged' to the students.

A few weeks later, Sandra, Alan and Colette were interviewed and recorded on videotape as part of the debriefing process. This no doubt helped in the writing of production logs. The following comments give some idea of what the students think they learned from the project:

Sandra: My own performance was main coordinator and force behind the group. My dedication could have been stronger, but compared with the group it was brilliant. I learnt a lot from this project.

Firstly, do not always start off with a hard idea, as you can see due to lack of research they do not always turn out as you had expected. Do not depend on group members, because it is not always their fault but sometimes they can let you down.

We should have had the ideas for the video planned out properly. But most of all, don't waste time!

[Production Log]

Colette: We learned how to put a music video together. I would think of doing it again, I could do it better.

Alan: Yeah. If routines were worked out properly, locations found, if there were enough lights . . .

Sandra: If it was more rehearsed, more stylized.

[Interview]

In the interview, the students were asked to think about where their ideas had come from, and whether this was from the other work on the course.

Colette: . . . when we had that work on camera shots, the different angles that you look at through the camera, the different shots — to make up a story, things like that. I think that helped, that played a big part as you can see from the end result.

Alan: . . . from other videos, other Hip Hop videos. The dancing mainly, like from American Hip Hop . . . you can see them on *Night Network* and you can buy them at certain shops.

Sandra: You can see them on cable TV.

Colette: MTV — a special slot just for Hip Hop videos.

When asked if they were simply copying the Hip Hop style, the students said no, because of the subject matter. It was difficult to write a rap on 'Springtime' and to find images.

Sandra: We tried to get a unity — everybody's happy and it's the rebirth . . .

Alan: Of love!

Sandra: It needed more women in it. They just weren't around on a Friday afternoon or they wouldn't appear. We wanted to do a scene with a couple but we couldn't persuade them. We also had a scene outside but it rained and we couldn't use the video. We would have like to use more of the tennis but the colour balance wasn't right.

Alan: Teachers stopped us filming because of the noise.

All three were well aware that they had wasted time and that if they had prepared properly the result would have been much better. At this stage they were still thinking through the process:

Sandra: The research was the hardest — we didn't really want to do it.

Colette: The most important thing was to get the to the core of the problem — getting the video together. It's no use doing the research without the finished video.

Sandra: But it's no use trying the video without the research.

Colette: We did the research but it wasn't written down properly. You need to stick to easy ideas — the radio programme wasn't an easy idea.

Sandra: Yeah. Stick to an easy format and a main thing so you can research it.

Colette: If you had chosen the video first you would have done far more and you would have carried on right to the end.

Sandra: That's true but I was on my own most of the time. I was forced to be director — I had to go and find people.

Despite its faults, this group's production was successful, especially in terms of reaching its audience.

Group B

This group had a more confused history. It began as a loose grouping of the less able students in the class who came together with little common purpose. At the last moment, Stuart, the most able student in the class (and the only one to gain an A grade for Media Studies), abandoned his own project and joined the group. Although not a forceful personality like Sandra, Stuart nevertheless provided a firm centre and the project was finally completed.

The project drew on two of the themes on offer, 'In Vogue' and 'On the Street' and ended up with the title 'Street Sophistication'. Gordon, Gerry and Gina were all taking Photography GCSE and they each set out to produce a magazine style portfolio of fashion photographs. They made slow progress in planning and preparation and eventually came together with Roger who had the idea of exploring the world of rap videos (which he collected). Roger's idea was to edit a compilation of rap videos in such a way as to make a statement about the importance of rap as a youth movement. The photographers were then to provide still images of the fashion accessories to the rap scene. Many weeks were spent discussing these ideas but little material emerged. Stuart, who was very much a computer specialist (and taking Computer Studies GCSE) suggested that the group make use of the electronic titling facility available using the college Amiga computer. He was invited to join and agreed. In the week before the deadline, the group realized they were in trouble and borrowed equipment in an attempt to emulate Group A and record the best college dancers as an image track to mix with the rap compilation. In the event they were reduced to recording themselves (Roger proving to be an embarrassed but extremely skilful dancer).

For the last class the group appeared (minus Gerry) armed with a stack of rap videos, still photographs which had been transferred to video, video footage of the group attempting rap dances and a script which was intended to link the items via computer text. Stuart, with some assistance, was able to edit the material and add text via the Amiga, but this was a long process and Gina added some of the text as a voice-over. I intimated to the group that without a bit more explanation through a voice-over, I wasn't sure that an audience would understand their argument. They agreed and decided to end the tape by recording a discussion amongst the group members where they would make quite explicit statements about what rap meant to them. The discussion worked very well, showing perhaps that the group members knew what they wanted to say, but had found it difficult to work it into a functional script. The final product pleased the group and although it didn't receive the same number of screenings as Group A's, the general reaction was favourable: other students were impressed with Roger's knowledge of rap and the comments made in the discussion.

Group B were interviewed in the same way as Group A (except that Gina was not present). Stuart, Roger and Gordon found the interview process quite difficult but Stuart used the experience to good effect in his log. This extract shows a clear understanding of the production process.

I felt that the video we produced was of a fairly high standard. I was genuinely pleased with the results and I though that we had achieved most of our targets. However, there are many points, which in retrospect, could have been better organized and improved. Our initial planning did not go into sufficient details, so we had good ideas, but no real concept of how difficult it would be to implement them. Although I had the most experience on computers, I had no idea how long the video text process would take, having not done it before, and eventually ran out of time, because I had underestimated the difficulty of the task. This was true of many of the other problems; we chose to do things which we were not experienced in and did not try them out first to see if they were possible.

Time management was badly handled. Since the group had no clear leadership, timetables for rehearsals and shooting were not followed and there was a lack of discipline, which meant that a lot of time was wasted.... The group was very disorganized when I joined, with a definite lack of commitment on the part of certain members. However, being a late-comer I did not join in discussions as much as I should have, nor make suggestions which I felt would conflict with the decisions which the original group had already made...

From the interview, it is possible to gauge some of the organizational and motivational problems the group faced:

Gordon: I planned to work on 'In Vogue' myself but I didn't think I could do it on my own — I couldn't manage all the words and the layout as well as the pictures. I joined Roger's group.

Stuart: I was going to work on my own on the Channel Tunnel issue but I lost some of my newspaper cuttings and I couldn't get the equipment when I wanted it so I joined Roger as well.

The three students recognized that they needed a group (Roger claimed he could have done it on his own, but there was little evidence to support this). They also recognized that working in a group was fraught with problems.

Stuart: People not turning up...

Roger: ...or not doing what they said they would do — like going out with a camera and coming back without the shots.

RS: Why do people fail to do things?

Gordon: They aren't organized properly.

Roger: They just don't want to bother — it's the difference between school and college. They don't have to be here. They can't be bothered. They don't care if they let others down — they don't think about it like that. They would come in if there was an incentive — if you paid them!

The interview ended with an extended discussion about how the students in the college (i.e. mostly those on 'low-level' courses) were motivated or not by their work, the need for qualifications, their expectations etc. There was a concrete basis for the group's dissatisfaction but there was also some over-reaction. In general, the students in the Media Studies class were well motivated, more so probably than in most other GCSE subjects. They all wanted to succeed but they found it difficult to organize themselves in these open-ended projects. There were four other groups working on the project and all four struggled to meet the deadline and suffered similar kinds of problems. But none of them gave up and most felt pleased with their efforts. My feeling was that students with often low expectations had grappled with a practical project demanding unfamiliar skills and understanding and had achieved some success.

Conclusion: Rethinking 'Creativity'

The pedagogy adopted here was chosen to complement the closed exercises in rule-breaking or analysis of codes undertaken elsewhere in the course. So what are the benefits of such an approach and how might they be judged against the 'orthodoxy' represented by Ferguson and Masterman? Do they fulfil Hornsby's criteria?

The key term here appears to be 'creativity'. This term has often been used pejoratively to describe activities concerned with a mere expression of 'feeling'. It does have another meaning, however, which seeks to embrace all the skills and understandings that might be involved in any form of practical activity.

It was only when I began to reflect upon the experience of teaching on the GCSE course that I realised the importance of the curriculum debates around Vocational Preparation[13] and specifically CPVE in developing my own ideas on practical work. I have intimated above that the orthodox approach to practical work in media education was partly influenced by a recoil from the development of skills-based curricula during the early 1980s. Indeed, I shared in that concern[14] but I felt then as I do now that vocational education is important and that retreating towards a purely analytical 'subject discipline' would not help to promote media education more broadly.

That retreat or more correctly refusal to occupy the battlefield was misguided and misconceived for a number of reasons. Firstly, the force of curriculum change was too great and GCSE itself is heavily imbued with ideas of resource-based, active learning. Secondly, the new curriculum model was not monolithic. It is possible to discern a considerable difference between those documents emanating from the educationists within the Further Education Unit (FEU) of the Department of Education and Science and those with an FEU label but a parenthood in the Manpower Services Commission (now the Training Agency).[15] Here for instance is an extract from an FEU Discussion Paper of 1985[16] promoting a 'creative curriculum':

The creative curriculum is one in which:
There are opportunities for students to develop their creative abilities

by pursuing their individual skills and interest in an environment which values experimentation;

A premium is placed on self-directed learning, in which the teacher and the learning environment are seen as a resource;

Learning activities are negotiated and renegotiated and new and original ideas are welcomed, subject to disciplined evaluation and rigorous criticism;

There is recognition of the value of groupwork, where the strengths of different members of a team, as well as the talents of the individual, are drawn on;

There is an emphasis on problem-solving approaches, in which the processes of learning by doing, working and reworking, drafting and redrafting are valued as much as the finished product;

A creative curriculum is not only concerned with transmission of accumulated knowledge, but also with generation — with enabling students to take the initiative for their own self-development and to acquire the skills, understanding and flexibility to hand new situations with confidence.

This appears to me to be a very constructive framework for practical project work in GCSE Media Studies. It is not specifically designed for media education and in this respect can suggest ways in which common practice with other cross-curricular activities can be developed. In developing this argument, I propose to add my own observations relating to the specificities of video production.

'An environment which values experimentation' is precisely what is required where students are asked to study a range of media texts, to understand how narratives are constructed and coding systems are developed and are then required to produce their own texts. I would contend that both the projects described above show evidence of students grappling with forms and techniques, not in slavish imitation of broadcast media, but in an attempt to find an appropriate means of making a statement. In both cases there is also a recognition of different individual skills and contributions.

'Self-directed learning' is only possible in some form of workshop environment where teachers are genuinely resources available to each student and not primarily agents who construct problems for students to solve. The extended nature of video production allows for groups of students to be engaged in different activities at different stages of the production process (providing, of course, that there is enough equipment available). Again there is evidence in the projects described of a degree of self-direction, although it must be admitted that it is not a form of learning that young people who are used to a traditional relationship with a teacher-director find easy to handle. There was some evidence in my class that the traditional 'good' student found this more difficult than the student who found the formal classroom alienating. There is an opposite problem which I have encountered with adult students, where the teacher may be monopolized by a single student who fails to recognize that the teacher is a resource for everyone in the class.

'Negotiating and renegotiating learning activities' is an attractive ideal, but one which may prove difficult to implement. For the GCSE project the parameters are already set and in that sense the potential for renegotiation is limited. However I was happy that students changed their ideas as long as they discussed the reasons for changes. As long as practical work includes some formal process of self-evaluation and reflection it need never be simply an 'expressive' act. It is possible to posit evaluation as the final stage in video production, especially if it is directly related to screenings for the target audience.

'The value of groupwork' in video production is of paramount importance. In the range of different types of skill and understanding required, video and film production have few parallels. They require collaborative work within which individuals might be expected to display communication, presentation or performance skills in front of camera, technical skills in operating equipment, social skills in organizing a crew and performers and on top of that to develop ideas as to the form of the finished product. It is no wonder that students of average ability find it a daunting prospect — quite a few teachers find it difficult as well. Why then have media educationists paid so little attention to this specific problem?

In a society which promotes the individual so assiduously and an education system which remains based on individual achievement, it is not surprising that some students find collective enterprise a bewildering experience and 'let each other down', as the students in Group B discovered. Here is an argument for linking evaluation of practical work with analytical work on TV as an institution, as Jenny Grahame suggests in the next chapter. In the same way that students may learn about narrative structure by constructing their own narratives, so may they learn about institutional structures for collective work by attempting to organize themselves into a production team. This is how the 'professional emulation' argument should be articulated. I'm not sure that the students discussed here reached that point and certainly I was not able to make those links. I am convinced, however, that an extended project is the best way to explore such concepts.

Groupwork requires a high level of social skills. Not only do students have to develop working relationships but they have to do so under pressure: the production has a deadline, equipment failures and mistakes by other members of the group can mean repeating work several times leading to a build-up of frustration. Students who have 'succeeded' in their contribution have to accept the 'failure' of others and support them in producing a group achievement. For students who are not used to success this is a tall order and can be a real learning experience. In contributing ideas to a group project, students have to unlearn the notion of ownership: they must release their ideas to the group and see them criticized and amended. All of this requires a degree of maturity which marks the apogee of the learning process. The students in this study struggled to form teams in which members had distinct roles. Despite the pressures they succeeded collectively and in the evaluations offered by Sandra and Stuart it is possible to discern some acute observations about the development of relationships.

The notion that 'drafting and redrafting are valued as much as the finished product' alerts us to the primacy of process over product. This links to the self-evaluation in emphasizing that although *completing* the process is important, the recognition of what has been learned is what students should take from it. The students here did not draft and redraft as they should have done, largely because of their poor time management, but they solved problems and offered evidence of evaluation of process.

'Enabling students to take initiative' should be a central tenet of media practical work. The concept of education as empowering is coming back into favour at the start of the 1990s, and several Local Education Authorities have produced 'entitlement curriculum statements' which offer clear opportunities for media education. In an extended project students have the chance to take risks and to look outside the classroom and traditional skills. The rap performances of Sandra and Alan are a good example. Other students in the class organized productive interviews, one student with the Guardian Angels and the London Transport Police (successfully recorded over the telephone!). Another group gained access to a local recording studio and recorded a video interview with a record producer.

The creative curriculum provides a framework to which must be added those elements of video production which relate directly to the 'core concepts' of media theory. There is evidence here that the students made use of their theoretical knowledge in relation to three of the core concepts — namely forms, audience and institution (they had not yet undertaken work on representation, even if they do show awareness of some of the issues).

In formal terms it is clear that the two productions both draw upon knowledge of a relatively specialized television genre, that of the rap video in particular and graphics-orientated youth programming in general. The approach is not 'alternative'. Rather it is consciously chosen to appeal to a specific audience and it is clear that the students are well aware of their construction of the style. Gordon, who has difficulty articulating his ideas, spoke about the use of graphics in such programmes as 'making things you might not know about appear interesting'. In fact, of course, the student productions were concerned with a culture which both producers and audience knew very well. It is worth noting that both videos fed into and commented on a college culture which has been promoted successfully over the last few years by means of a Student Union Fashion Show which has been recorded by media students and circulates on videotape. Several of the GCSE students played prominent roles in these shows and I am sure that there is a whole exchange system of cultural codes operating in these videos which is beyond the ken of staff in the college who wouldn't know a Troop training shoe from a Clark's sandal.

The appeal to a 'college culture' also raises the issue of resistance to the 'official culture' of the college as an institution and the peripheral and subordinate nature of black youth culture within broadcast media. The discussion at the end of Group B's production offers an effective refutation of the dominant representation of rap as a degenerate form — a clear example of Hornsby's 'progressive content' in an appropriate form.

The extended projects described here have at least the potential to confound the misgivings of the Ferguson/Masterman orthodoxy on practical work and to meet the more optimistic objectives of Hornsby and Arthurs. I have argued for an extended notion of 'creativity' which sees students developing a practice based on experience in a specific institutional context and which leads to a real understanding of the process of production and the development of useful skills and knowledge which in turn inform and feed on theoretical work. An approach which offers extended project work, carefully integrated with practical exercises of a more closed nature, is a model which not only leads to effective learning in Media Studies GCSE but is also a powerful argument for media education across the curriculum.

[I would like to acknowledge the work of my co-tutor on the course, Joan Marshrons, without whom this research would not have been possible.]

Notes

1 Masterman (1985), p.26.
2 City and Guilds of London Institute (CGLI) and Business and Technician Education Council (BTEC) are the two main vocational education examination and validation bodies. They both offer certification of media courses and in 1984 they were jointly responsible for the launch of the Certificate in Pre-Vocational Education (CPVE).
3 Ferguson (1981).
4 See Ferguson (1969).
5 Masterman (1980), Chapter 8.
6 Masterman (1985), pp.26–27.
7 See Buckingham (1987a) and Grahame (1990).
8 Hornsby (1984).
9 Arthurs (1987).
10 Simons and Bethell (n.d.).
11 All the video production work described in this paper utilized the following equipment:
Panasonic M7 Camcorder, 2 x Panasonic F10 Cameras and N180 Recorders, Unitron Mixer/Edit Controller/TBC, Tascam 8-track Mixer, Amiga A500 Computer.
This represents a level of equipment provision now increasingly available in Further Education colleges.
12 Students' names have been changed.
13 'Vocational Preparation' is a generic term to describe the curriculum development of the late 1970s and early 1980s which attempted to create provision for young people unqualified for entry into

traditional vocational education courses at a time of high youth unemployment. *Vocational Preparation* was the title of an FEU publication of 1981. See also note 16 below.

14 Stafford (1983).
15 See *A Basis For Choice*, FEU (1979), a proposal for a progressive educational initiative in Vocational Preparation which was effectively scuppered by the rapid implementation of the Youth Training Scheme. *Basic Skills*, FEU (1982a), is indicative of the impact of the Manpower Services Commission.
16 FEU (1985). This document represents an intervention by the FEU in the debates surrounding the implementation of CPVE.

Chapter 5

Playtime: Learning about Media Institutions Through Practical Work

Jenny Grahame

Introduction

Among the many conventional wisdoms underpinning the practice of media education, the claims which are most fiercely defended are often the hardest to evaluate. For example, the 'best' classroom practice has tended to be based on assumptions about the intrinsic value of active learning and of practical work as a means of understanding the processes and institutional structures of media production. These assumptions mark a transition from a text-based lit-crit approach to media study to the concept-based experiential model which now informs GCSE and TVEI courses; and they have increasingly characterized the changing shape of classroom practice, curriculum planning, and examination syllabuses.

Yet evidence of the value of hands-on experience of media production is notoriously difficult to assess. Having for many years trusted intuitively in — and argued interminably for — the importance of practical work in media education, and the need for a structured curriculum for it, I had begun to feel increasingly uncertain about how to evaluate its many outcomes, and how those outcomes were perceived and evaluated by the students themselves. When I undertook a piece of practical work, I knew what I wanted the students to learn, and had developed a range of strategies to ensure that they took away with them a variety of experiences and questions according to my own pre-determined agenda. But I had become increasingly aware that my agenda was not necessarily synonymous with theirs; that my meticulously pre-planned learning objectives were often redefined or amended according to the dynamic of the group; and that my observations and assumptions about what students had understood from the process frequently diverged from their own explicit analyses. I wanted to look at this more closely, to examine the factors that seemed to be important in shaping what and how students learned from practical work.

Like many teachers, the area of the media curriculum I had found most difficult to teach was that of media institutions. Teaching young people about the structure, ownership and economics of media organizations had always proved a less than motivating task, viewed from both sides of the blackboard. The pedagogic problems of transmitting vast quantitities of data about broadcasting legislation, patterns of power and influence, or the economic infrastructure of media production have been well documented,[1] as have a range of valid and accessible ways of exploring the area through more specific, localized study.[2] Nevertheless, the complexity of the topic, and my own very limited access to information, had led me to feel more confident about teaching it through practical activities.

In undertaking some classroom research, I was seeking to discover whether students' understanding of otherwise difficult or 'boring' areas of knowledge could realistically be developed through hands-on experience of media production. I wanted to monitor the social interaction of students during the negotiation and planning stages of a practical exercise, and the ways production roles were allocated and handled, in order to identify the factors which determined both technical performance and students' abilities to draw conclusions from it. I also expected to investigate a few half-formed hypotheses based on previous observations, intuition and gender theory — for example, how far aspects of the technology were annexed by the boys, whether girls really did take responsibility for editorial decisions and for the 'look' of the work, and how far qualities of physical coordination, confidence and assertiveness contributed to effective group learning.

But somewhere along the line, my focus changed — not once, but several times. At various stages, I found myself shifting from an evaluation of simulation as a methodology to an examination of the significance of social interaction, to an analysis of gender differences, and ultimately, to reflections on the process of students' own self-evaluation. These changes underline the significant problems involved in monitoring, evaluating and drawing meaningful conclusions from practical work — particularly where technology adds an extra dimension to the complex dynamic of group interaction. In fact these are precisely the issues faced by any Media Studies teacher attempting to evaluate students' practical work. They highlight both the contradictions and limitations of assessment practices, and the understandable problems experienced by students in evaluating their own work. In this respect, my account confirms the very real anxieties about evaluation voiced continually at all levels of media education and most frequently at GCSE moderation meetings. Ultimately, it will argue for more flexible and student-centred criteria, and for a broader redefinition of exactly what it is we are trying to assess.

Practical Simulations in Media Education

Simulation has been extensively used as a teaching method in media education to explore a range of processes, systems and practices. It is a logical extension of an enquiry-based, student-centred pedagogy which seeks to develop cognitive understandings of the media rather than define a prescriptive body of knowledge. It allows students to engage actively in decision-making and problem-solving in areas of the media to which they would not otherwise have access.

To a lesser or greater extent, most forms of simulation employed by media teachers relate to the concept of institution. Indeed, it could be argued that any practical exercise exploring the way meaning is produced is a form of simulation of professional practice: most practical media work aims to investigate the collaborative processes, industrial constraints and conventions which shape and determine media products.

There would seem to be three broad types of media simulation: those which are text-based and focus on the formal conventions by which meaning is produced; those which investigate specific production practices; and those which explore the processes of media institutions as systems.

The first category would include photoplay exercises such as *The Visit* or *The Station* or those contained in the *EyeOpeners* booklets.[3] These involve the selection, sequencing, captioning and contextualizing of still images, and are designed to examine the role of editing in constructing mood, atmosphere, genre and meaning. Students typically work in pairs as editor/directors to construct captioned photo-sequences. The tasks are sufficiently flexible to allow for a number of different perspectives or briefs, and result in a range of finished texts, which in turn lead to analysis and discussion of the effects of particular editorial choices.

The second category employs more complex material and structured working practices to examine the institutional constraints of media production. Here, students are organized into larger editorial groups with more specific production roles. In *Choosing the News*[4] for example, groups of students construct newspaper front pages from a range of pre-prepared news stories, headlines, and photographs to conform to different editorial stances. The activity centres on issues of representation, readership, newsworthiness, and editorial policy rather than accurately replicating the time or financial constraints of newspaper production. Other simulations such as *The Front Page* or *Radio Covingham*[5] seek to offer a more 'realistic' hands-on experience of news production. In both cases, pre-written news items have to be edited, redrafted, prioritized, and presented within a specific time-scale by production teams corresponding loosely to their real-life counterparts. Students thus experience how news is determined by constraints of time and space, and by (often unquestioned) 'news values', rather than simply by a pre-determined editorial viewpoint. Here again, the limited selection of material available allows for intensive comparison and a more focused range of outcomes.

The third category of simulation addresses more complex institutional issues, such as television scheduling,[6] the structure of the film industry,[7] or the marketing of pop music.[8] Generally these activities take longer to perform, and require participants to enact one or more specific negotiating roles in order to follow through a process from the initial idea to a notional finished product, which may be a text, a schedule, or a contractual arrangement. Thus, a film industry simulation might require students to participate in role as members of a production company devising a package for a particular film, or a distribution company planning its priorities in terms of target audiences, budgeting, and future marketing plans. The two groups will negotiate an appropriate deal, contract, and budget, and work towards a detailed treatment, script, publicity campaign and promotional materials. Within the participant groups, roles might be further broken down to allow individual students to experience specific elements of the production process, and to negotiate with each other. Unlike the previous categories, students are offered a structured brief for which they must generate original material, rather than selecting and re-editing pre-determined material; there is a wider range of institutional variables which offer a wider range of outcomes. Here again, the focus is on the process of negotiation and problem-solving as they constrain and determine the final outcomes, rather than on those outcomes as ends in themselves.

Playtime: the Task

Playtime, the production simulation I chose to research, is a development of this last category which draws on elements from the other two. While it uses role-play, problem-solving and group interaction techniques to explore the institutional systems which determine a particular genre of television programming, it also incorporates structured experience of production itself, and requires selection from pre-determined options to address issues of representation and audience. It also results in an end product in the form of a specific media text. It is therefore considerably more elaborate than many of the examples described above, and although its central focus is the concept of institution, it raises a number of other complex and inter-related issues.

As its name suggests, *Playtime* involves the production of a pre-school children's television programme along the traditional lines of *Playschool, You and Me, Rainbow* and, latterly, *Playbus*. Its author, Hugh Morris, has for many years run a Television Studio Workshop in the ILEA which, as well as facilitating student-devised productions, offers a number of structured production simulations and activities. These include news production simulations, exercises around sports coverage, narrative construction, the logistics of studio drama, selection, editing and captioning. As an experienced teacher, Hugh Morris has a pedagogic commitment and an understanding of young people unusual outside the classroom: this informs both the conceptual base of the activities on offer, and the quality of students' experiences of production, which are almost invariably positive, whatever the finished outcomes.[9]

Playtime was devised in response to teachers' demands for work which directly addressed the concept of institution. It involves students working in departmental groups to produce an episode of a fifteen-minute magazine programme for under-5s.

The team is given a tightly controlled budget, and required to select from a series of options, each of which is costed. Each department is responsible for the selection, scripting, *mise-en-scène* and finance of one or more contributory items, which are co-ordinated and approved by a producer with overall editorial responsibility for the programme. Thus, the 'department' (i.e. two or three students) responsible for songs must choose from a selection of nursery rhymes costed out in terms of performer, copyright, presentation, and visual elements: for example, a straightforward version of a finger-rhyme performed by the programme's presenter miming to a pre-recording costs nothing, but if toys, graphics, pictures, video extracts or additional singers are introduced, the cost is proportionately increased. Thus the department is forced to reconcile the need to make the item visually interesting and appropriate with both the demands of a limited budget and the editorial requirements of the producer, who can veto decisions on the grounds of expense, aesthetic interests, or a thematic approach.

Playtime includes departments for songs, stories, activities, video extracts, the programme's title sequence, and overall presentation (including number and role of presenters, the appearance of the set, and any regular or visiting toy characters). The material on offer has been selected to offer a number of possible links and themes (animals, families, transport, noises, etc.) which an astute producer can exploit. In each case, the departments' decisions are affected not only by their own specific costs but also by the requirements of other departments. Debates about appropriateness to the age group, education versus entertainment, and what makes 'good television' are thus located within 'real' industrial constraints of finance, time-scale, and editorial accountability.

As well as being responsible for the financial viability of the programme as a whole, the producer is required to judge this in relation to a projected series of ten programmes. S/he must weigh up the feasibility of over- or under-spending on this particular programme, and the implications for the rest of the series. Is it justifiable to exceed the budget for a first episode in the interests of attracting the audience but at the expense of later episodes, or is it wisest to play safe and stay within the budget no matter how televisually limiting? A fall-back strategy allows the possibility of injecting extra funding for selling the series to other channels, which can be exercised by the producer at the discretion of the class teacher.

Playtime was designed for groups of between ten and eighteen upper secondary students and takes a day to complete. The only advance preparation required, apart from basic familiarity with the working of the studio, is the screening of examples of pre-school children's programmes in the classroom prior to the studio visit. The day itself falls into two distinct stages, each taking about two-and-a-half-hours. In the morning students are briefed, volunteer for (or are nudged into) production departments, and plan their individual items. By lunchtime, the producer has approved or amended their selections. The rest of the day is spent in production; the original departments are dissolved, a studio crew is formed, and the overall programme is rehearsed and recorded. The crew consists of three camera operators, two sound engineers, a vision mixer, floor manager and a variable number of floor assistants, caption-changers and dogsbodies. Although the brief is open, most groups choose to have two on-camera presenters, who are the only non-crew personnel. Thus, every student is involved in both stages of the process, and encouraged to work on a variety of tasks in different groupings.

Conducting the Research

As a peripatetic advisory teacher, I was without a teaching group of my own and unable to undertake the sort of long-term obervation and follow-up I'd originally anticipated. However, I was able to gain access to a number of other teachers' classes, and could thus observe a single activity being conducted in a number of different contexts and at different levels across a range of teaching groups. I expected to be able to draw conclusions from a variety of evidence: from close observation of the groups at work; from an analysis of the decisions taken, and the reasons for them; from the finished products; and from students' own evaluations.

I observed *Playtime* with six different teaching groups, representing a broad spectrum of age, ability, context and institution. I adopted a fly-on-the-wall observer's position throughout the different versions of the simulation. The level of activity in the studio was invariably so intense that my presence was ignored, although I was occasionally approached for technical or linguistic advice by students, and during the final recording I sometimes assisted an under-staffed crew as caption-changer or general dogsbody. However, when the final programmes were screened for debriefing, my views as an 'objective outsider' were solicited and listened to attentively.

During the simulation I recorded my impressions in note form. I recorded as accurately as possible who did what in both stages of the process to see if there was any correlation between the sorts of tasks students opted for and to analyze their groupings. I itemized decisions taken by each department, and the basis on which they were made; and listed the points at which I saw evidence of particular sorts of understanding.

With one fourth-year all-girls group, whose work will be described in greater detail below, I developed what was probably the most useful combination of approaches. I was able to work in much closer collaboration with the class teacher, for example in devising a helpsheet for written evaluation of the exercise, and a follow-up assignment designed to apply their experience. I also attended and recorded the debriefing session back in school where they reviewed and discussed their finished programme. In fact the most interesting issues raised by this group were generated by an analysis of their written work, perhaps because this is a more familiar and measurable form of evaluation, but also because it is at this stage that the tensions between an active pedagogy and a pre-determined theoretical framework often become most significant. It is this issue that I will be concentrating on in the final section of the chapter.

Analyzing an exercise of this kind poses enormous research problems. Purely logistically, the range of different activities involved made it extremely difficult to monitor. At any one time during the production stage, for example, there were six sub-groups, each engaged in reviewing material, calculating expenditure, debating the value of their choices, scriptwriting, or arguing over the distribution of labour. The following account therefore offers some general observations on the main stages of the exercise.

Planning the Programme

To observe the process of allocating roles in any sort of practical work provides many insights into the dynamics of collaborative work: how and why students select particular roles (or fail to volunteer for them), the basis on which they form partnerships, and the criteria by which they assess their own production abilities are intimately related not only to their own self-image, but also to their perceptions of the activity itself — and clearly have a direct effect on its outcomes. This is particularly true of *Playtime*, where learning about the institutionalized division of labour is a central aim of the exercise.

The way all six groups selected their individual roles seemed to indicate considerable understanding of the production process. The notion of departments, and their functions, needed little explanation, and students generally opted quickly and enthusiastically for particular teams, making their choices on the basis of perceived skills and abilities. However, in most cases the producer was the final role to be allocated, and students expressed considerable reluctance to take on its responsibilities.

There were also considerable gender differences here. Departments tended to reflect friendship groups, and were frequently single-sex. Boys tended to volunteer more readily for departments involving hardware — such as the title sequence department, which involved computer graphics, and the video department — while girls opted for the activities, presentation and songs departments. Similarly, in discussion, girls tended to focus far more frequently on the needs of the pre-school audience, both in choice of material and presentation, and in debate about the learning functions of their items. In general they had a clearer sense of how items could be presented visually, and how they might be understood by young children. Boys on the other hand appeared to be more interested in the technical effects they might be able to achieve through vision-mixing and camera-skill — many of which seemed inappropriate for their audience and ultimately did not materialize in the final programme. These observations may simply reflect the fact that young women usually spend more time than their male peers caring for younger siblings and may thus watch more pre-school TV. But the production stage of the simulation revealed similar differences in terms of the division of labour and performance, which suggest that this is an area worth investigating more rigorously.

An interesting feature of every group I observed was the intensity and articulateness of discussion about the nature of the programme and the choices to be made. I had feared that these discussions might be laboured and disaffected, given the conventional nature of the material groups were working with; however, they were lively, motivated and full of personal anecdote, fond memories of childhood viewing, and sparky ideas for alternatives. Significantly, however, I did not once overhear any reference to work that had gone on in the Media Studies classroom, to the pre-studio viewing, nor to the key concepts of representation or audience, although these had been raised explicitly at the start of the day. The fund of personal experience of pre-school television, and the ability to mimic and parody programmes they could not possibly have been old enough to have seen themselves, were staggering. But if there was any application of Media Studies understandings, it was implicit rather than conscious.

Perhaps even more crucially, however, these discussions turned out to be quite unimportant in terms of the production itself. The most striking feature of the way sub-groups worked was the overwhelming priority of keeping to a budget, which for most was the central factor (and for one or two, the *only* factor) in their decisions. In this sense, the simulation was successful in encouraging students to think of the programme as a product. However, the extent to which financial considerations dominated their planning often outweighed their considerations of audience. For example, none of the activities departments really managed to reconcile their educational aims with their concern to work within their budget: despite intense discussions about the learning needs of under-5s, when it came to the crunch their interesting and often imaginative ideas were dropped in favour of the cheapest alternative. At the same time, the departments constantly tried to break out of the constraints of the simulation, usually by attempting to liaise with other departments to influence the shape and theme of the programme — which according to their brief was clearly the producer's responsibility. In three cases, individual departments decided that the items should be linked by an animals theme, convinced their colleagues, and then presented the producer with a *fait accompli*. Two other groups arrived accidentally at a similar focus.

These attempts to unify the programme came from heated and intelligent argument about the nature of pre-school television. But somewhere between the negotiation process and the final recording, these considerations got lost. It was as if students could only think through the intention of the programme as a whole by deviating from the constraints of the simulation and the professional practices it replicated, and this in turn inhibited their ability to conceptualize their own individual items. There seemed to be an underlying conflict between two opposing aims within the structure of the simulation itself. On the one hand students were experiencing the constraints of working institutionally in a hierarchical structure, to major budgetary restrictions; yet they were also confronting issues of representation, and being expected to think through 'alternatives' to conventional children's TV — an impossible task under such circumstances.

Similarly, the time-schedule and the intensity of the activity left students little space for explicit reflection or analysis, so that many of the insights of their planning discussions were not shared with their peers, and sank without trace, never to resurface in the programme or in their final evaluations. While this was an intended reflection of professional practices, there was a sense in which the students were inhibited by precisely those factors which had been designed to generate conceptual understanding and enquiry.

The end-of-day debriefing session, the first point at which teacher intervention and analysis was possible, was thus an essential moment in the learning process. But by the time students came to watch their final product, they had worked under such intensive pressure to complete in time, and had become so emotionally involved in the logistics and performance aspects of their programme that evaluation almost invariably focused on technical issues, how far departments had worked within their budgets, and comparisons with the professionals, rather than on the process itself. The last thing students wanted to do was to re-examine their decisions, their objectives and the implications of working in this way. Any explicit analysis of such institutional factors would have to take place back in the classroom, at some distance from the experience of production.

A further — and less intentional — complication to the departmental structure was the crucial importance of the producer's role. Although this was most clearly articulated in the all-girls group, none of the producers was able to divorce the demands of this authoritative role from their desire to retain the approval of their peer group. In every group, the producer ultimately acceded to the decisions made by departments, rather than risking personal unpopularity. However able, well-organized and assertive individual producers were, there seemed to come a point at which the realities of group interaction, and personal anxieties and histories intruded on the simulation process. Often, the desire to avoid conflict resulted in an artificial consensus which worked against the interests of both the final product and the conceptual objectives of the simulation.

The Production Process

In the second stage of the simulation, the departmental structure is abandoned, and students are recruited into roles as studio crew and on-camera presenters. Here, as before, the process of role allocation seemed to relate intimately to issues of gender and peer pressure. This was particularly apparent in the case of two key production roles — the on-camera presenter and the director, which despite their prestigious status (indeed, perhaps because of it), were extremely difficult to fill. In the case of the presenters, this was perhaps predictable, given the exuberant wackiness of their professional counterparts. Many boys explicitly refused the role on these grounds, although, as was noted acidly by several girls in mixed groups, this also seemed to relate to the pre-school nature of the audience, which was far more inhibiting for boys than for girls. In contrast, there was competition for the role in the all-girls group, where students seemed far more confident about public performance and the perceived demands of the role. Similarly, students were wary about volunteering for the role of director: they were well aware of its authority and unpalatable responsibilities, and unwilling to risk failure. Most frequently the role was accepted by whoever had been producer, on the grounds that s/he had already acquired an overview of the programme and its requirements: most programmes ended up with female directors.

Despite the focus in this and other simulations on process rather than product, the final programme represents not only an important outcome for students, but also a public exposure which many seem to find unpalatable. This tension between the desire to make a good programme and the reluctance either to accept responsibility for it or to be seen by one's peers to be fronting it may be an understandable consequence of adolescent insecurity. Yet it is a major influence on the outcomes of much Media Studies practical work, and hence on students' perceptions of what they have learned and achieved.

Crew roles, too, were divided along lines of gender, although again not always in predictable ways. Boys overwhelmingly opted for the relatively undemanding but apparently high-tech jobs of camera operator or sound engineer. Interestingly, girls rather than boys volunteered for the challenging role of vision mixer, which requires considerable coordination and concentration, and employs the highest-tech equipment. However, they also monopolized the unglamorous but essential position of floor manager, liaising between control room and studio floor, cueing presenters, organizing caption-changes and set, and maintaining a working atmosphere, often in fraught situations — generally carrying the can for the performance element of the production. This role was openly spurned by many boys for its non-technical nature, but again perhaps also because of the responsibility it carried. Girls seemed more aware of its importance and more confident with the organizational and diplomatic abilities it requires.

The allocation of roles was obviously significantly different for the all-girls group.

Here, there was fierce competition for cameras and vision-mixer, while the floor manager was hard to recruit and resentful of her position. The technology appeared to constitute little threat, and students were not only more critical and perfectionist in their approach, but also more interested in the process of the production than other groups. They also collaborated far more effectively and supportively as a team; their confidence as crew members, and the sympathetic way they dealt with each other's mistakes and miscues throughout the production stage was quite different from the behaviour of mixed groups, which was often accusatory and occasionally abusive as tempers grew frayed. These girls had had four years of single-sex schooling behind them, and despite a highly disciplined convent-school environment, they had not been inhibited by the institutional parameters, curriculum expectations, and male peer-group pressures of their co-educational counterparts. Superficially at least, their performance would seem to confirm the value of all-girls groupings in areas of technology perceived as conventionally male.

Finished Products

I have described the production process in some detail because in many ways it was far more revealing than the resulting programmes, which were devastatingly similar, despite differences in age and ability. On one level, this was only to be expected, given the parameters of the simulation, its limited range of material, and its broadcast models. Within the limits of departmental budgets, students had the option of experimenting with alternative voice-overs to video extracts, importing images to accompany songs, or constructing personalities round toys or animals. Yet these options were tightly constrained by time and money, resulting in almost identical sequences and selections from programme to programme.

The material provided — Old Macdonald, Puffing Billy, cuddly animals on video, etc. — had been selected to offer conventional, familiar qualities which could be challenged by the inclusion of a multi-cultural story or high-tech graphics; yet it set a particular agenda for the final programme which did not encourage students' creative or analytical abilities, and lent itself only too well to parody. It was hardly surprising that the activity often appeared to be reinforcing, rather than questioning, students' existing assumptions and prejudices about children's television.

Thus, while there were opportunities for variation, innovation, and subversion, very few groups made use of them. Although the brief specified a particular combination of items for the programme, the presentation, sequence and delivery were left deliberately open, as was the activities slot. It was hoped that this would offer room for students to exercise creative choices, to exploit performance skills, and to make the programme 'their own'. However, in each case, these 'open spaces' were completely unplanned, unscripted, and unorganized even up to the final rehearsal.

This resulted in improvised performances, at best relying heavily on pastiche and parody of the Joyce Grenfell variety, and at worst, mumbled embarrassment. In part, this was due to the universal failure both of the planning departments to think through their ideas in the face of financial considerations, and thus to brief the studio crew and performers adequately, and of the directors to take responsibility for the creative aspects of the production. But primarily it seemed to be because the simulation failed to offer sufficient spaces for reflection, in which institutional pressures and creative ideas could be reconciled.

Despite the improvised nature of the presenters' performances, it has to be said that they were at times extremely funny, usually intentionally so. Interestingly, the humour seemed to derive from a fund of shared references to a pre-*Playschool* form of children's TV nearer to *Watch with Mother* than anything else. This was parallelled by particular choices of music and commentary which seemed to come straight from *Uncle Mac* and *Children's Favourites* — programmes with which they could not possibly have been familiar. How far these references were inherent in the choice of material, or derived from contemporary parodies, or purely random, was unclear. Certainly there was ample room for mickey-taking in the original source material, and the obvious pleasure and familiarity with which the presenters acted out their parental roles suggested a great affection for their own pre-school viewing.

Nevertheless, there seemed to be a considerable discrepancy between the serious and intense discussions of intentions at the planning stage, and the delivery of the final product. The embarrassment of being seen by one's peers to be fronting a kids' show may well militate against a straight delivery, particularly for boys, whose performances were much more parodic. In contrast, only the all-girls group managed to play the presentation straight: they elected two presenters, whose performances were very much extensions of their own personalities, and who were able to bluff their way blithely through various technical hitches without resorting to parody.

These discrepancies between planning and performance seemed to offer ample illustration of the points we wanted students to learn about. But for students themselves, the issues were less clear-cut. The evidence of the complex processes they had negotiated was invested in a single fifteen-minute tape, towards which even the most articulate and reflective students expressed ambivalence in the debriefing sessions. In the absence of objective criteria for assessing the process, it was impossible to avoid evaluating their performance.

Post-production debriefing sessions are never the most illuminating experiences: students are too wound up with the tensions of production to look analytically at the implications of their products until much later. Every session followed a similar pattern: initial hilarity and praise for presenters, whatever their weaknesses, followed by intense scrutiny of technical errors, skilful vision-mixing, dodgy camera work and so on; barbed comments on the relative professionalism of the programme and its presenters; and finally self-congratulation for having achieved any result at all under the circumstances. At the beginning of the debriefing, the groups were presented with a financial statement, which Hugh Morris later itemizes and sends back to school for further evaluation; during the sessions this was frequently referred to as the justification for any perceived inadequacies in the programme, rather than an organizing principle for their work. It was clear that they had gained an implicit understanding of the processes they had worked through; but what they talked about was their product.

Part of the rationale for simulation as a teaching method is the assumption that the process is an end in itself, and that the outcome or product is only as important as the learning it exemplifies. From my experiencce of *Playtime*, this begs a number of questions. Firstly, it does not take into consideration the significance that products may have for students. How far students are able objectively to evaluate the processes underpinning their production may ultimately depend on what they perceive as the 'quality' of that production, when compared with professional standards. Yet if the end product of a simulation is intended to reflect a learning process, by what alternative criteria should we evaluate it?

In a highly structured simulation such as *Playtime*, there may be few opportunities for students to exercise personal choice or develop creative responses, and this may ultimately inhibit real analysis. In this case, the limited material was intended to distance the students whilst allowing them to draw on their own cultural and media experiences. But on the evidence of their final programmes, the agenda set by the simulation militated against innovation or challenge. The only real option for students to make use of their own experiences was through token resistance — through parody or pastiche.

Learning What's Been Learned

This section focuses more closely on the all-girls group mentioned above, in order to investigate the final — and most crucial — stage of the simulation: the evaluation process. I have already outlined the difficulty in identifying the conceptual learning which takes place during the course of a production, and the inadequacy of the finished product as a measure of its effectiveness. Similarly, my experience of conventional self-assessment strategies — diary-keeping, log-writing, group discussions and presentation — has been that these frequently reveal more about the limitations of the simulation itself, and the social interaction of the participants, than the media learning that has taken place. Teachers have always assumed the acid test of practical work to be the extent to which it enables students to transfer their conceptual understandings to other media processes and institutions. Yet recent experience of GCSE assessment has revealed only too clearly the difficulties students face in articulating and applying their learning within the limitations of existing forms of evaluation.

In the double lesson immediately following the studio visit, the students reviewed their work far more objectively and analytically than during their initial debriefing. The first part of their discussion focused almost exclusively on the technical weaknesses of their programme, of which they were both proud and critical. Each image, camera angle and line of dialogue was deconstructed and accounted for, initially anecdotally, but increasingly in relation to the meaning it might hold for its pre-school audience.

This close scrutiny revealed two contradictory features. Firstly, it was immediately apparent that their understanding of their audience had in fact informed their programme, however flawed — and that they were very aware of the ideological nature of the material. For example, their story had been selected because it was the only item in the programme to offer multi-cultural images; yet in evaluation, they were critical because there was no girl in the narrative, and the women were represented in conventional domestic roles. Similarly, they had consciously decided against the use of a doll in the programme because they wished to avoid sexism. The songs had been chosen for the physical activity and repetition they entailed, but students were highly critical of their middle-class settings and performance. Discussion of the sequence and variety of items revealed a sophisticated understanding of the concentration-span and needs of their audience, and considerable dissatisfaction with both the nature of the material on offer, and their own use of it.

At the same time, only in close analysis did students begin to realize the range of choices that had been open to them, and the opportunities they had missed. For example, their story, which was presented as a series of illustrated captions, was the most difficult of the alternatives to record, and they shot it very badly, misframing particular images, moving others, and so on; it was also far too long to hold its audience. The episodic nature of the story would have enabled them to edit it into a far tighter and more manageable unit, but this possibility did not occur to them until after the event. It was immediately clear to them how much this was a function of the institutional context: the division of labour, time-scale and financial constraints had militated against clear thinking and forward planning.

Threading through the discussion was a sense of bringing to the surface and making explicit knowledge and understanding about television which students had not previously recognized. Analysis of their botched story led into a discussion of rostrum camerawork; an inspection of the way they had spent their budget raised questions about the economics of series production and scheduling; there were constant references to the *mise-en-scène* of Wogan, the conventions and constraints of the News, and so on. Clearly the simulation had activated a fund of experience and knowledge they already had but had never valued. The most frequent comment was 'I sort of knew but never really thought about it like that before'.

What also began to emerge was the way in which they perceived their work to be inhibited by their interaction as a group. Although this group was much more conciliatory and cooperative than other groups, it did not always function effectively.

Nevertheless, the students' loyalty to each other precluded direct criticism, just as the group's desire to maintain equilibrium in the studio worked against the coherence of their programme. This sense of shared responsibility and unwillingness to apportion blame was unique among the groups, and must in part have derived from their unusually strong sense of group identity. But the priority given to social interaction and collaboration in both oral and written evaluation is typical of many students' responses to practical media work. For many students it may be far more significant than the conceptual learning it is designed to encourage.

Following this discussion, students were asked to produce a written evaluation for their GCSE coursework folders. In comparison with the class discussion, however, these seemed to tell a rather different story. They were invariably descriptive, anecdotal and bland. Although we had provided a carefully structured helpsheet, the majority tended to be chronological accounts detailing the minutiae of the production process, involving interminable lists of who did what, what the choices were, and what the end result looked like. This was entirely compatible with all my previous experience of log-writing, which I have always found a profoundly disappointing exercise. Several students ignored our guidelines altogether, and all bar the two most able girls omitted the more difficult questions about what they felt they had learnt from the process. None of them reflected the excitement, intensity and pleasure of the experience; nor, for the purpose of assessment, did they offer much explicit evidence of how their understanding of media institutions had developed during the simulation. In the main they focused squarely on the limitations of their own product, but far less analytically than in discussion.

However, a few students did attempt to identify what they thought the experience had taught them. In the hands of a more academically able student, the account reads like this:

> My experience of producing *Playtime* taught me a lot about the television industry. I never realised how much work went on behind the scenes, how much preparation and time was spent on the programme before the actual filming. I also never realised so many people, departments and money were involved in just one programme. The fact that more time was spent on preparing the programme than the actual filming shocked me, I think now the filming is quite easy and quicker. I think it's a shame that the presenters are so well praised and looked up to for the job they do and that no attention is directed towards the people behind the scenes as they do a very hard and important job.
>
> (Sharon)

On one level, these are fairly mundane insights, but they do indicate a genuine sense of demystification directly related to Sharon's personal investment in the experience: she had been responsible for the choice of story, and, as camera operator, for recording it

— perhaps the weakest moment of the programme. Although throughout her log she attempts to predict how the programme might have looked without constraints of finance and time, her focus is strictly on the parameters of her own experience. When she attempts to make more general points, her writing sounds like commonsense knowledge rather than the analysis she was able to apply to other forms of television in group discussion.

> From my experience any TV programme is affected by having to produce within a very tight budget because their choices are limited in each department, with more money you could improve the set, have better standard videos, more enjoyable songs, cartooned stories etc. On the whole have a much better standard of programme, but the reasons why programmes are strictly organised is so that the series has been fairly put together, it could be stupid to spend a lot of money on one programme leaving only a small amount for the following. So with these strict rules each programme is equally produced.

In fact, this rather laboured and generalized comment implies considerable understanding not only of the constraints imposed on the genre, but also of the economics of series production; what's missing is an ability to reference other examples, to make broader comparisons, and to raise questions about how and why the industry works in this way. But isn't that ability an awful lot to expect from a 15-year-old, no matter how able? How many teachers could articulate more clearly their understanding of a complex and inaccessible system of power relationships and industrial practices from the basis of a simulated experience?

The following extract from Ann's log seems to epitomize the difficulties many students experience in trying to meet the agenda we as teachers set for them. Ann was the presenter who carried the show and improvised through the various disasters. A Band Three student, described as academically weak, she was a lively and committed participant throughout the production process, quick to improvise, and intuitively responsive to the needs of her audience. Her contributions to the group follow-up discussion were bright, funny, and intelligent. But committing her experiences to writing resulted in work like this:

> [The producer] had made decisions that I disagreed with because she said that I should use paint which I would like to use colour pencil. She should had made a decision on useng the toys and showing it to. The Producer role is important to the programme makers because if there was no producer everyone will not know what to do and will be uncontroled and confused ... The decision were not made sensibly they just happened. There was a lot of teamwork help in this programme ... The professionals only stick to one job because if they swop around something can go wrong

so they need to know who made that thing to go wrong to make things right.

Ann's writing suggests a struggle to make sense of her own experience and articulate it in a form with which she is not at ease. She wants to make connections between what actually happened and what she thinks we want her to have learned; but she is doubly handicapped both by her limited writing skills and by the limitations of her own intensely-felt experience. We can read her learning from between the lines, but not on the page itself.

In some ways, the evaluative skills we expect in log-writing are not dissimilar from those required in a conventional 'A' level English Literature essay — a form which many teachers have found deeply unsatisfying in itself. The field may be different, but the skills are not: 'objective' deconstruction balanced against personal response; a body of conceptual knowledge about how language works, whether literary or televisual; and the articulation of personal experience, whether of reading or production, into an acceptable framework in appropriate language whose parameters are defined according to criteria far removed from those of the students. Add to this the extra dimensions of writing in literary mode about experiences which are essentially audio-visual, and the influences of the group dynamic on what is learned, together with the informational and technical aspects of knowledge about media institutions and processes, and it is hardly surprising that students' work so rarely meets our expectations. Reading these laboured accounts of *Playtime* has confirmed my view of the inadequacy of written self-evaluation, whether as a means of assessing what students have learned or of helping them to identify and articulate their own learning. There has to be a better way.

An Alternative Production

In addition to the written log, we designed a follow-up task which attempted to gauge how far students were able to apply the institutional understandings they might have gained from *Playtime*. This involved devising a proposal for a Channel Four pre-school programme, without financial constraints. The submission was to include a detailed outline, a title sequence, a storyboard for an opening sequence, and rough costings, together with a detailed rationale. By deliberately reducing the importance of the financial element, and by prioritizing the question of audience needs, we hoped students would produce very different types of programme, and that they would then be able to reflect on these differences and on the institutional factors which gave rise to them.

Furthermore, we wanted to offer students the opportunity to develop their ideas creatively, to draw on their own cultural experiences and identities, and to set their own agendas for pre-school learning. We had been unhappy about the white middle-class bias of *Playtime*: while it was necessary for the purposes of the simulation, we were concerned that it might have reinforced rather than challenged dominant conventions and representations. So we were relieved when students actively took up these issues in their discussion and began to articulate critical notions of representation, rather than simply resentment.

The writing which the students delivered was of a very different order from that of their logs. It was unequivocally subjective, full of anecdote and personal reminiscence:

> For starters I remember when I was a child, I enjoyed making things like paper airoplanes, plastersine models, etc. These are fun to do and also teach the child how to use their hands. . . . I enjoyed creativity. I like creating my *own* things. Paper collarges with different substances such as milk bottle tops, feathers, different coloured paper is a creative activity so I'd include that.
>
> (Sharon)

This informal, direct mode of address was evident in most of the students' work. It was obviously an assignment perceived on one level to be much closer to autobiographical writing, and therefore less threatening; but it was also clearly much more pleasurable as a task.

In addition, the writing invariably demonstrated a meticulous sensitivity to the concerns and educational needs of their target audience. Among the topics mentioned were items about the arrival of a new baby, a whole range of lively strategies to develop an understanding of road safety, and — surprisingly frequently — activities designed to promote books rather than simply to develop reading skills. Notions of 'everyday life' recurred throughout the work — in pointed opposition to what students perceived to be an unrepresentative view of the world constructed by adults for children in existing programmes. And everyday life, for several students, was far from the world of leaping penguins and *Alex and Roy* games represented in *Playtime*:

> So for my programme I would like a story to do with a child going out to different places. I'd like the story to describe the surroundings of the child, the busy roads, the big buildings, the people they see, etc. And for the video, the dangers of their surroundings. I think the video should show the dangers of children straying from their mothers, the dangers of the roads, the dangers of children going off with strangers . . . a child so young and innocent and I feel that is vital it knows the dangers around it.
>
> (Sylvia)

Here Sylvia may be voicing her own adolescent anxieties and privileging her preconceptions about children's vulnerability over her sense of appropriate content.

But these sorts of issues emerged throughout the students' work, indicating a very different agenda from the one determined for them in *Playtime*.

Despite a completely free hand in terms of programme content and structure, most students' work remained fairly close to the magazine format of *Playtime*, but significantly made it their own. Most felt that a combination of short varied items would be most appropriate for pre-school children's concentration span, but then constructed elaborate and often innovative variations around it. This was the point at which they began actively to make use of what they had learned from the *Playtime* experience. For students almost invariably emphasized the importance of a theme to each programme — a direct reflection on their own problems in achieving this in the studio:

> For example if one week they were doing something on farms, there will be a story read which would relate to farms, there would be videos shown of children who live on farms talking about what they do and what it's like on the farm. The people reading the stories would dress up in a costume that would go with the theme like dressing as a farmer, a stereotype of a farmer with straw and hay sticking all over them, something that would keep the children watching amused.
>
> (Adeswa)

Adeswa's work relates to a further issue raised in their own experience with *Playtime* — that of the identity of the programme's presenter. Her projected programme was a theme in itself — aimed at 4-to-6-year-olds 'who are showing signs of intelligence and like to read . . . . It would educate them and show them how to pronounce words and read sentences also a little about punctuation so that they would understand a little about why they have to use it.' But her *pièce de résistance* is:

> A funny little assistant called Bookworm. The programme will include a book club where the children can write in and obtain books at a reasonable price, and a story session . . . . The story will be short because it will be read again with the words coming up on the screen, Bookworm will go underneath each sentence pronouncing the words for the children and encouraging them to repeat. At the end the Bookworm will ask the presenter questions and the presenter will answer them.

Her work is lavishly illustrated with full-colour pictures of Billy the Bookworm.

While other students were less earnestly educational there was a range of genuinely inventive presentation ideas. Several opted for animated characters or puppets, including Sylvia, one of the *Playtime* presenters, who invented Freda the Space Alien glove puppet,

> . . . who'd look all green and fluffy but very lovable. The person operating

this puppet should sound gentle and happy. I'd like my programme to be called *Stop, Look and Listen to Freda*.

This implied connection between the programme's identity and the persona of its presenter relates directly to their experience of *Playtime*, where they had rejected the use of the toys on offer, mainly on grounds of gender and ethnicity. Interestingly, few of the presenters suggested here were human, and most were more or less androgynous, apart from their names.

Two further features reflected students' awareness of TV as an institution. In the rationales submitted with their proposals, many students argued coherently for appropriate budgets for their series, adjusting these according to the technical sophistication of the programmes. This was the section of the assignment which was not always completed; it seemed to indicate how far students felt confident with the concept of institution, and predictably, students such as Ann, who had enormous difficulty expressing her ideas coherently, omitted this part of the work.

The second indicator was the detail with which students conceived and visualized their work. Although not all students produced a storyboard, in almost every case the 'look' of the programme, its *mise-en-scène*, and the sorts of conventions it would observe were recorded lovingly in minute detail. Many students included colour illustrations of presenters, logos, titles and floor plans. Adeswa's work included a convincing representation of the presenter (a black woman) sitting in the studio surrounded by cameras, monitors and microphones, to illustrate the effect of Billy the Bookworm's sub-titles. This work suggested not only a sophisticated understanding of television conventions and industrial practices, but also a clear development from the random and un-visual way in which they had approached the production of their own programme. To this extent, *Playtime* seemed to have transformed the ways in which they thought about the construction of television.

What might we conclude from these different attempts at evaluation? Of all three approaches, the formal log-writing exercise seemed the most problematic, for reasons outlined above. The *Playtime* simulation — and much other production work — is often most valued by students for its difference from other kinds of learning, its connections with the real world of professional broadcasting, however tenuous, and the opportunities it offers for both individual responsibility and collaborative enterprise. It is also conducted outside the normal context of school, its pips and lesson-changes, and its conventional classroom hierarchy. Yet the form of log-writing which is required for examination purposes cuts across these differences: it brings it all back into school, into a conventionally teacher-directed context, where personal experience is ultimately secondary to a series of pre-determined learning objectives. This may devalue what for students was a genuinely radical learning experience; and judging by the evidence of students' logs, it almost certainly defuses the excitement and pleasure of the experience.

This may account for the curiously flat and impersonal tone of many students' logs, which in my previous experience is characteristic of formal self-assessment. It may also account for the enormous differences between the responses made in informal group discussion and those which surfaced in the *Playtime* logs. Perhaps this illustrates a mismatch between what students themselves perceived as appropriate language for examination assessment, and what they saw as classroom 'chat'. Certainly the interpersonal dynamic, which they identified in their discussion as one of the most significant areas of learning, was not adequately reflected in their writing; their perceptions of the nature of exam assessment may have discouraged them from explicit comment which might have reflected unfavourably on other members of the group.

The kinds of learning demonstrated in the more open-ended follow-up task seem to offer a far more positive approach to evaluation. The task enabled students to move outside the economic and ideological constraints of the original simulation. They were able to set their own agenda and to build upon their extensive and active experience as an audience — an aim which is frequently voiced by media teachers, but rarely fully addressed in practice. By offering a range of forms — storyboards, scripts, visual aids, as well as descriptive and transactional writing — it offered a wider range of opportunities for students whose skills are not conventionally literary. It made space for oppositional or innovative practices without actively penalizing those who feel safer in replicating conventional modes.

What this sort of task does not entail is an explicit account of the production process or an abstract definition of the concept of institution. Yet, as previously noted, these may be aims which are ultimately unrealistic and even counter-productive. So why do we routinely demand them — and demand them in a written form which experience has proved to be inhibiting, unrewarding, and undermining for many students?

One major function of 'objective' written evaluation is to enable us as teachers/examiners to identify the contributions of individual participants, and on this level it is a potentially useful recording strategy. Yet there is also a sense in which we demand it because we need evidence to justify practical work in traditional academic terms — and perhaps also because we are insecure about what students might be learning from it. However open-ended the project, we seem to need strategies which bring academic knowledge back to us in a safe and acceptable form. But by insisting that students must locate their individual accounts within a pre-determined 'objective' framework, we may be putting several important learning outcomes at risk. It may be that only by allowing students to write freely and subjectively about their own personal perceptions of the production process can we begin to reconcile *our* notions of appropriate learning with what *they* perceive as important to them. Perhaps it is at this interface between 'our' theory and 'their' practice that a new agenda for media education may be constructed.

Jenny Grahame

Conclusion

Despite carefully structured learning objectives, there were tensions inherent in the *Playtime* simulation which are typical of much practical work in media education. We were requiring students to work within tight institutional constraints, in unfamiliar working relationships, with intimidating technology. At the same time, we sought creative or innovatory responses to the brief which were incompatible with the hierarchical division of labour we had imposed. In effect, we had three distinct aims: to develop students' technical and production skills; to offer them the experience of working within institutional constraints; and to generate creative programme-making which questioned existing practices. While all of these were touched upon during the simulation, it became clear that these aims were both too demanding and potentially contradictory.

The evidence of *Playtime* suggests that however structured a framework, the physical intensity of production work militates against explicit reference to 'theory', and that previous analytical work may not simply transfer into practice. On the other hand, the students' final evaluations and follow-up work offer clearer evidence of a movement in the opposite direction, from practice to theory. What *Playtime* and other media simulations tend to lack are opportunities for reflection during the process itself. This might have been aided, for example, by introducing interim production meetings at various points to create space for reflection, for judicious teacher intervention, and for conscious consideration of their working practices, both in terms of the 'institutional' questions and in terms of the group dynamic. Relatively small organizational strategies would thus serve to contextualize the production experience for students and offer them a clearer sense of the purpose of the exercise, as well as enabling us as teachers to monitor more effectively what is actually being learned. We cannot assume that this sort of learning happens by osmosis; we need to actively construct the conditions and practices which will make it explicit for students.

Clearly, for many students, the most memorable and valuable aspects of the production process were to do with the experience of collaborative group work.[10] Yet this aspect of production work has never been fully acknowledged by Media Studies theorists, and is explicitly omitted from assessment practices, which are geared towards evaluation of the individual rather than the group. It is as if this crucial aspect of students' learning is considered part of another order of knowledge, subject to other criteria, unrelated to the conceptual framework of the syllabus. Yet the potential learning outcomes of practical work are multiple and diverse: we need to devise strategies which will enable both teachers and students to evaluate these, without reducing them to a set of abstract skills or understandings.

I would like to thank Eddie Lobo for his collaboration on this research.

Notes

1 For example, Masterman (1985), pp.72–77.
2 For example, Branston (1987); Alvarado, Gutch and Wollen (1987).
3 *The Visit* (Simons and Bethell, n.d.) and *The Station* are published by the ILEA English Centre. *EyeOpeners One and Two*, Bethell (1981).
4 *Choosing the News* is published by the ILEA English Centre.
5 *The Front Page* is published by the ILEA English Centre. *Radio Covingham* is published by the ILEA Learning Materials Service.
6 Masterman (1980), Chapter 7.
7 For example, Jenkins and Stewart (n.d.).
8 Blanchard, Greenleaf and Sefton-Green (1989).
9 The Television Studio Workshop was closed down in 1990 with the demise of the ILEA.
10 Interestingly, advocates of practical work within a broader media education approach have long recognized the importance of collaborative learning in terms not only of language, communication and social skills, but also of subject-specific skills: see Lorac and Weiss (1981).

Part Three
Reading Representations

Chapter 6

Teaching and Learning about Representation: Culture and *The Cosby Show* in a North London Comprehensive

Julian Sefton-Green

Many a media studies course begins with the concept of representation. It seems a natural place to start. It arouses passion and personal conviction; why can't the black characters in Albert Square escape from a life of crime; is the average adolescent boy a hooligan and a drunken slob; why does the average TV family comprise of a middle-aged middle-management executive, a housewife and a girl and a boy? Media studies teachers are often drawn to the subject precisely because of a sense of injustice in the way they feel the media 'represent' minority ideas or interests, and outrage at the evening's edition of *EastEnders* often gives rise to the lesson the following day. However, the idea of representation is deceptively simple. Although it is enshrined as a key concept in all media studies syllabuses and could be seen as a piece of specialist jargon it is also a very common idea. Any discussion of these issues in any classroom will instantly reveal a level of opinion and a range of example that can rival the staffroom. So how do our students understand and use the concept of 'representation', and what should we aim to teach them about it?

It was with this very large and abstract question that I began to explore the popularity of *The Cosby Show* within the particular context of a North London comprehensive school. I wanted to see how its enormous following in the school at large, among both black and white students, might be related to the fact that it features almost exclusively black characters. I hoped to examine the kinds of understanding about race and representation on TV available to upper school students, with special emphasis on the meaning of positive images and the significance of role models. It seemed to me that the programme was very 'up-front' in its message about how black people are usually represented on TV and I anticipated that this would act as a kind of prism to reflect students' understanding of the conceptual issues.

The Cosby Show: A Positive Image?

The Cosby Show is an American sit-com, now in its fourth series, revolving around the Huxtables, an affluent professional black family with five children living in a New York brownstone. Interestingly, both in its inception and reception *The Crosby Show* seems to have keyed into a fierce public debate about the representation of blacks on TV. There is an enormous amount of mythology surrounding both Bill Cosby's utterances and the supposed intentions of the programme itself. Nevertheless it seems to be generally agreed that there is a political purpose, a hidden agenda, to the programme. This much is clear from the kind of press coverage it tends to receive:

> 'The old image of the black family as a social problem is not simply conspicuous by its absence, it has been overturned.[1]
>
> The Show has broken new ground in British Television as an all-black situation comedy that dispenses with racial stereotypes and portrays blacks in comic, but non ethnic situations.[2]
>
> . . . one of the nicest things about it is that although it concerns a black family nobody ever makes a fuss or even refers to the fact.[3]
>
> . . . perhaps it has social significance too. For it conceivably represents black middle-class aspirations towards upward mobility — and away from alienated resentment.[4]

This kind of press coverage attempts to depoliticize race and somehow separate an idea of blackness from ethnicity. Yet it is precisely because of the ease with which the programme can be incorporated by racist critics (according to the *Daily Telegraph*[5] it was South Africa's most popular show, with high ratings among whites), and its success with all sections of the audience (it received *The War Cry's* approval in 1985), that it has been condemned by left and liberal critics alike.

Writing in *Channels*,[6] an American magazine, Brian Winston poses the liberal double bind. 'Is it better that *The Cosby Show* in redressing some of the damage done by a long line of stereotypes, creates a spurious picture of black privilege?' And deeply concerned about Cosby's popuarity 'with the American housewife', *City Limits*[7] claimed that the fabulous success of the show is 'only possible because of his [Cosby's] safe sanitised status. This isn't a comedy about black families or class, it's a comedy about the kind of black families with which white audiences feel comfortable.'

Thus both right and left popular criticisms of the programme focus on the alleged impact of the positive representation offered by the Huxtable household. Yet it is not just a one-way debate; stories about the programme's inception also reveal a desire to meet this popular awareness about stereotypes and positive role models : 'To make sure the show does not use negative stereotypes about race, women, or older people, Cosby has as consultant Dr Alvin Poussaint, the noted behavioural psychologist at Harvard.'[8]

Dr Poussaint explains his mission as follows: 'Part of what [Cosby] wants to change in American society [is] the negative image of blacks in the media and in this society in general. And he wants to provide hope and positive images to black children . . . in terms of expanding the concept of what blackness is.'[9] Yet the argument isn't just an aesthetic or political issue: it is also argued that the programme is a reflection of contemporary America. Poussaint again: 'There are plenty of middle class black families. But TV has given the impression that if it's not black it's not in the ghetto.'[10] And Cosby himself, playing out the myth beloved of American reviewers that the Huxtables are the Cosbys (and thus providing the perfect *post hoc, propter hoc* rationalization of this position) maintains the same argument: 'This is a black American family. If anybody has a difficulty with that, it's their problem not ours.'[11]

We will come back to this question of the ideal versus the realistic later, but Poussaint's main role seems to have been more on the former side of this dichotomy, as illustrated by the following stories, taken from *Newsweek*.[12] The first relates to a scene in which the little girl Rudy keeps squealing in pain when she is having her hair combed. This 'strikes the black psychiatrist as a reinforcement of the racial stereotype that kinky hair is somehow undesirable' and so the scene is cut. The second concerns the jokes Cliff makes about his son's messy room and poor performance at school. The jokes were toned down because they seemed in 'Poussaint's view, a perpetuation of the cliche that black males are less responsible and effecutal than black females.' The final anecdote from this article encapsulates what Poussaint calls above 'a new concept of blackness' and also refutes the *Daily Mail*'s[13] claim that nobody ever refers to the fact the programme is about a black family. Asked by NBC to remove the sign in Theo's room that reads 'Abolish Apartheid' because the network cannot endorse controversial positions, Cosby retaliates: ' "There may be two sides to apartheid in Archie Bunker's house" he fumes. "But it is impossible that the Huxtables would be on any side but one. That sign will stay on that door. And I've told NBC that if they still want it down, or if they try to edit it out, there will be no show" '. Given Cosby's reticence on racial issues (a fact that has irked all liberal/left commentators) the anecdote is even more revealing because it shows a concern with calculated effect — albeit on an unconscious level, rather than by direct statement.

However reliable these reports may be, it seems fair to say that part of the meaning (both social and textual) of the programme is the image of blacks that it offers, and that this ideological dimension is quite explicit in popular debate. It seems very likely that questions about the intent and realism of the programme will be an integral part of the way it is received, interpreted and talked about.

Teaching about Race and Representation

These concerns with the potential 'effects' of 'positive' or 'negative' images of black people are also at the heart of the traditional ways of teaching about race. Yet the debate about 'positive images' hinges on an unresolved double bind. As Poussaint says above, part of the aim of the programme was to 'provide hope and positive images to black children . . in terms of expanding the concept of what blackness is,' and to offer what *The Times* described as 'affluent role models in America'.[14] Yet this aim is always open to the criticism that it encourages an unrealistic idealism — that it is, in effect, a dangerous form of political utopianism, which neglects the realities of inequality and racism.

Furthermore, the notion that one can replace negative images by positive ones implies that both kinds of representation will have an equal and undifferentiated effect on audiences. Not only does this ignore the fact that audiences will read texts in different ways; it also implies that reading itself is a mere response, that it is an effect of the text. Poussaint's singling out of children as beneficiaries of this process if symptomatic of this approach: it rests on a view of children as particularly susceptible to the influence of powerful images and role models. Yet as we shall see below, many young people may well realize that idealized representations are unrealistic, and reject them for this reason — although, like many advocates of 'positive images', they may be unwilling to give up the idea that they may influence *other* people.

The notion of the stereotype is at the heart of most conceptualizations of positive and negative images. It is central to theories of what is vaguely and very grandly called 'the power of the image'. However, can we really say that TV programmes have the kind of power once attributed to the camera? A TV programme employs a variety of sophisticated codes in order to communicate: it does not work by 'exposing' meaning onto the 'silver-backed' paper of our minds, imprinting single uniform interpretations. The idea that stereotypes work in this fashion patronizes any viewer; the idea that children are especially prone to this form of brainwashing is one that can only be entertained by people who don't listen to children. In effect we need a new understanding of what people do with stereotypes rather than what sterotypes do to people if the idea of positive image is going to have any effect beyond that of good intentions.

Yet these assumptions about the power of the media have permeated most teaching in this area. Andrew Bethell's article 'Negative images, positive talk'[15] is a case in point. In the tradition of Barthes, the aim is 'to look at the way ideology works in the image, particularly in images of blacks and Asians, and then to suggest a few ways in which we might be able to redress the ideological balance of the classroom through trying to build up an awareness of how ideology dominates the meaning of the image.' The idea of 'redress' with its connotations of deficit schooling places the (ideologically sound) teacher in the hero's (gender intended) role, stripping the scales of ignorance from working-class kids' eyes. However this scenario is premised on a view that images have a special power, 'an immediacy and an intensity,' that children 'identify' with what they see and that therefore they are psychologically and ideologically at risk until teachers can create an awareness 'of how the dominant

ideology works so persistently against the development of Black identity.'
Deconstruction as a pedagogy requires this uneven balance of knowledge between
teacher and taught and rests on unfounded assumptions about the power of the media.
This particular tradition of teaching about race and representation hypothesizes the
object of intervention, working-class students, as passive readers, absorbing the
dominant ideology like a sponge and thereby having their identities moulded and
corrupted. There is of course an inbuilt rationale for the role of the teacher in this
position and as such it perpetuates the power relations of the school and validates the
knowledge of media studies as a subject discipline.

It is also fair to say that much of the media output discussed by this 'school' of
media studies is not contemporary; it often fails to connect with the material students
actually enjoy, or for that matter with the agenda set by the black film and video sector
today. Obviously historical material can provide pertinent sources for study, but it is
important to be aware of the constantly changing nature of the debate. Teaching about
more 'liberal' contemporary representations of black people, such as *The Cosby Show*,
will require a more complex, less propagandist approach.

The Research

In setting out to investigate these issues, I hoped to get beyond some of these
unsatisfactory assumptions about 'positive' and 'negative' images, about the 'power'
of the media and about the role of teachers as moral or political guardians. As I have
implied, we need to pay attention to the understandings that students have, rather
than the ideas we want them to have. We need to examine how those understandings
are formulated, developed and changed, rather than trying to impose a naive and
vacuous idealism.

It was with these considerations in mind that I began this research. I conducted
half a dozen interviews, some with individuals, some with small friendship groups.
Some were conducted over a period of time, with the conversation continuing
between the actual interviews. The interviews were free-ranging about *The Cosby
Show* and included a series of questions about when, how often and in what context
the programme was watched, as well as questions aimed to elicit opinions about the
social meaning of the programme and its political import. The questions encouraged
reference to other TV output. They took place in lunch breaks so an informal
atmosphere predominated as we all ate our way through the discussions. I tape-
recorded and transcribed these interviews in full.

Subsequently I taught a four-week unit of work on *The Cosby Show* to a mixed-
ability fourth-year English class. One of the interviewees was in this class. I tape-
recorded and transcribed two of these lessons. I also made notes during and after the
lessons and collected all the written work set, which included rough notes as well as
formal essays required for the GCSE course.

The school and the local community were of course very important influences on the ways students thought, felt about and expressed themselves; indeed, reacting to the specific ideas and culture of schools and relating those to the larger picture is part of the problem every teacher faces. I thus include the following brief sketch to give a flavour of the context for the students' discussions.

The school is a mixed, purpose-built comprehensive in Tottenham, in the London Borough of Haringey. About a third of the pupils are black, chiefly Afro-Carribean, a third Greek or Turkish Cypriot and a third white; about 5 percent are Asian, usually Bengali or from Mauritius. There is an absence of adequate and up-to-date indices to describe the social deprivation of the area, but in terms of employment, housing and single-parent families it is customarily regarded as one of the poorest areas in the country. (Only one of the fourth-year class had a parent or parents employed in conventional middle-class occupations). The local communities are varied and fragmented but especially since the Broadwater Farm troubles of 1985 the black community has been an important, well-organized and ideologically significant pressure group. Local Education Authority initiatives have been responsive to this pressure, but both locally and nationally there has been a backlash against anti-racism, and Haringey has featured quite prominently in this conflict.

The next three sections of this chapter provide a detailed analysis of the data I collected. I have focused on three themes: realism, the family and pleasure, and teaching representation. Because this kind of research is so detailed and the topic is so complex, these themes are no more than fragmentary insights into the whole picture.

Modality and Realism

'The 'Cosby Show' is recorded in front of a live studio audience.'
'That family, that family, they're just so unrealistic.'
'A reasonably believable family . . . true-to-life episodes.'

The first two comments here are immediate responses by students to even the briefest of references to the programme; the third comment is taken from Channel 4's official programme previewer. Taken together they open up one of the key questions of this study: how discussion around the notion of realism is crucial to both how and what the *Show* represents. For in deciding whether *The Cosby Show* accurately or misguidedly reflects a 'black reality', we have to engage with the interpretative codes and conventions of realism. Thus, judgments about the representation of black people on TV contain implicit references to a range of cultural, aesthetic and modality criteria.

Modality is a term derived from linguistics to describe the ways we judge the reality of things.[16] The phrase quoted above, 'a reasonably believable family', is a classic modality judgment. If a family is 'believable' what does the qualification 'reasonably' mean (reasonable to whom anyway?) and what does it mean to have a believable family in the first place? We make these judgments all the time, yet we have to learn to do so, and the more experienced we are as viewers the more complex these judgments will be.

Since comments about modality range from the pedantic to the politically sophisticated, I have attempted to construct a taxonomy of such judgments derived from my interviews. I am not suggesting that this structure possesses a linear developmental pattern, (that would be of use in constructing learning progressions for example), but that a study of these different kinds of judgments signals different forms of understanding. Working out exactly what students mean by these judgments will be necessary if we are to explore the full potential of a concept like representation.

1 Comparison with Literal Reality

Michael: You never see them go shopping.

This kind of judgment is often deployed within certain kinds of discussions. Here it arose in response to my comment that the family is well-off because the fridge is always well-stocked. It lacks reference to a generic framework, i.e., it is part of the conventions of (some) sit-coms that you wouldn't necessarily expect to see a family go shopping. However Michael presumably knows this, as the context of this utterance shows a deliberate desire to provoke.

2 Comparison with Referenced Reality

Melanie: ... I don't believe in them real American Families is like that anyway. It's hard to believe.
... I don't know what American schools are like, whether they have things like that but I think quite a few of them are realistic, like them going to the college.
... I can't tell you she's a typical black American wife 'cos I don't know what they're like.

These kinds of comments were frequently invoked to explain or justify difficult judgments. Obviously our readings of (representations of) fundamentally different social worlds require certain kinds of knowledge to explain them. Much of this knowledge is derived from other texts, though there was always reference to the *Show*'s American-ness rather than its use of other generic conventions.

The use of hypothetical knowledge, about American families for example, in order to make judgments about what is realistic can serve particular functions in the context of discussion. For example the third extract above occurs within the following sequence:

> JSG: Tell me what kind of image Mrs Huxtable's got?
> Melanie: . . . I can't tell you she's a typical black American wife 'cos I don't know what they're like.
> JSG: Yeh.
> M: But I don't think you get many black women acting like that anyway.

I think Melanie wanted to make the last point in answer to my question, but care not to make sweeping generalizations forces her into referencing her knowledge of black American wives.

3 Comparison with Experienced Reality

> Melanie: . . . there's one thing about it, they never argue in the house . . . I don't think that. I think that's the only unrealistic thing about it, they never have arguments or anything.
>
> Charlotte: They have arguments, but I don't think it's anything like people, brothers and sisters would really argue about. It would be much more, you know; when brothers and sisters argue it's really intense, you know. You just wanna kill each other and that's how it is, but this is not that. There's not that much hatred in it, guess that's not how it's supposed to be or come across. But yeh, it's good and funny.

The goings-on of the Huxtable household contrast with both these young women's experiences of family life and this calls into question the modality of the programme. Different interviewees picked out different facets of their experience to act as a 'reality control' as it were. Here contrasting *No Problem* to *The Cosby Show*:

> Kay: Yeah, cos *No Problem* was real.
> Nkasi: Yeah.
> K: Cos I mean it was real, when you see that house.

The straightforward comparison between experience and representation creates an immediate aesthetic judgment. However this kind of judgment is a selective mechanism. It does not throw into doubt the whole programme, it is an acceptable difficulty that can even be used to make more sophisticated interpretations. Charlotte's comment 'guess that's not how it's supposed to be or come across' reveals her incorporating her judgment about the programme's unreality with an understanding of its aims, and even implying how the programme-makers might use her kind of judgment for larger strategic purposes.

4 *Affective Reality*

Michael: I reckon there are some people like the family, yeh.

JSG: ... um ...

M: But like say, they're not as well-off or don't have two kids in college and that stuff, but they've still got the 'attitude' of Bill Cosby and the other woman.

Here there is a distinction between an economic or social reality and an emotional truth. The external trappings of the family's affluence can be set aside as fictitious but the programme still possesses credibility on another level. The separation between feelings and economic reality is interesting because the interviewee here has hypothesized a concept of the liberal family differentiating between class and attitude, a reading not necessarily implied in the programme.[17]

5 *Unreal Models*

Nkasi: The 'Cosby Show' is just a programme and everybody knows it's just a programme.

Charlotte: That man, he's a good husband, he's the kind of thing I'd like, he's a hard-working, loving, blah blah. But everybody's different, he's just acting, nobody knows what he's like in real life at all.

JSG: Could be a real bastard you mean?

C: Yeh, nobody really knows. So I mean if people think about it properly, you know, then they'd know you can't really use things like that to compare, unless he's real life you know. It's from something real life reconstructed or it's a real life thing ...

Nkasi's statement categorically assigns a particular value to the programme. It is only a work of fiction, of entertainment, and has no status in any discussion about role models. She separates real life from any representation and uses judgments about the modality of the programme as an argument against any social or political meaning. Charlotte's deliberate obstinacy, referring to Bill Cosby the actor rather than *Bill Cosby* the star or even Dr Huxtable, emphasizes this point. She clearly contrasts 'real life reconstructed to real life' in order to reinforce her judgments of the modality of the programme. However it is interesting that she continues in a way that blurs her previously sharp modal awareness. She continues: 'and this is not so, but it is good in a way, so some people would follow the examples and try to get good jobs and, you know, be a good family man and help in the house.'

She is employing what discourse analysts would call logically exclusive repertoires here;[18] she is forcing together contradictory sets of ideas from different positions in the argument . . . . The notion that people will copy positive role models is really at odds with her high modal awareness; 'if people think about it properly', they would be wrong to compare the programme with real life. Her phrase 'but it is good in a way' forces what is in effect a contradictory link between these two perspectives.

6 Intertextual Reality

> Kay: To me the Brady Bunch was more real.
> Nkasi: Yeh.
> K: because . . .
> N: Because you see it all the time, it's common to see white middle-class families.
> K: Yeh.
> N: But it's not common to see a black middle-class family in high position.

This exchange refers not to a hypothetical knowledge about the real world but to the codes and conventions of the way the middle class are represented on TV. The 'real' is normative, it's what 'you see all the time'. Uncommon representations like the Huxtables throw into doubt the modality of the programme. The 'progressive' representation of blacks is simply not acceptable to these young women, not just because it contrasts with their own experiences (see 3 above), but because within a politicized discourse about representation it adopts an idealized and untenable position. Yet the generic expectations of sit-com are really ignored; a particular form of social realism is dominant here.

> K: OK when you watch American films, the *Cosby Show*'s still there; . . . how do they show black people in American films living in New York or a bad part of America?
> N: Mum's pregnant with a million kids round her. Dad's missing.
> K: There ain't no Dad and the kids are teefs, just put it that way.
> Despina: On drugs etc.
> N: On drugs, eldest daughter pregnant.
> K: In gangs.
> JSG: Does this make?
> K. That's why we don't think the *Cosby Show* is real, do you get what I mean, all the black things.

The sense of reality here is intertextual (derived from other texts) and although no specific texts are mentioned there seems to be a consensus about a kind of representation which can perhaps best be defined in terms of a political position rather than in specific characters, films or TV shows. There is an assumed, commonsense, shared understanding; I get the sense that Kay's 'we' in the 'we don't think' of her last utterance may well stand for more than just the three participants of this conversation. But for *The Cosby Show* to be seen as not real it has to be read as implicitly 'black' and operating in the way that these other texts are, for it to be judged by the same standards. There is thus a distinct repertoire, or shared understanding, about what constitutes a 'black' show (whether this means with black characters or about black issues or whatever) and this is defined primarily in terms of a kind of social realism.

7 Unreality

Nkasi: Number one, right, the things in it are so fake, right, that the whole thing just probably seems a big fake and so it makes no effect on society at all.

Kay: . . . it's not real that programme it's not real.

N: You know it.

Despina: Better if it was.

K: It's coming like *Hart to Hart*, you remember *Hart to Hart*.

N: They're so fake, they're so perfect.

The sequence from which this extract comes continues to repeat itself and there is a sense of frustration in the ritualized 'it's just not real', more detectable in the original recording. Part of the frustration may stem from the limited vocabulary available: 'real' and 'fake' seem inadequate terms to cover a variety of different kinds of judgment. Comparison with *Hart to Hart* is pejorative. The anger here seems to be directed at a reading of the programme's *intentions* to be real. This is surely a revealing misreading which discounts its genre, format and internal modality markers. If not directed at this kind of preferred reading, the criticism must be of other (ignorant) people who might mistake the programme for the real thing. Again, it is revealing that it should matter so much that people at large might mistake a sit-com for a slice of life. There is obviously a profound mistrust of the media inbuilt into this position, although this is contradicted by her comment 'so it makes no effect on society at all.' Later in the discussion Nkasi makes the same move that Charlotte does in 5 above, moving between repertoires:

N: It's not realistic, it doesn't happen, it's not a common thing. I mean it's not natural, right, it isn't. It's not natural but it's a role, you can't change the fact it is good. It is. It is good.

D: What, *Cosby Show*?

JSG: The role model?

N: Yeah the image, everything about it. I just think it's good, it's unrealistic but it's good.

There is a contradiction here, denying the effect of the media but believing in the importance of role models. Whereas Charlotte can concede strategic value to the programme, Nkasi is anxious about its claims. She tries to find different ways of expressing her concern; 'natural, uncommon, doesn't happen' and 'unrealistic' are all different ways of defining 'unreality'. Yet while she will easily concede the worth of the role model, she doesn't want to do so at the expense of her low modal awareness of the show. It's only an image that is good, not an example for people to follow. She refuses to grant the programme high modality status. It remains distant, ideal and artificial.

As these extracts show, the students' judgments about the modality of *The Cosby Show* are complex and flexible, both because of the wide variety of (potentially contradictory) criteria available to them, and because the judgments themselves may be strategic, part of other arguments, or part of an interpersonal dynamic. At least some students here are clearly making political judgments about 'representation', although *The Cosby Show* doesn't neatly fit into this, being ambiguously 'real' and 'ideal'. Similarly they speculate about the intentions of the programme-makers but these too are seen to be ambiguous. In many respects their discussion acknowledges the fundamental contradictions which surround debates about race and representation: while they are ambivalent about the potential 'effects' of the media, they implicitly reject any simple polarization between 'positive' and 'negative' images.

Families And Pleasure

Ideas about the family, and particularly the black family, are crucial to these students' understanding of the programme both in terms of the representations it provides, and in terms of the context of 'family viewing'. The black family has long been a 'cause for concern' for both progressive and reactionary social policy-makers.[19] *The Cosby Show*, we have to assume, must have responded at some level to this debate as it provides almost a mirror image of the pathological model, with an active father, employed parents, etc. Indeed part of its 'positive' image simply is the 'loving family'. On the other hand the programme has been widely criticized for its reactionary sexual politics[20] and seen as a manifestation of Reagan's right-wing pro-family backlash. There is thus a point of conflict here between those who might find its representation of blacks progressive and those who are unhappy with the fact it can be endorsed by the Salvation Army's *War Cry*.

However both responses are trapped in the positive images dilemma analyzed above, with its limited notion of media effects. In interviews, students were aware of how the ideal might function as a mechanism for pleasure whilst remaining distant and artificial, just as they negotiated such pleasures within an understanding of their personal circumstances. They perceived their own families as problematic, but whilst this might make *The Cosby Show* enjoyable, it was not seen to deceive or set false hopes.

Watching at Home

As David Morley[21] has shown, the viewing context is often the site of conflict or harmony within families and may contribute to the social meaning of watching TV in general. This could be extended towards an explanation of the meaning of particular programmes. It could be that the viewing context holds the key to the pleasure of *The Cosby Show.*

> [1]JSG: . . . do you watch it by yourself or with your family?
> Melanie: Well, there's three televisions in the house, right. Well my step-dad watches it downstairs.
> JSG: Yeh.
> M: Sometimes me, my mum and my sister's in my sister's room watching it or usually I'm in my room watching it and they're in Michelle's room watching it.
> M: Yeh, it's about family life, cos on telly there's a lot of white programmes and it shows they, what they are like in the house. But there's one thing about it, they never argue in the house . . . I don't think that. I think that's the only unrealistic thing about it, they never have arguments or anything.
>
> [2]JSG: And when you watch it who watches it with you?
> Michael: Me, just me . . . in the bedroom.
> JSG: Does Helen [sister] watch it?
> M: Yeh.
> JSG: Where?
> M: In her bedroom.
> JSG: And do you ever talk about it; or do you all just sit in your separate rooms and watch it?
> M: Sometimes, sometimes . . . I like the way he treats the children, he makes jokes with them, like when he's punishing them he sort of makes it into like a joke sort of thing, instead of shouting at them and all that. It's good.

Both Melanie and Michael bring out the separate and isolated nature of their lives, yet respond warmly to the togetherness of the programme. It doesn't take too much imagination to connect the pleasures of the programme with the difficulties in their lives, and Michael in particular emphasizes the way Cosby acts a model of paternal discipline and explicitly contrasts it to his own circumstances. Likewise Melanie's argument about the programme's 'unreality' is clearly based on a contrast with her own experience of family life. Whilst both respondents might enjoy this representation of family life, they are aware of its 'utopianism'. Melanie criticizes it for this reason (as do all the other interviewees) and although at one stage Michael claims 'that's how parents should be', he selects particular examples of the father/son relationship which revolve around communicating with each other, rather than a blind fantasy acceptance.

Representation and the Black Family

JSG: Why do people in this school watch it?

Nkasi: It's the family, I think: it's because there's a mother and a father there. Because a typical black family there is no Dad. The Dad is missing, true or false Kay?

Kay: True.

N: The Dad is missing.

K: OK, when you watch American films, the *Cosby Show*'s still there, . . . how do they show black people in American films, living in New York or a bad part of America?

N: Mum's pregnant with a million kids round her. Dad's missing . . .

We have examined some of this segment before but the introductory elision between reality and representation sets up a real tension. But what is the basis of their argument? Is the programme popular because of its counter-stereotypical images or its counter-real ideas? Is the programme appreciated for the way it appears to refute traditional *images* of the black family or what it does for real black families; or has this distinction become irrelevant? Indeed the incorporation of 'ideas' about the family is indistinguishable from representations of the family.

JSG: You were talking about black fathers.

Nkasi: Yeah, missing, missing . . .

Nkasi then describes in some embittered detail her particular family circumstances (which interestingly enough the Greek student picks up as being caused by 'prejudice and that over here', but this point is ignored by the two black students). This is followed by a discussion of Tottenham and its large black population and reasons for the programme's popularity in this locale are explained as follows:

Kay: Because it [the programme] different, you know what I mean,

because as we can see as rough, downgraded, no dad in the family, like that.
But when you sit down and watch *Cosby Show* on the television where
they've got a father.
Nkasi: Yeh Bill Cosby's a safe Dad as well, not just a Dad, a safe Dad.
K: And the mother is a lawyer . . . and they live in a nice house.
Despina: And near enough happy
N: Yeh.
K: Black people want to be like that.
N: Yeh.

Again, I'm struck by the joint understanding and fluency of this interview group:
much of the meaning must reside in the conversation's social function. However the
segment is complex. There is a sense of wish-fulfilment — that the programme
provides solace for absent fathers ('safe', in school dialect, is applied to people) — but
this is mediated by intertextual knowledge — a sense that the programme fills needs
defined by the absences in other media output. In addition it is a general community
wish, not a localized individual fantasy. Kay doesn't say 'I want to be like that,' it's
'Black people' who want to. So the programme is perceived as speaking to her and her
family in as much as they are constituted as a special audience: the black family. She
responds to the programme not as an individual but as a member of a social audience.
She perceives its address to her through the utopian father but externalizes or
generalizes that pleasure to the social importance of the programme:

Kay: A black person doesn't normally have that.
Nkasi: They haven't got that role model to look up to normally, not in
their own image.

These two refuse identification with the pleasures of the programme, but
acknowledge that those pleasures fulfil needs.

Kay: . . . you don't say 'Oh I wish that was me living in that house with
that family.'
Nkasi: With that family. (spoken with mixture of envy and distancing.)

The family in family programming cuts two ways. It can produce a sense of
pleasure, warmth and togetherness.

Kay: Yeh, everybody in my family watches it. *Cosby Show* and everybody
runs for the TV boy, get best seat, sitting there, 'Cosby Show Cosby
Show.' (imitates excitement).

But the content of the programme is problematic on a variety of levels as we have seen,
and whilst these interviewees think the Huxtable family is a good thing 'as a role
model' they recognize the limited meaning of such representations. As Kay continues,

it's not real that programme, it's not real.

Yet if the programme isn't real, the watching is! 'Reality' isn't the issue at stake here however; the ideal or utopian is an equally valid criterion of critical appreciation, and pleasure often resides in the tension between experience and fantasy. The programme offers an uncertain and contradictory pleasure for these young black women and the status of the black family is at the heart of those uncertainties.

Teaching Representation

In this final section I will consider extracts from two lessons, taken from a four-week unit of work around *The Cosby Show*. In the first of these, we examined the programme's explicit representation of 'black issues' with a detailed study of a particular episode that dealt with a homework assignment about the civil rights march on Washington, which Theo (one of the Huxtable children) had been given. This is one of the rare occasions on which *The Cosby Show* has directly addressed black concerns as content. The final sequence in the episode comprised a family gathering, with both sets of grandparents recalling in a 'moving' fashion the civil rights march, which included large chunks of Martin Luther King's 'I have a dream' speech. It ended with Grandpa singing, while Theo's voice-over commented on the significance of the day for his family and America.

> Charlotte: This . . . was about a serious matter in history and how the family was involved in changing their country . . . it wasn't just black Americans, but also others fighting for equal opportunities at the time.
>
> Cathy: Grandpa sings a song at the end to remind everyone that the march was not just a day for people to enjoy themselves and meet new people, but a day that was a march of protest against injustice and that they were all there for a meaning.

In fact the programme scrupulously avoids phrases like 'equal opportunities' or a march of protest against injustice'; this discourse is implicit in the programme. Yet Cathy and Charlotte have read the underlying discourse and have preferred it to a simpler surface interpretation, such as:

> Simon: Grandpa sings the song at the end in memory of Dr Martin Luther King.

King is an important referent in the discourse of American civil rights and is mentioned in the programme. But to make the kind of connection Simon has, shows a kind of interpretative leap: if he is making the same point as Cathy and Charlotte, he is doing it in an elliptical fashion. I would speculate that he has drawn on the way the school curriculum elevates Martin Luther King to a heroic individualistic status and substituted that (perhaps as a kind of metaphor) for the meaning of the programme, despite the way the episode stresses the people's involvement. Thus both these answers reveal different ways of expressing the same understanding.

However, understanding is not just a question of decontextualized interpretation, for example of the importance of Grandpa's song. It frequently requires a level of what we might call 'meta-understanding', in this instance relating to the broader pedagogic structures of the series rather than the events of a particular episode. Thus, understanding the broad intentions of the programme enables a more sophisticated understanding of specific incidents. For example, most of the class though that the most important character was Theo:

Simon: . . . because it was all to do with his paper.

In contrast to this fairly literal response (though whether to the question or the episode I don't know), Charlotte interprets the same question with an understanding of agency: she reads the programme's pedagogy as part of her response.

Charlotte: There is no important character in the scene because it doesn't
take one person to tell of the past event, everyone puts their points forward
and Theo probes them to bring out more.

Because Charlotte sees the programme as didactic she sees the characters in terms of role and function, rather than as self-motivating entities or bound by 'realist' constraints of plot. The key question here appears to be whether this understanding precedes her fluency in the rights discourse or whether her understanding of the politics of the episode influences her understanding of its structure. On the other hand it may simply be that she is capable of expressing what I want (in terms of demonstrating an understanding of the obvious). Simon may have 'understood' what Charlotte makes explicit, but he doesn't make the point clearly. In this kind of classroom interaction, linguistic competence is crucial to the ways we evaluate students' understanding.

There is yet another kind of reference to this rights discourse which shows awareness of the discourse, yet steps back from endorsing the same position:

Raymond: . . . everybody believes in equal rights for everybody in America.

Similarly in response to a question about whether you view the Huxtables as different after this episode, we find:

Wayne: That is what you would have expected them to have done anyway.

or

Edith: Because they seem the type of family who are concerned about issues
like this. And who are willing to take part.

The discourse exists but elsewhere, 'in America'. It pertains to people's needs and lives, they are 'the type of family who are concerned about issues like this': yet it affects other people rather than people like us. (Because Edith is usually a more outgoing black student I have to interpret her comments as demonstrating a cynical disinterest in the topic. If she wasn't I could construe a different interpretation). It is not simply that there may be some racist resistance, but that the resistance may well be framed in the same conceptual terms as a positive rights discourse: after all 'equal rights' is the right phrase for this situation, even if it is rather morally undermined by the qualification 'for everybody in America'.

Indeed, we can't assume that any resistance will be racist, because this work has been produced in specific circumstances which may foster its own resistance (like the fact that Raymond virtually refuses to do any work in school at all). Yet if approval and disapproval are allied merely to the repetition of certain phrases as opposed to demanding deeper exploration of the issues, we can expect empty understanding.

> Raymond: Grandpa sings the song at the end because the adults were there
> with the Washington march and it brings back old memories.

The problem with this kind of work is how to make the obvious clear. Raymond 'understands' equal rights, but on what level? And how does this understanding come about in the first place, since it isn't from a complex reading of the programme? It seems as if the pressure of the classroom exerts its own influence on demonstrating understanding.

This was even more apparent in the discussion that formed the conclusion to this unit of work. The class had 'researched' how black people were represented on TV, and were collecting all the information in categories, 'good'/'bad/'criminal'/etc., to see how *The Cosby Show* fitted into the picture. A class discussion took place after all the evidence had been collated on the blackboard and I reproduce the discussion in full with a parallel commentary. The most obvious point to note is that only two students (black, female and articulate) actually participated, and they clearly set out to make their own point, namely that the media and the people who control them are racist. The extract opens after the class had pointed to the predominance of middle-class 'realistic' blacks on TV, and shows the ambiguous way the two protagonists accept this, at the same time as asserting a monolithic theory of media racism.

JSG: If that's what we think how come the evidence doesn't fit with that?

There is a problem with the idea of evidence here. Does forty minutes' class discussion drawn mainly from anecdote and memory constitute fact?

Yvette: They disguise it very well.

Charlotte: They don't they want you to

First of all who are the *they*? Does the *they* pre-exist the discussion or is it invented to believe what they want, like right, they, them people high up, those people up there. They don't really want the colours to mix, they just disguise it, they just say things are changing, things are getting better but they don't really want them. So when you tell the truth, right, like when somebody comes and tells the real truth, they don't like them, they say they're anti-white and all that business. But they know the person is telling the truth and they try to make them out to be bad, but it's not like that.

fulfil a conceptual need, a strategic function within the argument?

There is a model of ideological transmission in the way *people high up* use the media *to disguise* reality as well as a notion of public debate; that the media can be used as 'evidence' to describe social relations. This argument implies that the media are transparent and disregards any notion of a reader (like themselves) selecting and interpreting. The idea of the *colours mixing* suggests that TV is a potential force for change, that it does matter who is represented and how.

There is a sophisticated understanding of contemporary racist anti-racism, being *anti-white* and a rather self-validating heroic role for the *somebody* who *tells the real truth*. Isn't this understanding being implicitly claimed by Charlotte? If she can analyze the situation as such, it self-justifies her critique.

J: So how would all these pictures, these images of the good, realistic, middle-class blacks on television fit into what you're saying then?

Why does nobody challenge her and Yvette? Is there a sense that the argument is practised or rehearsed? Why is the teacher's question (an attempt to shift the agenda) ignored? There is a sense of laying down the law here. Vociferous black pupils are not going to be challenged on issues which are perceived to be 'their' territory and if the 'evidence' doesn't fit, the argument can be manipulated, especially as the notion of the falsity of the media derives from an honourable tradition. Ironically as white and male, I am totally powerless to challenge them unless I want to risk a great deal.

C: That all, that is just, the . . . whatever

There is a need to hypothesize a racist

they say, right, is just the truth behind it. They just put in what they want. They're just what do you call it showing what they want us people to know. Because a lot of people like we were talking about somewhere in Kent or Devon or whatever, they believe it, they take everything they see on the TV in the newspapers or whatever, the truth.

British audience who are white, rural and stupid enough to *believe it*. This is not supported by these students' direct experience but central to their formulation of racism within the discussion, a formulation which may have few points of contact with their actual experiences. The students claim they do not believe the media and that they have a privileged access to the truth. There is also a limited view of white, middle-class power. *They're just ... showing what they want us people to know.*

J: OK, if that's the case, then people in Kent or Devon seeing all these good realistic middle-class people on television, black people, are going to think 'Oh well, black people are good realistic and middle-class,' are going to think 'Well that's fine. We're all going to get on well together'.

The students reject this idea of a liberal establishment responsive to debates about representation, in favour of the idea of a totally racist establishment — though whether this is to make the point or what they really think is unclear. For all their forcefulness, they don't know how to argue with a subtle liberalism.

C: No, cos half the time that's not what comes out.

J: Is that a fault in what we've done in this lesson then?

C: No because we're telling, just saying what we know, innit, what we think, but others don't want us to think so we'll do whatever they want. But we've got our own ideas and that is what we think ... Cos when there's a black person in a show, right, there's only one or two, there's not a whole lot of them. Then, then a few, ten white people and there's one black person so you don't really take much notice of the black person so much.

There is a contradiction inherent in their model of the audience. They privilege themselves, yet maintain that the media will affect others.

The students effectively change the terrain of the debate from a qualitative to a quantative argument. In order to maintain the consistency of the category 'racist media' they vary the debate to fit the pattern. It is a sophisticated point they are making here, but how do we use it in class?

J: Would that be true for *EastEnders* and ...

C: Yeh, they're just trying to say 'we're not racist, we're trying to mix people in' but there's only about one Indian family in there, that girl, and how many black people, they just come once in a while.

J: Right, *The Cosby Show* is obviously different from that, isn't it, cos everybody in the show is black usually.

C: We used to have a black London Jamaican family but it's gone.

[I am criticized for getting the name of the programme wrong and summarize the discussion so far to steer it back]

J: Does this mean that images of black people are changing?

?: No.

C: No, the only thing is the BBC have brought out new programmes like *South of the Border* and they've got a nearly black person in the role ... But it's still all more white people in there than black. It's like, she is like the leader of the detective thing. That is it, it's still not that much thingy ... I don't know. It's not based on black reality, it's still around things more on whites than blacks. They just use the black thing so people can say 'oh that's good they're changing'.

J: Does anybody agree or disagree with Charlotte? ... How does *The Cosby Show* fit into this pattern?

Y: Right. The people then, they think putting these programmes on, what's really going on right.

Again the teacher is not answered. What the students say is perfectly true but they are unwilling to relinquish any power within the classroom (the rest of the class were virtually silent for this whole exchange) or within the debate.

The rather petty criticism over the name of *No Problem* is symptomatic of this struggle for power.

The unwillingness to allow that in the media race relations have improved or changed is clearly contradicted by the evidence of the previous discussion, yet the students do not possess a vocabulary or a discourse to cope with the change.

The meaning of *black reality* is unclear. It is an important and resonant idea but it may have argumentative rather than empirical weight.

They are also anxious that change in the media will not be mistaken for 'real' change. Is this because their discourse would have less power, that their role of spokespeople for the oppressed gives them immense status and authority in the classroom and indeed without media

147

J: Yeh (indicating she should carry on)

Y: And they put *The Cosby Show* on to make it look like they're the opposite of what everybody expects them to be like, they're well off, they're (prestige)

C: Can I ask something?

Y: No

C: No, you know, they've got that on, right like they're well-off. They've got everything, right, and they're happy right, so like if somebody somewhere, if somebody somewhere...heard that black people were arguing, 'oh we ain't got no money, we need for this and that', they're gonna argue that, what about that programme? They're gonna use it like, but they're well-off you know. There's a big problem here for black people and in America as well.

misrepresentation their case would be in some way diminished? Is there also not a sense that there is displacement from housing, crime, education, etc. to the media, where it seems much easier to make forceful arguments about racism?

Compare Charlotte's awareness of the programme's modality on page 133. Why is she so concerned about the effect of the programme here in this particular way, when we know she possesses another understanding of the way the programme works? I suggest that there is a public discourse about race and representation which she is mobilizing in this particular situation because of the political will to control the school as a social institution, and the curriculum. Silencing the rest of the class is a form of intellectual control. Speaking on behalf of a deeper truth, and for *black people* in general, is irrefutable. Again she mobilizes a racist other, the *somebody somewhere*, to give her discourse full power. This is however a particular discursive strategy and should not be confused with knowledge about the media or the processes of representation.

There is much to be admired in the foregoing discussion. The young women are forceful and clear. They have a consistent and articulate position which is obviously linked to a wider political perspective. Yet, for all its radicalism, I find the presuppositions of their argument depressingly conservative. First of all there is the contradiction between the 'facts' we had gleaned as a class, that many representations of blacks were progressive, and the desire to state the radical position, that the media are uncompromisingly racist. There is also an emotional and political consensus revolving around conspiracy theories of the media and the notion that the media possess 'fabulous powers' over audiences. The complexity of liberal representations, as in *South of the Border* and *The Cosby Show*, or their sensible interpretations about their own, and each other's understandings, are jettisoned for the rhetorical flourish and classroom power.

It is not that I wouldn't have wanted these students to speak out in the way they did: it was an enjoyable and provocative lesson questioning important issues. But what learning is taking place here? To a large extent the rest of the class are excluded. Even for the two speakers I don't see an understanding of a concept here, just the rehearsal of a position in a debate (in fact not a rehearsal but a performance!). As I hope the commentary shows, the politics of the classroom and the issues surrounding the topic supersede the contradictions in the argument. In the context of the earlier understandings, we have to assume that either these young women are making a choice as to what they say they believe in, or it could be that they don't have the vocabulary, the ability to position the more liberal representations they have discussed within arguments available to them. If the latter is the case it points towards a need in media studies to equip students with these kinds of understandings, to make arguments and debates themselves a topic of study. It also suggests that we need to utilize students' own capacities for interpretation in a way that builds theories of media power up from honest self-reflection rather than with the wholesale adoption of prevailing political positions.

Conclusion

So in the end how do we assess the quality of conceptual understanding, and of learning, that has gone on in the discussions that I've tried to dissect? All the extracts discussed above show an understanding about race and representation *in the process of being systematized* into arguments and ideas; being turned from feelings and viewing experiences into personal, sociological and political theories and explanations. This process of transition is accomplished through language. As they talk or write, justify to each other, share and compare viewing experiences, explain to their peers or rant and persuade, we can watch them, if only for a second, in the act of thinking.

Yet what is absent from the teaching here is a moment of reflection, where the learners acknowledge that their views and ideas belong to other structures of thought. They need to understand not just where the ideas and the language come from, but the political interests invested in certain positions. To what extent would a specialist discourse or vocabulary enable them to compare these different positions, and to develop a conceptual awareness of the issues at stake? How can we develop their language and the contexts for its use in such a way as to enable that comparison to occur? Clearly we need to build from what our students bring to our lessons rather than appear to know all the answers. However we also need to find ways to get our students to question explanations that don't challenge them and to enable them to conceptualize independently, rather than neatly define our concepts, like a kind of painting by numbers. We need to mobilize the experiences and understandings they do have in a way that enables them to find relations between different patterns of thought. All we have to do now is work out a way of assessing that in the next ten years!

Notes

1 *New Musical Express*, 5 April 1986.
2 *Today*, 21 March 1986.
3 *Daily Mail* 21 March 1986.
4 *Daily Mail*, 16 February 1985.
5 *Daily Telegraph*, 8 September 1987.
6 January 1985 edition.
7 1–8 May 1986 edition.
8 *Guardian*, 7 May 1986.
9 See Adler (1986).
10 *Tube*, 1985.
11 *Ibid*.
12 *Newsweek*, 2 September 1985.
13 *Daily Mail*, 21 March 1986.
14 *The Times*, 16 February 1985.
15 Bethell (1985).
16 See Hodge and Tripp (1986) especially the chapter entitled 'God didn't make yogi bear'.
17 Ien Ang (1985) refers to this kind of interpretative process in her discussion of 'Dallas'. Her attempt to account for the pleasure that the programme affords, especially to an audience theoretically oppressed by the ideology of the series, hypothesizes what she calls a 'tragic structure of feeling' whereby one can enjoy the programme on an emotional level, irrespective of the 'unrealistic' nature of the content.
18 See Potter and Wetherell (1987). They describe interpretative repertoires as 'recurrently used systems of terms used for characterising and evaluating actions, events and other phenomena . . . often . . . organised around specific metaphors and figures of speech.'
19 See Lawrence (1982).
20 See for example, *City Limits*, 1–8 May 1986 edition.
21 Morley (1986).

Chapter 7

Intervening in Popular Pleasures:
Media Studies and the Politics of Subjectivity

Chris Richards

Introduction

This chapter focuses on the difficulties and resistances encountered in bringing forms of theoretical knowledge to bear upon objects of everyday popular pleasure. Whereas, clearly, the regular watching of television constitutes a popular practice, media education, as yet, does not. Television has been an important and pleasurable element in the lives of almost all those students who, in this case at the age of 16 in a tertiary college, come into a Media Studies class for the first time: they have an extensive knowledge of what television actually presents on the screen and, though their knowledge is bounded largely by the recent past, they do draw upon a shared cultural repertoire. But *as an object of study*, television is entirely new to them and that object of study has somehow to be located within their already established common sense about what education is for, and within such common sense, what a subject entitled Media Studies might be about.

The process of 'locating' television as an object of study cannot be limited to gaining it a place within what happens to be the prevailing common sense about education. The process is problematic and, as such, is a primary object of investigation here. Does opting for Media Studies indicate an already established distance from the prevailing common sense about education? Does working through a Media Studies course produce a 'troubling' of that common sense? Or is there more of an incorporation of media education within its terms? If television is to be an object of study, then is the object of such study just another GCSE, a means to a vocational end, a matter of displaying an appropriately 'modern' knowledge? And, further, what alternative sense of television as study object might be made and argued for?

Teaching is necessarily an intervention of some kind. Many subjects might be defended on the basis that they intervene in 'areas of ignorance' to establish the basic means to conceptualize and become orientated within particular domains of the material, natural and social world. Natural sciences and geography, but also sociology, economics, history and politics, can be thought of in this way. It would not be difficult to assimilate Media Studies to this perspective: it designates one domain of the social

Chris Richards

world and, like other such domains, has a disciplinary specialization appropriate to it. However, no discipline ever addresses the kind of empty subjective space implied by the term 'ignorance'; on the contrary, there are always pre-existing forms of knowledge of some kind, of varying degrees of density, coherence and tenacity. Physics or geography may intervene in some forms of commonsense knowledge, initially disturb such knowledge, but eventually come to be a co-existing, if incompatible, knowledge which is equally without proof or confirmation in experience. However, the kinds of interventions which Media Studies appears to make are likely to be more troublesome as they address the constitutive elements of everyday life and, therefore, 'personal' domains of subjectivity. Media Studies intervenes in those forms of discourse in which students locate themselves as having freedom, pleasure and an identity or place. Media Studies, or more broadly media education, is exceptional in its consistent engagement with elements of immediately contemporary popular experience and in addressing those for whom that experience is seen not as an object of educational enquiry but as a formative and on-going dimension of themselves. There is, necessarily, a conjunction here of theoretically developed conceptual frameworks and obvious, situated common sense about the media. This is often a problematic conjunction, but it is always also a *political* relation between a specific body of academic knowledge and a more diffuse popular knowledge, and between those who develop, promote and advocate that academic knowledge and those who have no necessary commitment to it. The meaning of 'intervening' in popular pleasures is then a point of intersection and conflict for all those involved in the various levels of research, teaching and learning which constitute media education.

A GCSE Media Studies Class, 1988–89

These broad issues were raised through a detailed study of one GCSE Media Studies class, which I taught during the academic year 1988-89 at a tertiary college in Outer London. The detail of what in-coming students were told about the course during the process of enrolment, in September 1988, is beyond the cope of this study. But a set of formal questions presented to the students during the first Media Studies session did at least provide an outline of what they could say about what they expected to do and why they had agreed to do it. None had any prior experience of Media Studies, though some second-year students may have derived some knowledge of the course from other students. Most identified the course as encompassing a variety of objects of study (newspapers, magazines, television, radio and advertising) and these tended to be associated within an overarching definition of the media as providing or communicating *information*; only three listed films as objects of study, one of whom was a second-year 'A' level Film Studies student. Some did specify exclusions which I understood as belonging to the category of 'serious cultural objects', but not objects of study for Media Studies — for example, books, novels, records, tapes, movies, cinema and theatre. Other cultural products didn't seem to be accepted as objects of serious study at all — such as comics, *The Sun* and its reporters, and television interview shows such as *Wogan*. The first category might be understood in terms of a distinction between the media (as either information or entertainment) and high culture; the second may also derive from a similar distinction, though the exclusion here is of what is trivial, or low taste, and perhaps not to be emulated or accepted as properly belonging to the media professions. In this latter case there is a convergence of a popular discourse, ridiculing *The Sun*, with a more middle-class discourse which, for one student, made possible a distinction between *Brookside*, as 'quality' drama, and 'soap opera'.

Of course within this formal educational context it is unsurprising that a division was made between serious, legitimate objects of study and those which are either beyond educational discourses altogether or are located within other areas of the curriculum. A later request for information about what they *enjoyed* generated lists which seemed to exceed the 'positions' required by the first set of questions. Clearly, the educational setting and my relation to them, as teacher to student, necessarily framed their responses. Nevertheless there was a great deal that they did enjoy but which they did not expect to encounter within formal education, even within Media Studies.

To understand their responses to my questions I had to find out more about how they defined themselves and, when it was possible, I engaged them in discussion around this issue. It did seem that their self-identifications in terms of class, ethnicity and religion were quite diverse but it emerged that their institutional categorization as 'young people' coincided with what was also their most unequivocally shared self-identification. Furthermore, age marked the clearest distance between them as a group and myself as their teacher: between eighteen and twenty years separated them from me and we were therefore placed in radically different ways historically. If, on average, during the Autumn of 1988, they were 17, then they were 5 in the Autumn of 1976 (James Callaghan's Ruskin College speech), less than 8 in May 1979 (election of the first Thatcher government), and less than 11 at the time of the South Atlantic War in the spring/early summer of 1982. Their experience of middle and secondary schooling thus lay entirely within the period of Thatcherism.

These observations, though schematic, do suggest the possible difficulties which arise in presenting courses which derive from an intellectual formation which, at least in its earlier moments, belongs to a period preceding the birth of many of the students. Concepts so well-used that they might almost constitute the 'common sense' of media education were highly unlikely to coincide with the more 'spontaneous' concepts[1] which the students brought into play. My attempts to investigate what they already knew, and what meanings they might attribute to 'Media Studies', produced some evidence of class-differentiated discourses about the media but did not initially enable me to identify the significant generational difference which made establishing a shared account of Media Studies seem so difficult. Engaging in more specific work around advertising produced more evidence of distance between teacher and taught, as it became apparent that our discursive repertoires were not at all the same. It was not possible to assume shared 'fields of reference', shared repertoires of cultural, political and social knowledge, and this led me to question the value of adopting an entirely self-assured position in presenting a 'critical' body of knowledge about the media.

Of particular concern in my attempts to grasp what was happening in this classroom was the way in which gender further complicated the relation between 'academic' and commonsense knowledge. There is evidence, from discussions with the students, that gender significantly shaped what it was possible for them to say about education in general, and Media Studies in particular. Two boys drew upon discourses which constituted education as 'useful and serious work': 'Media Studies is an important subject', 'that helps you', and in which watching television is 'work', 'the way we watch it', 'actually breaking it down', where 'you obviously read between the lines', see 'how advertising could really manipulate the public' and get 'quite a good insight into how it works'. The girls also drew on such discourses but they were somewhat less constrained by a need to constitute either Media Studies or television as such 'serious business': 'she said it was really interesting and I'd enjoy it'; 'it's a nice relaxing subject', and 'I've told so many people about it'; and television can be 'sexy' and 'raunchy' and 'I've always loved television'.

The issue of how students conceive of the relation between Media Studies 'knowledge' and their experience of themselves as gendered subjects is clearly a significant element in the formation of their understanding of the field. Did they understand Media Studies as a course which offers them 'public' skills and knowledge, or were they perhaps more inclined to see it as offering, enabling, or possibly intervening to produce, changes in their understanding of themselves, beyond the domain of public knowledge, as 'personal' subjects? Perhaps their common sense about education included a belief in a necessary separation between formal learning and the domestic, familial sphere; education might then be a means to separate the 'self' from that sphere and to locate it in terms of an equation between educational success and achievement in 'professionalized' occupations. If this was the case, then to define Media Studies as addressing social, familial and affective capacities would tend to place it, for them, with 'girls' subjects' such as Child Development or with non-academic and moralistic elements in the curriculum.

The ways in which these students made sense of the course itself constituted gendered negotiations, both of those concepts which are specific to Media Studies and of the more broadly referenced political concepts which I introduced. These gendered understandings, registered through group discussions somewhat apart from the usual routine of lessons, will be examined further in this chapter. However, there is a broader theoretical debate which needs to be outlined at this point, and which should clarify what is at issue here.

Gendered Subjectivity: A Problem for Media Studies?

Traditional approaches to teaching about gender issues in media education tend to assume that the media directly and powerfully form subjectivity through from early childhood. Thus, there are feminist critiques which deplore the wide ranging promotion of highly gender-specific forms of behaviour on television and, especially, see these as defining socially available roles for young children. Media education might then be conceived as intervening to challenge such representations and to free subjects from the positions in which they are placed by them. Judith Williamson's oft-quoted essay[2] represents a sophisticated version of this position.

Williamson's argument for a combative pedagogy rests primarily upon an understanding of her own teaching as provoking a decisive rupture in the obviousness of everyday knowledge. She argues that promoting a radical cultural relativism, a belief that all social reality is constructed, can liberate students from what seems natural and inevitable. However, she offers few adequate explanations of why particular relations of exploitation and inequality persist and are reproduced. The conviction that 'things could be otherwise' cannot itself produce change and cannot, even if successfully transmitted to her students, liquidate the force of the social, familial and economic relations in which they live. Attributing too great a fragility to social reality does little to explain the more common experience of its permanence and predictability.

Williamson's teaching is concerned with the deconstruction of the 'self', particularly, in this case, the male selves of the students towards whom she adopts an adversarial stance. The importance of her argument that teaching questions particular formations of 'experience' and 'identity' is not in any doubt here, but the terms in which she defines such an activity do require some consideration:

> The value of ideas is ultimately in their use for changing things — not necessarily material things, but for changing ourselves. The only point I can see in teaching is to make this possible . . . . [W]hen they grasp the idea that everything they took for granted is in fact relative, that everything they thought was natural is constructed, that everything they are can be deconstructed — they freak out. (p. 85)

There is here an assumed separation between 'material things' and 'ourselves' which over-simplifies the multiple and complex ways in which subjectivities are formed. The assumption that one can move from an investigation of the power of 'social discourse' to form subjects to the assertion that such discourse is the sole determinant of their formation leads Williamson to believe that she is 'hacking at [their] very roots'. Certainly teaching can involve the deconstruction of those discourses in which subjects may 'locate' themselves but such selves, or subjects, are not reducible to the points of intersection of the multiple discourses by which and in which they are positioned. Subjectivities are not simply produced in discourses and cannot be reduced to 'only discourses and categories'.

A psychoanalytic approach, to the contrary, would suggest that the most crucially formative moments of subjectivity precede the positioning of subjects by the discourses of the media and would thus implicitly question the view that gendered subjectivity can be substantially transformed through education. This contention has been given a feminist and explicitly historical elaboration in the work of Nancy Chodorow.[3]

Her work is a sustained attempt to comprehend the reproduction of gendered subjectivity, and notably the desire and capacity to mother, without resorting to models of social learning prominent in social psychology. Her argument derives from 'object-relations theory' within the psychoanalytic tradition but is carefully qualified by an emphasis upon the historical specificity of forms of the family and of childcare. The main thesis of Chodorow's study is that the desire of women to mother, to provide care, is constructed in early childhood and cannot be explained sufficiently in terms of role training, identification, instruction or coercion. Her argument is complex but central to it is the proposition that:

> Women's mothering reproduces itself through differing object-relational experiences and differing psychic outcomes in women and men. As a result of having been parented by a woman, women are more likely than men to seek to be mothers, that is to relocate themselves in a primary mother-child relationship, to get gratification from the mothering relationship, and to have psychological and relational capacities for mothering. (p. 206)

She argues that men experience themselves as 'more separate and distinct from others' and that their development involves locating themselves as 'opposed' to their mothers. For Chodorow, the primary formative processes of subjectivity are not those identified in critiques of the gender differentiation of toys, books, clothes, or television but are rather to be located in the historically specific structure of families and of the relational dynamics within them. This would suggest that the relational contexts in which children grow up and encounter television may be a significant focus of enquiry for media researchers.[4] Moreover, if media education is to evolve an adequate politics of subjectivity and is concerned with intervening in processes of social reproduction which sustain forms of inequality and oppression, it cannot be limited to work on text-reader/viewer relations abstracted from the full complexity of the social/familial relations within which subjects are formed. It is necessary to ask how media education can engage with such a 'recalcitrant' dimension of identity.

Questions of this kind are a necessary means of reassessing priorities in teaching Media Studies and of investigating the ways in which students make sense of the knowledge they are offered. To pursue this further I have selected fragments of practice which allow some empirical evidence of gendered negotiations to be considered.

Classroom Practice 1: Understanding 'Feminism'

The following 'interlude' from a Media Studies lesson allows some more detailed attention to the social relations of a particular classroom and the discourses which were brought into play when the issue of change in gendered 'roles' was introduced. It is a tiny fragment but one which presents important problems. The session from which the 'interlude' has been taken was the seventh of the Autumn term and the third which I had taped. Sixteen of twenty-two students were present, six girls and ten boys, seated in a semi-circle facing a television. The tendency throughout the course was for girls and boys to group themselves somewhat separately and to interact with each other from within such gender-exclusive groups. On this occasion all but one boy was present and several girls, at least two of whom would usually speak quite consistently, were absent. The preceding six sessions had been concerned with introducing the course, the WJEC syllabus and modes of assessment, and with the concepts and methods of image analysis. The majority of work had involved directed analysis of images from women's magazines and, subsequently, presentation of magazine covers from the BFI *Selling Pictures* pack. Session seven was perhaps too overloaded with teacher-presentation of material from *The Companies You Keep*,[5] and of an item from *The Media Show* (Channel Four, date unknown) concerned with the currency of the 'New Man' in advertising.

The 'interlude' arose when students asked for time to make notes after viewing the item from *The Media Show*. The following transcript represents less than three minutes of discussion, initiated with the intention of clarifying observations made by the Fabergé Brut Brand Manager, Julie Catherall.

?:	Can you give us a few minutes just to copy a few, whatever . . .
CR:	Yeh alright [I'll give you] just a couple of minutes to note down . . . What was that Colin, you don't want to write down anything at all?
Philip:	It is actually . . .
CR:	What?
Philip:	He just said men and women are getting to be more sort of equal . . . [Never] . . . I said more equal not totally equal . . . they've come up a little bit . . . still a couple of notches below though . . . [Laughter] . . . I'm gonna get hit in a minute . . .

CR:	Why do you think they're still a couple of notches below you?
?:	Because the men're still chauvinist bastards.
Philip:	Yeh . . .
CR:	Oh I see, right.
Philip:	So are a lot of women . . .
CR:	In what way?
Philip:	Well some men are chauvinist and so some women are chauvinist . . .
CR:	What would a chauvinist woman be?
?:	Women are more hypocritical when they're chauvinist . . .
Philip:	Yeh.
?:	Very critical.
Yvonne:	Mind your head as you walk out the door.
CR:	Sorry?
Yvonne:	Mind your head as you walk out the door.
?:	Why?
Philip:	See, that is the sort of . . . [laughter] you're a chauvinist you are.
Yvonne:	Yeh I know I am.
Philip:	See!
Jonathan(?):	So are you . . .
Philip:	No I'm not, not as much.
Yvonne:	Give as good as you get, that's what I say.
Philip:	Shut up. [laughter]
Steven:	[inaudible]
CR(?):	Pardon?
Yvonne:	What did you say?
Steven:	Since all this women's lib and all that crap you don't really, you don't get as much sexism do you?
Yvonne:	Crap?
Philip:	You don't get men laying under lorries at Greenham Common . . . [laughter] . . . that'd be [Greenham?] common sense actually.
Simone:	I think men are [inaudible] above women personally . . .
CR:	What's that you're saying?
Simone:	I disagree with women's lib . . .
CR:	You disagree with whom?
Simone:	Women's lib. I think women should stay at home.
CR:	Really?
Philip:	Well said. [laughter]
Simone:	Seriously . . .
CR:	So that's what you're going to do . . .

Lee: I think women're, women're a jinx on society . . . you realize that the first time a woman went in the space-shuttle it blew up. [laughter].

Simone: . . . I would be quite happy . . . quite happy, I'm quite happy not to drive a car if a man will chauffeur me around . . . [inaudible] not going out to work . . . [inaudible] money to spend. I'm quite happy about that kind of lifestyle, not going out to work.

Philip: I'd be quite happy to have that sort of lifestyle as well. I wouldn't mind being driven round in a chauffeur-driven car either . . .

Though there had been some initial engagement with the item they had been watching, at least from Yvonne, this section of the discussion does not appear to dispute or even make much reference to it. The first comment here from a boy is to the effect that he doesn't wish to write anything down. Philip then intervenes, reflecting on a comment made by another boy, and appearing to be entering the discussion on the terms implied by the presentation of such issues as the object of serious educational enquiry. However, the interjection 'Never' marks a decisive shift away from such an engagement and initiates a series of exchanges between myself and Philip and several other boys. My questions and requests for clarification, which may have been conceived as moderate challenges, do seem rather to help secure the 'arena' for boys and to marginalize girls. There is no adequate effort on my part to encourage girls to speak or to allow them to define the terms on which this, admittedly unplanned, discussion might proceed.

Yvonne seeks to re-enter the 'arena' but does so by making brief threatening remarks rather than attempting to articulate a counter-position or challenge the anti-feminist discourse apparently shared by the boys. Her combative willingness to retaliate is taken up by Philip as confirmation of his observations which, from 'Never' onwards, have been seemingly directed towards securing the laughter and approval of the boys around him. Steven's utterance appears to be an attempt to refer the discussion back to the comment that 'men and women are getting to be more sort of equal' but to do so from a position of explicit self-distancing from 'women's lib'; yet he, unlike any other speaker, replaces 'chauvinism' with 'sexism', perhaps indicating access to a feminist discourse. Philip retrieves the attention of the group by mocking the Greenham women's action against Cruise missiles, construing it as absurd proof of the irrationality of women and the superiority of men.

Simone now intervenes, ignoring the laughter, to assert the superiority of men and her own apparent acceptance of their dominance. Simone appears to be resuming the tone and intent of Steven's intervention, though what she says is presented in terms of her own personal feelings and desires. Her main assertion is that there are advantages for women in not taking on responsibilities which she, at least, is content to leave to men. Philip persists in his attempts to centre the interactions around himself and his immediate male audience but also engages in a mockery of Simone's projected lifestyle: this is both perhaps a reflection on the unavailability of such an option to men but also, more particularly, to anyone excluded from the middle-class affluence Simone seems to assume. Meanwhile another boy, Lee, also attempts to win the attention of the group and to fracture the 'seriousness' on which Simone has explicitly insisted: 'women're a jinx on society . . . you realize that the first time a woman went in the space-shuttle it blew up'. The extent of the laughter at this point suggests that he has succeeded. Simone's subsequent comments are addressed more to me than to the group as a whole and no attempt is made to recover a more inclusive discussion from the situation.[6]

This 'interlude' is not unusual; it is like many others within classrooms and, it may be suggested, could have taken place elsewhere whenever students gather informally. However, it does present two kinds of difficulty which are of central importance to teaching Media Studies. First, the relations between the students and myself as their teacher constitute a powerful matrix through which any reading of texts has to be negotiated. Second, the meanings which I derive from and attribute to feminism are not necessarily shared by the students, for whom other more popular discourses locate feminism as 'other' and not therefore a part of their common sense.

Such an interaction was not too surprising as, during the third session with this group, I had distributed a large number of women's magazines, predominantly the more expensive monthly issues. Amongst them were two copies of *Spare Rib*, both of which were handed back to me, one by a girl ('I don't want this feminist rubbish . . . '), one by a boy ('I'd find it hard to be objective . . . '). One copy carried a cover photograph of Bernadette McAliskey, the other a photograph of Simone de Beauvoir in old age. My understanding of this slight incident was that these students were refusing texts which addressed them as political subjects and possibly also displaying a resistance to what they might perceive as a teacherly moralism. Certainly it was a warning that before assuming a common political vocabulary or alliance with one's students, it would be better to consider their already formed allegiances. Though both 'feminism' and 'sexism' were used occasionally, for them it did seem more usual to speak of 'chauvinism' or 'women's lib'.

Such terms, and the more extensive repertoires in which they are embedded, cannot be read simply as expressions of each individual's 'feelings' about the cluster of issues towards which each term points, but are indicative of the discourses to which they have access. Thus, it seems reasonable to explain the uncertainty and disjunction which characterizes the transcribed 'interlude' by the students' apparent distance from feminist discourses.

However, it is necessary to acknowledge a degree of uncertainty here. There is the possibility in reading this transcript of lapsing into observations which imply that this is a revealing moment, that this shows something of what these students are really like when they are not in the classroom and, further, that it is evidence of 'attitudes' which teachers need to engage with and intervene to change. But this would be to ignore the specific characteristics of the classroom — as a space in which such conflicts can 'legitimately' be articulated — and the interpersonal dynamics of the group. Indeed it may be that these students were indulging in a game of 'devil's advocate' and therefore made contributions which exaggerated conflict because it was more fun to do so, mocking, at the very least, the 'seriousness' of the educational context. It is this immediate social situation and the broader social relations within which they are placed which need to be grasped in their combination. In this context, it is not at all productive to think in terms of isolating 'problem cases' or to adopt the more confrontational form of intervention advocated by Judith Williamson — in effect, to blame and attack individuals.

In the broader debate around learning more emphasis does need to be placed upon the crucial role of *affective* preferences in 'acquiring' new concepts. Vygotsky argues that 'every idea contains a transmuted affective attitude toward the bit of reality to which it refers,'[7] and, clearly, there is more than a 'conceptual' difficulty in the apparent refusal of a feminist discourse here. The central problem is to find ways of connecting the more 'theoretical' and 'political' concepts of Media Studies with students' existing commonsense understandings rather than allow them to be confined in the repository of the 'academic'. It is essential to recognize the affective power of 'spontaneous' commonsense concepts and, if they are to be contested, to overcome the continuing isolation of educational discourse from popular pleasures.

Classroom Practice 2: Enjoying Power

I want to move on now to consider some aspects of the classroom presentation of a television advertisement for Shell petrol current in the autumn of 1988. An important issue here is that of the relation between 'conceptual learning' and 'affective' engagement with texts as they are read and reread both within and beyond the classroom context. Masculinity and the relations of power within which 'masculine' subjects are accorded positions of dominance were identified as 'issues' to be addressed in studying television advertising, seen by me as a source of problematic enjoyment. Advertisements which offered brief narratives of male 'self–possession' were given most attention: the currency of the Levi 501s advertisements opened onto the issue of how 'new' images of masculinity could be seen as nevertheless maintaining components of earlier representations. With repeated viewings, often in slow motion, the Shell advertisement emerged as an object of fascination. It became a common point of reference for the group and, for some, led into reading extracts from an article by Richard Dyer, 'Male sexuality in the media'.[8]

The method of analysis used with this material had been established through the use of *Selling Pictures*, and was similar to that derived from the early work of Barthes, described in Chapter 2. While this method served to direct students' attention to detail, it tended to assume that meaning was simply located in the text, rather than being actively produced by readers.

In a variety of ways concepts central to Media Studies — representation, mode of address, narrative and audience at the very least — were in use in the work that was done both by the whole class and by smaller groups within it. What disconcerted me was the uncertainty about how subjectivity was conceptualized and by what means a shared discourse around subjectivity could be established. Reading a few selected passages from Dyer's article perhaps provided an oblique means of recognizing the phallic excess of the images and the sexual connotations of narrative climax in the presentation of the racing car. Identifying an explicitly sexual discourse in relation to an advertisement promoting petrol did seem to enable most students to speak of what they already knew, but might not otherwise articulate, particularly in a classroom.

In a discussion which took place at the end of the Autumn term one girl, Simone, referred to her surprise in being presented with a 'sexual' reading of some television adverts ('I never realized how sexy they were . . .') but the boys present at the time avoided taking up this comment and tended to pursue a discussion of the course as offering an understanding of media in the public domain rather than connecting with affective dimensions of themselves or their familial experience. In the context of the discussion, which was being visibly recorded, the boys tended to maintain a relatively formal self-presentation, answering my questions and addressing their comments to me, whereas two girls, Sara and Simone, engaged also with each other, laughed and whispered and developed conversations of their own. When they did respond to the questions I was pursuing, the girls tended to offer far more personal accounts of their feelings about themselves and their relation to their families. Simone, in responding to pressure from me to offer some explanation of how Media Studies had changed the way she and her family watch television, suggested that her mother had become more aware of the sexual meanings in advertising: '[she will] send my brother out of the room . . . if she thinks something's a bit too raunchy in an advert or something'. None of the boys acknowledged sexuality in this way, nor did they situate their observations within the context of their relations to members of their families.

When the series of sessions including work on the Shell advertisement was evolving, several of the boys declined to accept photocopied extracts from the Dyer article which I made available as optional further reading. All of the girls took copies without hesitation. There was no overt denial of the proposed 'sexual' reading of the Shell advertisement from any of these boys though only one, Philip, made his agreement explicit, both verbally, and by gesturing with clenched fist and raised forearm. Possibly their avoidance of discussion and their subsequent maintenance of a stable masculinity in their coursework signalled a resistance to a perspective which problematized, even slightly mocked, the basis of their pleasure. It is difficult to know if this was a refusal to give up the enjoyment of power or a matter of taking refuge from the more threatening obligations of masculinity. Certainly it seems that for the boys Media Studies concepts could be accepted as defining skills and knowledge in the public sphere, whereas for the girls the course opened opportunities to investigate the construction of gendered identities.

Two girls working together, Sylvia and Madhumita, made this the central concern of their 'investigative production'. They produced a storyboard for children, centred on a girl who plays football and her brother who dances. They took their work into local primary schools, had it presented to the children and recorded both the reading and class discussion. Sylvia explained their project in her written production log:

> We set out to write a children's book which did not portray Girls and Boys according to their stereotypes. We chose to do this because we had studied stereotypes at the beginning of our media studies course, and decided that children are given their sex identities at an early age by the media.

Though the term 'stereotypes' and the proposition that children are 'given' their 'sex identities' by the media are attributed to the Media Studies course, this discourse, against which I have contrasted the work of Chodorow, was familiar to her within 'A' level Sociology. Media Studies provided an opportunity to investigate and reflect upon this discourse by combining production and empirical research.

It may also be the case that this was seen as a legitimate project because I didn't make the achievement of skill with 'high' media technology a priority of the course. Whatever the disadvantages of this, it did mean that little collusion with boys' confidence in handling technology was possible. Indeed, it is important not to allow Media Studies to be represented as in any sense a training in technical skills, for such an emphasis could make questions of subjectivity even more marginal, for both boys and girls. It is essential not to support boys in making of Media Studies just a public, impersonal arena. Of course both girls and boys should be enabled to develop skills with media technology, but not without contesting an instrumental common sense about education which excludes those issues central to a politics of subjectivity.

Classroom Practice 3: Sexuality

I have argued that in Media Studies the popular material of students' self-definitions is constituted as an object of study and that teaching about such objects must also be an intervention in the areas of subjectivity which are understood as the site of personal and private pleasures. Sexuality can hardly be excluded from the set of central concerns which necessarily arise there. The pleasures of the Levi 501s and of the Shell advertisements are hardly comprehensible without engaging questions of sexuality. It would be reductive to suggest that these questions are simply peripheral because the first advertisement is about selling more jeans and the second about selling more petrol, though it is of course essential to emphasize that these condensed moments of TV advertising would not be there if they did not have credibility as means of persuading people to buy.

Initially, my approach to teaching this material did tend towards an emphasis on the exploitation of forms of gendered subjectivity and sexuality as a means to sell more products. However, the direction of students' interests tended towards the representation of sexuality rather than the political economy of advertising. The imperatives of negotiating their own positioning as gendered subjects perhaps took precedence here, even if, in the subsequent storyboard exercise, they tended, though with exceptions, to withdraw into presentations excluding gender or apparently 'safe' male fantasies. It may be that the risks which might be taken in small-group discussion, where sometimes quite extravagant and amusing ideas developed, are not carried through into work which marks a return to the 'serious' educational processes of individual assessment. Writing, rather than necessarily bearing the 'truth' of the student's 'position', often seemed to acknowledge that the liberty allowed to groups had been withdrawn and that more formal educational objectives had to be realized.

The 'risks' associated with investigating gender and sexuality in a classroom context do need to be considered more explicitly. In the classroom being documented here, most of the students at least started out addressing me as 'sir'. Yet the materials presented and issues developed may be said to have addressed these students as sexually knowing. They had probably been accustomed to being addressed as 'children' and it may be, though I did not conceive of it in this way at the time, that the presentation of advertising and sexuality right at the beginning of the course implied a kind of break, a separation from the category of child and a repositioning of them as in, or entering, adult sexuality. When I read back through my notes on these sessions I found that I identified *Selling Pictures* as 'produced for use in schools', partly to explain the relative inattention to the range of men's magazines but perhaps also as a way of constructing the group as older, as distinct from and more knowing than their GCSE counterparts in schools.

The construction of sexuality within the 'family-school couple' may be seen as constantly defining it as elsewhere, never present as a constitutive element of one's subjectivity and of one's relations to others. Perhaps particularly for 'children' sexuality is also deferred temporally, again and again, and is thus conceived as an event or set of events which happen but do not enter, except occasionally, visibly and unacceptably, into either the public sphere of the school, or the private world of the family. Therefore to present the various advertisements, the *Media Show* item on the New Man and, more tentatively, extracts from the Richard Dyer article on male sexuality in the media, might be seen as defying this containment of sexuality elsewhere, as asserting its pervasive presence in an educational context, and as bringing into play a 'co-presence' of subject-positions which are defined as separate and unrelated. The 'pupil-student' and 'sexually knowledgeable adult' are positions which imply and allow quite different degrees of power and knowledge and, when such positions are articulated together, they clearly unsettle the relation between teacher and student. Much of this uncertainty and disordering of subject positions was evident in reading transcribed extracts from the end-of-term discussion, and in bits of the discussion that either could not be recorded or were perhaps censoriously omitted in my selection of material for transcription. Simone's overt references to the sexual meanings of advertisements were relatively infrequent, but the tendency of much of her conversation with Sara was towards matters of sexual interest. Though whispered, this surfaced through the 'legitimate' discussion in which boys addressed me, seriously, as did Jonathan here, telling me of difficulties with studying Chaucer:

CR: [addressing Jonathan] Does it 'click' with other people in the class in a way that it doesn't for you?

Jonathan: erm . . .

[Whispered conversation between Sara and Simone, not audibly recorded]

CR: You're not talking about my boxer shorts are you, by any chance? Don't whisper, I want to get it on tape; what're you saying? [Laughter]

Simone: It doesn't matter, it's not irrelevant . . . not relevant.

CR: Not relevant? It's interesting you said 'not irrelevant' . . .

My question about boxer shorts was an attempt to let Simone and Sara know that I could hear their comments on the just visible edge of the waistband as I leaned forwards to talk to Jonathan and, as such, was a familiar teacherly control strategy. At the same time, however, it brought sexuality into play in a way which disrupted the 'discussion' further. The basis of Simone's comment was, apparently, her surprise that a teacher should be wearing such once fashionable underwear.

Despite an apparent lack of explicit effort to render masculinity and femininity problematic in the students' practical 'experiments' with advertising, it is possible to argue that one consequence of this phase of work was a transgressing of boundaries between formal school knowledge and popular experience. Media Studies might therefore be understood by the students in ways which do not quite fit within the common sense instrumentalism which seemed to predominate in their comments on education. It may also be the case that boundaries differentiating and dividing knowledge within families, and between families and the college, are made more apparent to students and might therefore be identified as worth interrogating. The 'positioning' of students as 'children' within their families and as (almost) adults within the college does suggest a disparity between what they are assumed to know, and the power that knowledge implies, as they move back and forth between the two contexts. Simone, particularly, offered quite a detailed account of how her parents entered into her college work, something which she both enjoyed and resented.

Jonathan intervened to suggest that I 'give her mum and dad some lessons' but neither he, nor any other boy, offered more than the most minimal account of their own place within their families. Again, the separation of Media Studies from the 'personal sphere' was more clearly maintained by the boys than the girls.

There is not the space here for a more historically informed account of the professional ideologies of teaching and of the ways in which sexuality has been defined and regulated within them. However some general propositions can serve to indicate the importance of pursuing this further. Teachers could be defined as people with their sexuality in brackets; the sexual 'presence' of teachers and their 'self-presentation' as teachers within classrooms seems to depend upon a separation between the constitutive elements of their identities. This is hardly unique to teaching but it is a feature of that everyday regulation which maintains distinctions between what is and what is not legitimate where adults and children are brought together outside the network of intra-familial relations and the rules that govern them. The sets of prescriptions, and proscriptions, implicit in the placing of teachers 'in loco parentis' are presumably an extension of those familial rules: but from what kind of family, when and where, such rules are to be derived depends very much upon the particular historical conjuncture. The kind of family officially enshrined within Thatcherism has been invoked as setting standards for teachers, though since the latter part of 1986 whatever clarity those standards may have had has been blurred by the belated panic about AIDS and the consequent upheaval in forms of sex education. Certainly there is a continuing uncertainty about what forms of self-presentation are appropriate to teachers. Are they to be asexual subjects, skilled at addressing children who are somehow supposed to be neither sexual subjects nor sexual objects?

The work of Jeffrey Weeks[9] offers a promising approach to these issues. With reference to Foucault's work, Weeks comments that:

> The fundamental question, as posed by Foucault, is how is it that in our society sex is seen . . . as the central part of our being, the privileged site in which the truth of ourselves is to be found. (p. 6)

Perhaps the particular regime of pedagogic power in which teachers are positioned does require and depend upon a definition of sexuality as strictly private, and to compromise that privacy is, at the very least, to risk that power which teachers enact in classrooms. The history of sex education might well be read as one component in the construction and maintenance of pedagogic authority. Commenting on post-war developments, Weeks reports the occasional official acknowledgement of sex education (Newsom in the 1960s, for example) and its relative absence from schools or, where present, its role as a vehicle for moral instruction in the ethics of married life. It seems that the priority for education has been to refuse knowledge which might trouble the relations of power between children and adults, relations which are both required and reproduced within schools and colleges. Within such institutional relations, sexuality is not properly a legitimate region of subjectivity and neither teachers nor their students are assumed to allow sexuality to be a significant element in their self-presentation. My argument is that Media Studies, despite gendered differences in the way students make sense of the field, may disturb the customary exclusion of sexuality from what counts as legitimate classroom discourse.

Conclusion

In this chapter, I've offered a series of warnings that taking Media Studies to be a means of intervening to change subjects is to overestimate its radical power. It may be that I'm simply confronting my own past and continuing motivations and the real difficulty of classroom practice. In fact the difficulty is, in part, that of not knowing really quite what the outcome of all the effort might be. As must be obvious, the fragments discussed here don't contain the certainties or the reassurance that maybe I wanted to find. But these fragments come out of a sustained, and much more extensive, attempt to document the work of one Media Studies class across a period of eight months. To establish what kinds of learning have taken place is inescapably problematic and to attribute the status of truth to any bit of evidence is unwarranted. Equally, to expect a movement from the deconstruction of media texts to radical and permanent reconstructions of subjectivities migh well be seen as simplistic — or at least, to rely upon a reduction of historical processes to little more than the effects of representations. The marginalization of the formative social relations in which readers are constituted is perhaps a symptomatic weakness of disciplines which take texts as the primary object of enquiry. Further, to 'demystify' a text, as if it could be a matter of work upon a text which is somehow outside any particular set of relations and therefore outside the 'knowledge' of a particular subject, is indeed to become 'ensnared within the false concrete of the immediately given'.[10] Interventions which engage with the reading of texts cannot be limited to their deconstruction but must seek to locate and understand their place within specific sets of social and cultural relations, and particularly those which constitute the contexts of a text's consumption.

The argument that the construction of gendered subjectivity is not solely achieved through discourse should not be seen as insisting upon some kind of immutable gendered core. On the contrary, it directs attention to the social and familial relations within which subjects are formed, not apart from discourse, but as, at the same time, determining those discourse positions which are offered and assumed. The differential 'affective' relations theorized in Chodorow's work may offer some account of why critical work upon discourses does not, and cannot, of itself produce the changes it may advocate. Teaching takes place within conditions which are not of its own choosing and its power to intervene in the formation of others, though considerable, is itself historically variable and limited. Teaching about the media, as a political practice, has to address a much broader field of determinations if it is to grasp the full complexity of 'text-reader relations' and offer ways of opposing a commonsense instrumentalism about what counts as education.

Notes

1 Vygotsky (1962).
2 Williamson (1981/82).
3 Chodorow (1978).
4 See Morley (1986) and Walkerdine (1986).
5 From *Selling Pictures*, BFI Education (n.d.).
6 This is a provisional and tentative reading of a brief moment which has itself already been 'read' and worked upon in the production of the transcript. Such a text is produced within sets of implicit rules of 'scripting' and could be constructed in other ways from the available sound tape. The sequencing of utterances, as if each speaker awaits his or her turn, is not, for example, an adequate mode of transcription and may suggest a more cohesive 'debate' than a mode which stresses the simultaneity of utterances. With video recording a greater range of codings would also become available and might enable a more densely polysemic reading to be produced. The meanings which I attribute to this transcript must therefore be understood within the conditions, and limits, of their production.
7 Vygotsky (1962), p. 8.
8 Dyer (1985).
9 Weeks (1981).
10 Bennett (1979), p. 174.

Part Four
Media Education and the Curriculum

Chapter 8

Implementing a Media Education Policy across the Curriculum

Jocelyn Robson, Jonathan Simmons, Martin Sohn–Rethel

Introduction

The aim of this chapter is to describe in detail the experience in one school of attempting to implement a media education policy across the curriculum. On the basis of this experience, we draw some general conclusions and make some recommendations regarding the implementation of whole school policies on media education.

This study is of particular interest at the present time, for two main reasons. Firstly, Media Studies as a self-contained subject has been excluded from the National Curriculum. If it is to maintain a place in the school curriculum at all, Media Studies teachers will have to make links with teachers of other subjects and work across the curriculum to a greater or lesser extent.

Secondly, and more broadly, integration has become a strong policy objective of a number of bodies such as BTEC, NCVQ and the Joint Board for CPVE. Yet there has been much debate about the relative merits of subject-based and integrated approaches to teaching[1] and this chapter should give some basis on which to identify the strengths and weaknesses of each approach and to suggest future strategies.

Media Education across the Curriculum

The aim of this section is to examine some of the theoretical perspectives and rationales for promoting cross-curricular work such as media education.

It may be useful to begin by outlining some of the distinctions between Media Studies and media education, in terms of their aims and respective positions in the curriculum. The study of the media must be seen now to be both a domain (or subject in its own right) and a dimension (or aspect of all other subjects). Media Studies, the domain, exists as a discrete element on timetables, has its own object of study, its own set of concepts and pedagogy. It has its own history of development, its struggle for a place on the timetable and, like other subjects, its own struggle over form and content.[2] Media education, the dimension, may be viewed and taught as an aspect of all subjects on a timetable. Media educators are concerned to extend the insights of Media Studies to inform the use of media products in other curriculum areas.[3] This is not a new idea: there have been other such initiatives, most notably language across the curriculum[4] and more recently information technology across the curriculum.[5]

That a shift has occurred from Media Studies (as a discrete domain) to media education (a dimension of the whole curriculum) suggests that in the eyes of many educators certain key debates have now been won. There is a clear assumption that the debate over whether the media should be studied in schools or not has been won and a clear acknowledgment of the fact that teachers of many other subjects make substantial use of the media in their teaching. There is also an assumption that most children are watching a substantial amount of television and that, in the words of the 1983 DES Report *Popular Television and Schoolchildren*, 'all teachers should be involved in examining and discussing TV programmes with young people'.[6] Following the DES Report of 1983, a range of articles has appeared examining the role of media education in the curriculum.[7]

A starting point for secondary media education is this acknowledgment that a range of media products are used for teaching purposes in all subjects in the curriculum. These products often tend to be used as just another source of information (alongside textbooks) without any reflection on the fact that they are representations of the subject matter from a specific institutional perspective. For example, television programmes are used in Geography to give a more direct experience of another way of life, or in English as a stimulus for discussion or creative writing. In most cases, the ways these subjects are represented and the ways in which students make sense of them are not questioned.

One of the main aims of media education is to raise questions about the media text, using concepts developed in Media Studies such as narrative, genre, representation, audience, and institution. This activity would enhance the teaching of a subject by considering how the meanings that a text generates are constructed and how they relate to the expectations and prior knowledge of the pupils. The main problem with the unreflective method of using media texts is that it assumes that there is one meaning to a media text and that this meaning is the same for all viewers. From Media Studies comes the idea that texts are inherently polysemic and that viewers make sense of them in a variety of ways dependent on their prior knowledge and attitudes.

In the senses outlined here, media education is concerned more widely with how knowledge is mediated and constructed. It represents a challenge to traditional conceptions of knowledge because it is concerned with one of the processes by which pupils acquire information and understanding. Thus, coming to understand the selection and the choices made in the presentation of scientific findings in a programme such as *Tomorrow's World*, for example, may raise questions for the students about the selection and presentation of evidence in science as a whole, and about the nature and status of all empirical endeavour.

As with all cross-curricular initiatives (such as those concerned with language and information technology), media education needs an institutional base if it is not to lose its foothold in the curriculum. Integrating a subject across the curriculum requires that all teachers be familiar with the subject's central concepts and pedagogy and with the ways in which this process of integration affects the 'host' subject.

One way of supporting the integration of a subject is by issuing a policy statement. But it must be clear to most teachers that without other kinds of support (such as a post-holder responsible for the integrated subject, resourcing for staff development, pilot studies, representation on course teams, etc.), the subject will lose its foothold in the curriculum and be 'integrated out'.[8] As previous work on media education[9] has concluded, without such policies media education may be tackled in a piecemeal fashion or it may develop in an isolated way as a result of individual enthusiasm.

Our case study starts with a media specialist in post, and an agreed whole school policy for media education with some subsequent funding from an outside source. Recommendations regarding the implementation of media education policies will feature more fully in the conclusion to this chapter but it is clear that such cross-curricular initiatives are unlikely to succeed without their specialist base. A subject which is to be integrated across the curriculum still requires specialists to continue the development of that subject. It is also clear that the specialists who are most likely to succeed with this work are those whose interest lies in finding a broader base for their specialist insights, not just in promoting their own disciplines.

Context of the Case Study

Founded in 1980 from the amalgamation of three secondary schools in Paddington and Marylebone, North Westminster Community School was structured from the outset upon the notion of whole-school policies which were to operate across subject boundaries. They were to be written and implemented by responsibility post-holders whose effectiveness stemmed from their inclusion in the school's Curriculum Directorate. One of the first policies to be written and disseminated was the Whole School Media Policy, completed in January 1982.

This is an ambitious document stipulating far-reaching achievement objectives for each student in the school and setting out the analytic and practical skills they should learn in order to fulfil them. It is clear and uncompromising about the theoretical implications of such a programme, particularly in the stress laid on the 'non-transparency' of the media and in the recognition that 'all mass-produced images are *mediated*' and subject to 'industrial, aesthetic, professional and organisational constraints'. About the implications of this viewpoint on the media for every department, the document notes:

> The range of concepts and skills outlined above is clearly too wide and too complex to be achieved within the confines of a single discipline, or even a specialised Media Department. . . .
>
> Many departments teach about, with or through the media, each with its own disciplinary perspective and method of enquiry; thus there exists already a basis for a genuinely integrated approach to communications and the media.
>
> Certain topics, such as advertising and the Press, recur in several disciplines approached in a variety of ways and with considerable overlap. This diversity of perspective must be used as a strength on which to build; however, it must be monitored through stringent inter-disciplinary liaison and curriculum co-ordination to achieve coherence.[10]

The specific implications of the Whole School Policy for the Lower School curriculum are even more far-ranging:

> [Media Education] must develop a sound base of analysis and practice; it must remain in the core curriculum throughout our pupils' education. This inter-disciplinary structure involves:
> (a) highly structured media input within each of the major disciplines' core curriculum — whether in the form of short modular units, specific practical activities, project work or critical case studies;
> (b) considerable flexibility of teaching method, including possibilities of team teaching, . . . block time-tabling, inter-departmental collaboration and resource-sharing, and resource-based learning;
> (c) a substantial and essential element of practical work, supported by appropriate resources, expertise and equipment.

Martin (one of the co-authors of this chapter) joined the school in September 1985 with a dual responsibility for Media Studies as a single subject in the Upper School and for the implementation of the Whole School Policy across the entire curriculum. In this latter task he faced the following problems:

> (i) the school is divided across three sites: two Lower Schools, a mile apart, and one Upper School;
> (ii) resources for practical media work were based on just two of the sites; one Lower School had none;
> (iii) he was teaching a fairly full timetable exclusively at the Upper School;
> (iv) the strong union work-to-rule at the time meant no after-school meetings.

In addition, teachers' attitudes to the Whole School Policies were largely conditioned by a view of them as being imposed from above, by the head and management, and by the fact that timetable strictures, work routines and exam requirements constrained teachers to work day-to-day along single subject lines. Thus, work on implementing the Whole School Policies tended to be either non-existent or slow and piecemeal, although Martin's predecessor, Jenny Grahame, author of the Media policy, had taken considerable steps towards implementation, particularly in English and CDT. One problem she encountered was that with the departure of the head of CDT, much of the ground covered was allowed to lapse.

After a period of settling into his job, Martin decided to ask the Head for some remission from his teaching timetable in order to negotiate his cross-curricular role in a space freed from at least some of the constraints just mentioned. It seemed that unless he had the chance to work fairly concentratedly with one or two departments to start with, devising teaching materials and writing media components into departmental syllabuses, any implementation he might achieve would fall lamentably short of the aims of the original project. After persistent efforts and several applications to funding sources, INSET money was found by the ILEA English Centre and Martin secured a day and a half's remission per week for a year.

It was at this point, in May 1987, that the other co-authors of this chapter (who were fellow members of the Media Teachers Research Group) collaborated with him to set up the cross-curricular project as a properly researched and monitored exercise. A questionnaire enquiring about classroom use of and teaching about the media was circulated to every teacher in the school (see next section). The aim was to inform ourselves as fully as possible about school-wide use of media and the nature and extent of media education awareness in each subject area and to use this information to gauge where and how best to start in-depth work with particular departments. Ironically, however, the choice of subjects and teachers Martin worked with was ultimately determined by the split-site nature of the school and by the need to reach the maximum number of students in both lower and upper schools. These considerations effectively reduced the possible departments to three:

STAS (Science, Technology and Society), taught across fourth and fifth years in Upper School;
Lower School Humanities, taught across the first, second and third years;
English, a compulsory core subject throughout the school.

Using replies to the questionnaires as a basis, Martin conducted tape-recorded interviews with groups of teachers in each of these departments including the heads of STAS and English.

The English Centre's arrangements allowed for the half-day secondment of one teacher from each of the departments Martin worked with. This had the threefold aim of:

(a) effecting a genuine collaboration between two disciplines rather than mere one-way flow;

(b) establishing the other teacher as media expert in the department; and

(c) achieving more balanced and hopefully more permanent INSET provision, particularly in the event of Martin leaving the school.

Early Strategies

The Questionnaire

As explained, the questionnaire was intended to ascertain the extent to which teachers at North Westminster were using the media in their lessons. It was therefore intended largely to uncover current practice with a view to describing it and to finding a starting point for the project. It was also hoped that the questions posed might lead teachers to reveal the extent to which they were aware of the constructed nature of the material they were using (whether it was videos, photographs, audio cassettes or some other form of media) and that the questionnaire would help to identify key staff and departments who might be interested in becoming more involved in the project.

The questions were carefully framed by the group so as to encourage staff to describe their teaching strategies. It was felt that the questions should not appear threatening or intrusive and should not imply that certain answers would be 'unacceptable'.

In an early draft of the questionnaire, after a section which asked the teachers to identify the types of media they had used in the classroom, we asked 'Did you focus in any way on *how* the programme or film was made?'. These questions (and others like them) were eventually considered to be too indicative of a particular sought-after response and were replaced by more open invitations to staff to describe the advantages and disadvantages of the material they had used. We felt mindful, too, of the pressures and time constraints affecting teachers and so endeavoured to produce the questionnaire in a format that was spacious and attractive. The presentation is an important aspect of any questionnaire's design and we wanted staff to feel that this was an opportunity to contribute to the project rather than a subtle form of appraisal.

The questionnaire was distributed to about 140 staff at the school, and 36 completed forms were returned. The completed questionnaires indicated that a range of visual and printed material was in frequent use and that such material was in general more often used than sound-based media.

In general, the media were being used in classrooms for illustrative or directly educative purposes. Items such as films and videos were used to provide access to written texts (such as *Macbeth*) and to stimulate both writing and discussion. One Humanities teacher felt that part of his purpose in using a video he described as 'biased' was to train pupils to detect bias, that is to 'read' such videos critically. On the whole, however, the stated purposes for using these materials related to the perceived subject content of the part of the curriculum that the teacher was responsible for; they were related, that is, to 'getting across' a set text, a health education issue, or to illustrate the application and relevance of topics studied in class. Audio cassettes were used to develop listening skills, especially in language classes, and sometimes to provide creative work. Magazines, photographs and posters were generally used as visual stimulus for other activities (e.g. drawing or writing) and sometimes, too, as direct 'evidence' of an event.

The methods described for using visual material were generally based on the principle of screen or show first and then discuss, question and write. A few teachers did, however, introduce the material and one described the way in which he set tasks for completion (e.g. to spot the 'facts' and the 'opinions' in the video) before the students watched it.

More flexibility of approach was evident when the aim was the teaching of language; several language teachers described the way in which they played and re-played videotapes, used the pause facility and gave their questions out to the pupils before the viewing took place. These strategies were even more in evidence when teachers were using audio cassettes.

Teachers were asked next to state what they liked and what they disliked about the material in question. The answers given to these two questions often related to the constructed nature of the media and revealed that many of the teachers were, in fact, concerned about the 'hidden meanings' contained in the material they were using.

The things they disliked about the videos, magazines, slides or audio cassettes included, for example, the lack of multi-cultural awareness evident in the material; its heavy stereotyping; its lack of emphasis on class differences; its poor technical quality; and, on several occasions, the fact that the material was aimed at the wrong audience for their purposes.

The things they liked included good technical quality (of presentation, interviewing, filming or colour reproduction) and, on occasion, the representation of a particular viewpoint. (A video on South Africa was chosen and liked specifically because it showed black South Africans fighting back and avoided 'an Oxfam approach'.)

The questionnaire did not reveal the extent to which teachers alerted their pupils to these issues of representation, production, audience and mediation, if indeed they did so at all. It did, however, provide a basis for setting up interviews with several members of staff, details of which follow.

Tape-recorded Interviews with Staff

Martin interviewed staff from several subject areas (Humanities, English, STAS) as a follow-up to the questionnaires. The interviews lasted, on average, thirty minutes, and were tape-recorded.

During the interviews Martin outlined a brief summary of the central concepts of media education. The subsequent discussions demonstrated the ways in which people assimilate new knowledge by rephrasing accounts of new ideas, such as media education, in terms more familiar to them. For example, when Martin explained the emphasis that was placed on the concept of 'construction' to the STAS teachers they reinterpreted these ideas in terms of their syllabus, e.g. the requirement to 'distinguish between fact and opinion'; the Humanities teacher linked this summary to the examination of sources and evidence which was part of her syllabus.

The Humanities teacher expressed a lack of structured knowledge of genres in the media and a desire to learn more. The main issues discussed were the role of a media educator in relation to the 'host' subject and the implication of this for producing teaching materials.

One interesting point which emerged was that in previous Humanities work students had expressed a strong interest in making a video programme as an appropriate way of undertaking their assignment. As one teacher expressed it 'something seems to be going on because these students were not doing Media Studies and yet already knew about video'. It was not clear whether this interest was the result of the media education initiative or whether it came, for example, from the students' work in English, where a significant amount of work using various media was undertaken. Martin was able to advise this teacher on the need for supplementary material, like a student log, to enable individual assessment of group work such as video.

The STAS teachers proved most responsive to the idea of media education and were also the teachers who voiced more fundamental questions about the status of knowledge. The aim of STAS was seen as 'helping students to understand technical and scientific issues as they affect them and how they affect science and technology'. Extensive use was already made of articles from the *New Scientist* and the *Guardian* but staff felt that the language used was generally too complex for the students. All the teachers could see the point of using other media and particularly articles from the tabloid papers. In fact several of them illustrated this point by explaining how they had used articles from the *Daily Mirror* to demonstrate the way in which Chernobyl was reported. It was clear that the STAS teachers had used media material in their teaching. For example, in work on additives they had looked at food adverts and the audiences the adverts were appealing to.

The teachers did not see any conflict between their aims and those of media education, but it is interesting to note that discussion on this issue revealed differing viewpoints among the STAS staff. One member expressed quite a radical relativism, another a fundamental positivism. This debate illustrates how the status of knowledge is already an issue in some subject areas which media education can pick up on.

These teachers were quite searching in their questions: 'Are you trying to make the students aware of their responses (to visual images) or are you trying to get them to change their responses?' There was substantial discussion about the role of the teacher in imposing ideas on the students. Martin challenged the idea that teachers have no right to change students' ideas by questioning the underlying assumption that students somehow 'have' their ideas as if from nowhere. He argued that media education can provide a basis on which to examine the way ideas are constructed in the various media.

The interview with the English staff revealed another facet of a media educator's work. As was clear from the questionnaires, the English staff used media products a great deal. The discussion centred around the extent to which the English teachers' current methods were consistent with a media education approach. For example, they discussed the links that an activity such as writing a newspaper report from the point of view of one character in a novel had with a media education approach.

These teachers felt that there would not be enough time to do media education justice and cover all those elements which were important for the English curriculum. Martin suggested an approach in which texts were regarded as artefacts with production relations, a history, an audience or expected readership. The response from the staff was that it would be interesting to adopt this approach for a change but they did not think it would be appropriate to do this for every single text. The same kind of issues arose when they discussed the use of tape recorders for oral assessment.

Using questions and interviews in this way had a number of advantages. Firstly, these strategies provided Martin with a 'way in' and undoubtedly helped raise awareness in the school of issues related to media education. Secondly, they established him as an investigator who was concerned to discover (and not just to change) current practice. As a follow-up to the questionnaires, the interviews gave more opportunity for staff to question and challenge Martin in person and to explore the language of media education in order to accommodate this within their own subjects. Lastly, there was useful discussion, too, on the role of the media educator, and there were attempts to negotiate the next phase of Martin's work with him. Martin was able to ascertain how amenable staff were to media education proposals and to give useful advice on specific methods.

In the event, however, the logistics of timetabling determined the next phase in the implementation of the media education policy. These constraints became paramount, since they determined the availability of staff for collaborative work. We noted that intervention prior to timetabling is crucial if cross-curriculum activities such as this are to succeed.

Jocelyn Robson, Jonathan Simmons, Martin Sohn-Rethel

Media Work with STAS (Science, Technology and Society)

STAS was chosen as the first subject area for cross-curricular collaboration. As was suggested above, one reason for this was logistical and school-specific: all fourth-year and fifth-year students could be reached as STAS was a compulsory core subject for those years. However, there were several other factors which were important motivators for the collaboration.

STAS was constituted as a core subject equal in status and allocated time (three fifty-five-minute periods per week) to the students' own subject options. This is because it was conceived from the outset as integrating a variety of disciplines and approaches; in other words, it was itself a cross-curricular package. Initially this element was written into staffing and organization: teachers were drafted in from other departments and the subject content and syllabus were conceived and drawn up by an interdisciplinary subcommittee. Later, a core of four (then three) subject specialists were supplemented by non-STAS teachers (including the Head and one Deputy).

The central idea behind the course is the threading of issues such as nuclear energy, the environment, Third World technology and space research around a set of relationships (called 'themes' in the original syllabus of 1982), for example between the individual and science, technology and society, between people and organized groups, between materials and the products into which they are made. The issues are dealt with in discrete modules contributed by the various teachers involved and are designed so that 'the themes will be revisited in a variety of contexts and in a variety of complexities.' Also underpinning the content are a range of 'key concepts' such as *change* (subdivided into continuity, equilibrium, innovation, development, cause and effect), *influence* (also with its subset), *environment* and several others.

This course structure not only resembles the structure and approach commonly adopted in Media Studies courses, with such key concepts as forms and conventions, representation, institution, and audiences;[11] it also greatly facilitates the insertion of media elements into STAS issues and the dissemination and 'revisiting' of media concepts throughout the course. Indeed the original syllabus document foresaw as the second of three main functions that STAS 'will act . . . as a vehicle for appropriate parts of the whole school policies'.

Gardner and Young have persuasively argued[12] that television constitutes the general public's only significant source of information about science. Thus, in explicit consideration of the media in a subject expressly encompassing the public, popular aspects of science would appear to be of paramount importance.

To what extent was this the case prior to the collaboration described here? Media accounts of science did indeed form a significant, though not large, part of the materials used in the STAS classroom and in the examination (originally CSE Mode 3, then NEA GCSE Mature — see below) but they were entirely confined to 'up-market' sources such as the *New Scientist*, the *Independent* and the *Guardian* and were used predominantly as transparent windows on hard scientific fact. The mediating forces of bias, selection, presentation, editing and news values together with those of genre and narrative were never made the explicit subjects of study. This is hardly surprising: 'quality' science reporting, whether on TV or in print, is generally regarded as hard information by the public and by the vast majority of social agencies and as such is accorded high and uncritical status.

One of the main aims in planning the media education/STAS collaboration was precisely to prise open this seemingly transparent window on science. To do so, it seemed doubly advantageous to use examples of popular tabloid journalism: *The Sun*, *The Mirror*, *Wogan* and *Tomorrow's World*. Here mediation is far more full-frontal; moreover, these are precisely the media sources available to fourth- and fifth-year secondary students. It could be asserted that a 'hidden curricular' aim of STAS was to equip students with the skills needed to digest the *New Scientist*. To this extent, the down-market approach to STAS/media education work was clearly a challenge to the existing rationale. But the new direction was nevertheless readily accepted by the specialist STAS teachers; indeed, attempts have subsequently been made by the Head of Department to write a 'popular' media question into the NEA exam paper.

Prior to this, the NEA Mature certification of the course represented a rather uneasy compromise and was generally little suited to the needs of a compulsory core subject examined in the fifth year. It was actually intended as a one-year Mature course for sixth-formers and college students with an individual project receiving a 30 per cent weighting. (A Mode 3 submission by the STAS Department had been rejected by the LEAG as being insufficiently content-related — significant when compared with the near-total lack of prescribed content in the LEAG Media Studies syllabus! — and the NEA course was the only viable alternative.) Furthermore, and totally consistent with the transparent use of media described above, there were no explicit media elements in the exam paper. One or two regular question slots used *Guardian* or *Independent* science and technology reports in the guise of hard information — as comprehension exercises and for candidates to top up with their own knowledge. (In fact, these reports seemed often to have been significantly abridged, although this was not explicitly acknowledged.)

Overall, in the vital matter of GCSE assessment, STAS did not afford media-related work much scope for final certification other than in individual projects where students could clearly be encouraged to develop ideas in this direction. However, in the media education/STAS meetings convened to plan the main body of work, it was decided principally to produce materials for the discrete units described above, as they formed the substance of fourth- and fifth-year teaching. The most urgent need of the Department was for a three-to-four-week unit of media-related work on AIDS and HIV and this formed the first major component of the collaboration, the second being a unit on nuclear energy.

It was in designing the AIDS module that a very significant gap became evident in the school's whole school policy provision — one which called into question the cross-curricular aim quoted above. There was in fact no whole school policy for health education; any work done on sex, sexual relationships, sex-related diseases etc., was by default purely a matter for individual tutors; pupils were likely to encounter these highly emotive issues for the very first time in their STAS lessons. This constituted an acute problem for STAS teachers who needed to foreground the scientific aspects of AIDS and HIV rather than their sexual and attitudinal repercussions for the individual student — although clearly the two aspects can in no way be artifically separated. The difficulty was compounded by the high number of Bangladeshi girls who at home are almost totally sheltered from these concerns.

What then were the explicit, overarching aims of the media education/STAS collaboration and how were they translated into actual materials and teaching methods? One main aim has been raised already; to point students' attention to the many processes of mediation which operate when science and technology are treated by television and the press. This involves closer scrutiny of the media than of the scientific subject matter. However, this leads directly to a deeper aim, one directed at the very status of scientific knowledge itself; to identify scientific discourse as subject to and changeable by historical, political and social forces — in effect, as subject to ideology. The two aims fuse in the process of examining and questioning the media's representation of science as 'the truth'.

This aim uncovers a deep-rooted problem in the institutional demarcation of scientific knowledge within the school itself. By hiving off the human, social and technological dimensions of science into a different, albeit integrative subject, taught in near total separation from physics, chemistry, biology and general science, the school effectively sanctions the divide between social issues on the one hand and objective science as unimpeachable truth on the other: the very dichotomy which the media education/STAS collaboration was at pains to criticize.

In line with accepted Media Studies practice, the unit of work on AIDS offered a mix of analytical and practical activities, although in fact the former outweighed the latter, at least initially. This was due to an abundance of recorded TV material broadcast before and during AIDS Week in March 1987 and to an equal quantity of collected press cuttings on AIDS, both quality and tabloid.

The unit began with a small-group discussion encouraging students to pool what they already knew about AIDS, to evaluate it on a sliding scale from 'certain' to 'mostly rumour' and to locate its source: adults, their own age group or the mass media. In this way they were to identify themselves as the possessors of knowledge and more crucially as the potential controllers of this knowledge, not merely as the passive recipients of externally generated 'scientific' messages. A second small-group session asked students to discuss how they could tell from what they actually saw and heard that a TV programme was about science, then to name such programmes, say when they were on air and who they were intended for. The whole-class report-backs, with their airing of agreements and disagreements, introduced the specific mediating processes employed across a whole range of science programmes, hopefully including fictional genres too. By widening out, away from AIDS, to the whole of science, they also focused on the status of the knowledge they contained.

This prepared the ground for the main substance of the unit: a detailed study of the TV extracts — divided into those broadcast before and those broadcast during AIDS Week in March 1987. Here the work — divided between note-taking in pairs and whole-class discussion — was to follow three sequential steps:

(a) to record, separately, what was seen and heard (denotation), particularly the way in which the programme was organized (e.g., studio presenter, panel, invited audience, key phrases, important questions, music, etc.);

(b) to gather these impressions into a set of conclusions about the programme's schedule slot, genre and precise target audience;

(c) to speculate about the messages concerning AIDS that came across, both intended and not intended. How were they conveyed? Were any at odds with the rest? Lastly, and most problematically, what did these messages say about science, scientists, and their effect on society?

The extracts were selected so as to cover the widest range of TV genres. Here our choice of AIDS as well as the diversity of formats chosen by the BBC and ITV (acting in unison during AIDS Week) proved fruitful, in that the overriding concern to educate the viewers cast a quintessentially scientific topic into some media forms very far removed from the traditional 'hard science' ones such as *Horizon* and *Antenna*. For example, ITV's *First AIDS* was a hybrid, revisiting numerous TV comedy and pop music routines — including sketches, stand-up comedy, puppets (a *Spitting Image* sequence), a celebrity panel, promo videos and zany computer graphics. But outside this customized blend, the extracts included other 'non-scientific' genres: an interview with a clinical psychologist working with AIDS patients on *Wogan* and sequences from one narrative strand in an episode of *The Bill* where an AIDS patient throws herself from a hospital balcony after a policewoman refuses to touch her — a piece of 'scientific misinformation' which the show corrects only in a very understated and weakly acted doctor's aside.

Clearly to achieve meaningful learning in the three stages of the work on the TV and press material and to do justice to the aims outlined above, the lessons needed to be handled both with awareness of the potential media education outcomes and with the readiness to validate a very wide range of student observation about science in the media. That such observations might depart very considerably from the realm of 'hard science' is not necesssarily evidence of ignorance on the students' part, rather a measure of just how science is filtered through different media slots, genres and formats with their contrasting demands for entertainment, news or 'hard science' values.

The 'referent' for these varied forms of mediation, AIDS and HIV, is the focus of a social and political concern which much of the coverage has fanned into intensely homophobic hysteria.[13] This itself in part prompted the choice of AIDS for media education/STAS treatment: it is a scientific problem which has become a social and governmental one. At the same time the hysteria is not of course merely an objective phenomenon to be analyzed; it invades the ideological, subjective domain of the classroom and to this extent, it may be impossible to avoid student expressions of homophobic prejudice. This is true of any meaningful pedagogy which takes on questions of ideology. Here teachers needed to weave adroitly between subject and object positions: on the one hand exposing 'objective' scientific truth to subjective critique, albeit filtered through the recognition of different televisual forms (see above) and on the other guarding against excesses of subjective rumour and sexist vilification. The familiar problems of teaching about ideology were in this case further compounded by the personal and sexual address contained in much of the media coverage and foregrounded by the health education approach to AIDS which our approach could not always replace in the perceptions of the students.

The teaching materials endeavoured to promote sensitivity on these fronts by pointing student attention as much as possible towards the changing heterogeneous nature of the social and political debate around AIDS and by representing it as an area of active and urgent contestation. Shifts in social and governmental attitudes were suggested without, however, simply being spelled out: for instance between the first salvo of TV coverage in Autumn and Winter 1986/87 and the second of AIDS Week in March 1987; between the TV adverts, the 'falling mountain' and the 'iceberg' advert which followed it; and between both these adverts and those targeted at specific age and social groups. These adverts were studied primarily within the practical part of the AIDS package where students were asked to design their own adverts specifically targeting 14–16-year-olds, not yet sexually active but in imminent danger from the virus.

In this context, Tony Whittaker, the STAS teacher seconded for the collaboration, and Martin were able to present a considerable amount of background information and material gathered from an interview with Alison Rolfe, account manager with TBWA, the first advertising agency to handle the Government's AIDS campaign. The interview itself was somewhat 'contested'. As Tony's account puts it: 'Unfortunately, as one of the clients is a government department, Alison Rolfe was not completely free to give us all the information we may have wanted. In fact, clearance had to be obtained from the DHSS for our interview to take place at all.' Controversy clearly surrounded the first two TV adverts (universally condemned as ill-judged and ineffective), a major factor being government censorship: mentions of sexual intercourse and condoms were cut from the first advert by ministerial pressure. But also instrumental was the undeclared and constantly shifting stance of the IBA to the storyboards for commercials which had to be submitted for its approval. Teachers could follow this up by showing students *Diverse Reports*, screened on Channel Four during AIDS Week, which commented on the adverts and showed the far more hard-hitting, explicit examples made in France and Scandinavia.

A meeting called to review the progress of the AIDS package after its initial use in the classroom decided to balance the preponderance of media analysis in the work thus far by revising and designating specific lesson time to its practical component, *Design Your Own AIDS Ad*. This was now given a 'simulated brief' purporting to come from the Terrence Higgins Trust. We equipped this mini-project with precise teacher notes and a sample storyboard from a real advertising agency in order to make it relatively 'teacher-friendly' and avoid the pitfalls of the larger package which had been rather more teacher-directed. Nevertheless, the practical work depended for its true pedagogic success (as opposed to mere technical accomplishment and original copywriting) on the feeding back of insights gained from it into the analysis of the TV and press material that had gone before. It needed to be part of a cohesive programme both of teaching and of teacher-INSET. On an ad hoc basis, some of the necessary support was forthcoming from the very occasional sessions of co-teaching that Martin could fit into his timetable. The main advantage here was that inter-subject links could be conveyed as direct and tangible to the students themselves — by the actual presence in the classroom of two teachers from the different disciplines.

At this point it is necessary to move from consideration of the materials on AIDS and their classroom implications to the conditions of their actual delivery. It is clear in any case that teaching materials alone cannot guarantee success in the classroom — particularly in a 'two-pronged', cross-curricular project which aimed to get students thinking in new ways about how media coverage affects ideas about science, their own included. To prepare teachers to tackle questions of this depth, a systematic INSET programme is needed as well as the time to provide regular advisory back-up where required. How did the logistics of time and staff allocation in the collaboration affect the actual teaching of the AIDS package?

As was mentioned above, the media education/STAS collaboration incorporated the co-secondment of a full-time STAS teacher, Tony Whittaker, for one half-day per week. This proved to be very valuable, particularly in fostering a genuinely cross-curricular mode of working within the 'host' department. After an initial period of familiarization with media education concepts and methods, Tony assumed an increasing role in designing materials. Perhaps more significant was the sense of departmental commitment to new ways of working which his involvement brought about. He was of course ideally placed to liaise with his STAS colleagues and, in theory at least, to promote continuity of curriculum development after Martin, as media education Specialist, left the school. (In actual fact, he was redeployed and had to leave the following summer!)

The AIDS package underwent a chequered career in the classroom. The first materials (not the reworked practical component) were produced by Martin, the media education side of the collaboration, alone. The accompanying INSET, squeezed by restrictions on everybody's time into an overlong after-school session plus the odd snatched half-hour, was not adequate; some teachers lacked confidence and this, together with VCR breakdowns, led to rather piecemeal delivery of the package. Monitoring of the materials and their reception in the classroom, restricted as it was to following-up with individual teachers, was fragmented and inevitably subjective. The clear lesson learned was to allow enough INSET time for all participating teachers, on both sides of the collaboration, to view all the TV extracts and to tackle the student-directed questions and discussion points themselves. Only in this way could the deep structure inscribed in the aims and methodology of the package permeate through to the conscious critical understanding, and, if need be, to the fully articulated objections of those involved in teaching it.

Collaboration with Other Departments

Two further collaborations are worth noting, one with Lower School Humanities and the other with the English Department. Each of these involvements was different in some important ways from the work with STAS, and different issues arose for consideration.

Work with Lower School Humanities was much more ad hoc than with STAS and there was little or no departmental pre-planning of materials and method. Instead of working closely with a co-seconded member of another department on specifically commissioned materials, Martin sat in on selected lessons and designed a media input around what was being taught: in one case, the life and influence of Marco Polo and in the other, Islam, both as world religion and source of student experience.

Classroom study of Marco Polo centred around a video: the last two episodes of an Italian-produced series transmitted by Channel Four in 1986. Students were asked to complete a range of tasks, beginning with some descriptive work on major characters, and so on, based on clips from the video, and extending to some independent research on Marco Polo, followed by a second showing of the clips and a discussion about points of view. The final stage was to ask students how they could recognize the television industry's effects on the series.

In this way, students were led to question the historical authenticity of the television series' representation of Marco Polo, to debate the points of view expressed, and thus to debate the writing of history itself.

A similar approach was used in the treatment of the second topic, Islam. Again, the precise focus of the media input was to enquire into points of view and historiography through work on an educational video called *Islam through the Eyes of Muslim Children*. Work began, as usual, denotatively and students were asked to describe what they saw, as distinct from what they heard. Secondly, discussion was initiated around their own experience of Islam, in particular on gender divisions and prayer rituals, and thirdly, after a second showing of the programme, students were asked to speculate about the purposes and circumstances of its making.

The interrogation of this particular video and the questions as to who made it and for what precise audience were utilized and in turn reinforced by a practical activity in which the students outlined their own educational programme about their religion or beliefs and then scripted a short sequence from it. This work was linked critically with the preceding analytical work.

As with the intervention on Marco Polo, students were encouraged to think critically about the way in which history comes to be written and a challenge was offered to history's traditional understanding both of its content and its method.

The collaboration with the English Department differed again from those already described, as a consequence mostly of local, school-specific factors. Here the collaboration was confined wholly to writing media content and method at a 'macro' level into overall lower-school syllabus planning by the English Department: no 'micro' classroom materials were produced.

Media education/English work was considerably affected by the 'semi-familiarity' of many English teachers with media education methods and content that arises through the close historical and teacher training links between the two areas. (Many media teachers taught or still teach English.) Paradoxically, this was generally less productive for the collaboration than the unfamiliarity which media education represented for STAS and Humanities because, at the macro level mentioned above, it was almost impossible to identify how much media work was actually pursued within English itself. Whilst all English teachers used video at times and several included newspapers and magazines in their teaching, a few were resistant to media work, either to its conceptual framework or to practical activities.

A further factor affecting the collaboration was that Media Studies with its media education whole school policy had been pulled out of English and set up as a separate subject area to be an independent interdisciplinary force threading through the entire curriculum. Thus, somewhat unproductively, media-centred units of work had to justify and jostle for their place on the English syllabus in ways that would have been less necessary had media education continued as a fully constituted, uncontroversial part of English. (Now, ironically but predictably, the National Curriculum has confirmed a position for media education within English in the belief that 'this practice should be the entitlement of all pupils.'[14])

The following units of media and media/English work suggested at the macro level of syllabus-writing described above should be seen therefore as belonging within this problematic context. They were offered to fulfil the demands of a *syllabus* representing a media cross-curricular approach, not, as with STAS or Humanities, to integrate actual teaching materials and methods.

Each year of the lower secondary English syllabus was provided with a fairly self-contained unit of media work so as to give students (and teachers) a progressive foundation in media education approaches. To help teachers, these units were deliberately culled from published materials. For first-years, this was a unit of image study selected from Book One of *EyeOpeners*; for second-years, work on a photo-story such as *The Station*; and for third-years, work on either *Choosing the News* or *Comics and Magazines*.[15] Clearly, the last two involve considerable language work and might not necessarily be used to develop work in a media education direction.

The other units offered all call for a greater or lesser degree of English language or literature work, and thus may lead to similar difficulties: the very closeness of the fit within the subject content (newspapers obviously have everything to do with English) can work to prevent a media-critical line of enquiry.

This is particularly true of an idea for a first-year unit of work, 'What makes me laugh' or 'What makes me angry'. Here students collect their own examples from the media (print, photographic or televisual), mount them in a display and talk and write about them to classmates and the teacher. Clearly this work could easily sidetrack the whole issue of mediation and treat the examples as windows on the world. This danger is also present in a unit of autobiographical work where students use practical photography to present themselves to a real audience, perhaps to pupils in a school abroad or in a rural (or urban) area. Here there needs to be specific emphasis on the way in which photographs can be variously read and on how certain viewers will perceive meanings about ethnic, cultural or social identity that will not be read by others. In both units, captioning the images could play an important critical role.

Two ideas for second-year work attempt to build on these broader-based first-year ones, each leading in a specific media direction. An exercise on storyboarding a page, or at most two, from *The Eighteenth Emergency* uses, as an example, slides of a similar sequence taken from the film of *Kes*. These need quite detailed study and discussion, at an appropriate level, of how filmic language can capture the narrative and atmosphere of, say, a chase sequence.

Writing and recording a radio news bulletin to report amazing events in Hamelin is similarly based around a class reader, here *The Pied Piper*. This unit begins by exploring students' knowledge of radio and news in particular and then focuses on an actual Capital Radio news bulletin with students noting which stories are featured, from what angle they are written and then counting the duration of each item in seconds. They then base their own report on an imaginary Reuters press release — they are required to lead with a deliberately selected angle and to aim at a length of exactly thirty seconds.

The suggested third-year units broaden the focus once more with the comparative study of a genre such as Horror common to both literature and film. Here slides and film extracts are employed to direct attention to precise moments of narrative, which in turn reinforce detailed study of written texts. An important new dimension here would be consideration of who exactly is watching or reading and how the cinema and publishing industries cater for their tastes. Building on the earlier autobiographical use of photographs is a project charting in extended written form an imaginary (or real) campaign organized around a school or youth centre and culminating in the production of a publicity brochure designed to promote it. This is clearly an exercise in point of view: how to achieve a social aim through persuasive language and by judiciously taken, selected and cropped photographs. Simple graphics and layout can be added to the product; alternatively or additionally, the class could attempt to video a campaign-based version of the televised confrontation between opposing factions with a 'neutral' presenter attempting to keep the peace and maintain due 'balance'.

In conclusion, the main factors which affected the collaboration with English lay in the following areas. There was a lack of a systematically coordinated progression of skills and concepts through years one to three through which a corresponding spiral of media skills and concepts might be threaded. The National Curriculum proposals are now statutorily about to plug this gap for English, thus greatly easing the burden of responsibility for individual departments. Whether these proposals allow for a fully realized development of media education skills and concepts within English remains debatable. This problem might well not present itself in the same way for Humanities or for a science and society subject like STAS. There a media education dimension seems identifiable for almost any area tackled, the application being more integrally bound up with the precise subject matter under scrutiny than with English where, for example, students can be asked to produce newspaper or TV treatments on almost any topic from a school adventure to *Macbeth*. Such work becomes media education only when concepts such as 'audience' and 'institution' inform the questions which students are asked to address.

A similar approach can well be adopted for English. There are good reasons for studying the relationships between writers, editors, publishers, and readers, and indeed the whole social and cultural practice of English language and literature, in the same way that Media Studies addresses concepts such as 'institution' and 'audience'. And if Media Studies students can first consider media language denotatively and then interrogate it for metaphorical, connotative meanings, studying visual signs as social constructions, not as natural 'givens', then English students could productively analyze language, transactional and literary, in similar ways. The academic schools of post-structuralism and reception theory have already advanced such new channels of enquiry into texts; the stumbling-blocks are the many secondary and tertiary English departments that are tied to the traditions of 'Eng. Lit.' and by necessity, even with GCSE, to traditional patterns of English certification.

Since however both disciplines involve the study and use of meaning systems, it seems to make sense for English and media education to adopt an inter-related conceptual framework — if only to subvert the familiar refrain from alert students: 'This isn't English, it's Media Studies!' The present lack of conceptual fit makes the relationship between the two areas highly problematic. From a media education perspective, one would certainly want to question the sometimes 'transparent' use of films and videos to 'illustrate' literary texts. Altogether, the interaction of English and media education elements within one unit of work needs to ensure that the approach adopted for one element is not implicitly undermined by the approach to the other. For example, there seems little sense in drawing attention to genre in film and television while ignoring structures in literature which have very similar social and cultural causes and effects. Furthermore, a closer conceptual fit would facilitate the developmental progression of skills and understandings so important in formulating schemes of work for lower secondary and indeed primary English too.

Conclusion

What general conclusions for future practice can be drawn from this cross-curricular media education project that was by definition school-specific? What signposts point from this one account to an educational future dominated by the National Curriculum and its clearly articulated movement towards curricular integration and away from strictly demarcated subject boundaries?

Clearly one of the salient features of the North Westminster project was the pre-existence of a Whole School Policy for media education. However, this did not mean that management support structures were automatically in place to facilitate its actual implementation. Very considerable obstacles and resistances stood in its way, as described above; they all point to the strongest possible need in this, and any, cross-curricular innovation for post-holders with incentive allowances to carry direct responsibility for the effectiveness of teaching which crosses subject boundaries and thus by implication the parameters of virtually every classroom teacher's job and job awareness. The problem for management is to strike an effective balance between generalist post-holders holding fairly high-ranking responsibility for whole swathes of the curriculum (by definition not only media education) and specialists with direct expertise in the specific cross-curricular strand. The dilemma is that what generalists gain by virtue of their power base, they lose through lack of specific conceptual and practical knowledge; specialists with such knowledge lack the hierarchical clout to enforce curricular change and integration, often in the face of established departmental camps competing fiercely over shrinking resources of time and money. The North Westminster experience would seem to point to two general conclusions. Firstly, that the mere tacit support of Head and/or Deputy is nowhere near enough to ensure effective media teaching across the curriculum; and secondly, that moves to delegate cross-curricular responsibilities to mid-management generalists founder on the crucial need for a specialist who can empower the integration with coherent notions of media education theory and practice.

For these reasons, we see a Media Studies base, even if only vested in one person, as the essential prerequisite for effective media education across the curriculum. The on-going debate between media education and Media Studies[16] seems false and redundant, provided (and it is a weighty proviso) that Media Studies practitioners recognize and promote media education so as to enable *every* student to acquire media-related skills, not just those who choose Media Studies as a subject option. The two forms of provision are and should be mutually dependent on one another — to ensure dissemination of skills and knowledge and to promote conceptual rigour. Such a relationship should, moreover, effectively banish the insecurity that Media Studies specialists may experience in seeing media education skills and concepts disseminated and tailored to serve other areas of the curriculum.

Once a power base is in place to facilitate cross-curricular Media Education, three levels of delivery seem essential to ensure not only successful teaching by non-media-specialists but, crucially, continuation of the work when particular individuals leave an institution. These are, proceeding outwards from 'micro' to 'macro' levels:

(i) writing materials with and for a particular department;
(ii) teacher-INSET within the department;
(iii) overall curriculum planning within the department: writing media education work into the syllabus and determining modes of assessment and certification.

The first two are tied together particularly strongly. On those occasions at North Westminster where materials were presented to students without adequate trials and training, their full potential was wasted; teachers were unsure of the aims and of the underlying concepts and methods. Equally, to train staff of other departments without specific, purpose-prepared materials would just as surely undermine their confidence. It seems essential for the two collaborating disciplines to meet beforehand for a thorough preliminary discussion of both their conceptual bases. Quite apart from the benefits of teachers from different areas of the curriculum getting to know one another's teaching philosophies, this has vital consequences for cross-curricular media education in two particular directions.

One is that media education has to base itself upon cross-fertilization, not colonization of the curriculum. Each subject area makes different demands on a media education approach and method just as media education's conceptual base poses a challenge to each subject's traditional understanding of itself. Examples are the challenge to the neutral, white-coated 'objectivity' of science in the STAS collaboration and the exploration of how different historical accounts come to be written in the Humanities work. An example of the demands made on media education is the need for it to tailor its approach to suit the particular nature and syllabus of the collaborating subject and the circumstances of the institution's structures and processes. To degrade media education to the level of quick-fire, simplistic units aimed at varying modulations of media literacy is in effect to invite it to march with a repetitive colonizing tread across the curriculum rather than open itself and other disciplines to far-reaching epistemological scrutiny. Naturally, this makes for the exciting as well as the uphill nature of cross-curricular work.

The other consequence of thorough preliminary planning is to ensure that the media education input matches the host subject in terms of teaching methods, questions of practical as against written and oral work and the organization of time, although here as well the relationship should necessarily be a dynamic one capable of changes from both sides. In this respect some classroom observation prior to the collaboration would seem of benefit.

The third level of delivery, that of writing integrated elements into the syllabus and assessment, is in effect the essential response to the potential fluidity produced by the first two, comprising a considered progression of skills and learning as well as, in planning assessment and certification, an officially recognized rationale and justification to the collaboration. Without this level, cross-curricular work will always run the risk of surviving only as long as the energy and input of its individual contributors and will then amount to mere bouts of inconsequential curricular innovation.

The National Curriculum proposals and particularly those of the document *English for Ages 5–16*[17] suggest, at least on a generous reading, that cross-curricular teaching is anything but this — that it is, in fact, a very prominent part of every student's educational experience. However, the role ascribed to media education is very sketchy and as yet lacks any agreed map of attainment targets, levels or programmes of study. Nevertheless, what is of more immediate concern for the future of a media education genuinely integrated across the curriculum is whether the architects of the National Curriculum wish to see media education ghettoized entirely within English. Clearly, this would spell virtually the end of the kind of work attempted in the North Westminster project despite providing media education with a secure and reasonably familiar base. Analytical and practical work on media needs to be written into the National Curriculum proposals of all the core and foundation subjects if their ascribing of importance to working across subject boundaries holds any substance.

We were left with many questions after completing this project, not least of which were how the students' work in this type of cross-curricular initiative could be assessed and how the effectiveness of the different approaches used in the case study could be evaluated. We felt that many avenues were opened up for further research into student learning and collaborative teaching strategies.

Notes

1 Useful starting points on this topic include Bernstein (1971); Further Education Unit (1982b), Chapter 3; Heathcote *et al.* (1980); Pring (1976).
2 See, for example, Alvarado, Gutch and Wollen (1987), Chapter 1; Lusted (1982).
3 See, amongst others, Buckingham (1987a); Masterman (1983); Masterman (1985), Chapter 8.
4 Marland (1977).
5 See the RSA modular courses Information Technology for Teachers and Trainers and Information Across the Curriculum.
6 DES (1983).
7 See, for example, Blewitt (1988), Butts (1987), Hart (1987), McKiernan (1987), Reid (1987), *Secondary Educational Journal* (1985).
8 This term was coined in relation to the integration of General and Communication Studies on BTEC courses. See Waugh (1985).
9 See Cornish (1987), which is a summary of a conference organized in June 1987 by the South East Popular TV and Schoolchildren Group, one of the regional groups invited to participate by HMI after the publication of DES (1983). A previous conference, 'Television and Schooling', organized jointly by the British Film Institute and the University of London Institute of Education in November 1983, explored the wider implications of the Report's proposals; see Lusted and Drummond (1985).
10 Grahame (1985).
11 See LEAG Media Studies syllabus.
12 Gardner and Young (1981), p. 171.
13 Watney (1987).
14 DES (1989).
15 Bethell (1981); *The Station: An Experiment in Creating Mood*, ILEA English Centre; Simons and Bethell (n.d.); Leggett and Hemming (n.d.).
16 See Bazalgette (1989a) and Masterman (1989). The debate has been going on for some time: see, for example, Lusted (1985).
17 DES (1989).

Chapter 9

Teaching the Text:
English and Media Studies

Andy Freedman

As a teacher of both English and Media Studies, I have taken part in numerous discussions about the relationship between the two subjects. In some cases, a similarity in lesson content would suggest that the two areas are essentially united: for example, both English and Media Studies teachers regularly undertake work on advertising or the press. Yet at the same time, similar material might well be approached in quite different ways in the two areas. Beyond this, for example in syllabuses and more theoretical accounts, there is also a sense in which English and Media Studies tend to be defined and argued for in very different terms — although there is clearly a variety of versions of each subject.

This chapter examines the relationship between English and Media Studies by means of a small-scale case study, based on classroom observation and the analysis of students' work. In this study, as is often the case, the two subjects are taught by the same teacher, responding to the demands of two syllabuses. How are the similarities and differences between English and Media Studies manifested in classroom practice?

* * * * *

To some extent, English and Media Studies are concerned with different *objects of study* — and in particular, with texts in different kinds of media. Yet apart from this, what distinguishes the two subject areas? Why have the study of literature and the study of popular culture been seen, for many years, as inevitably in conflict? In order to answer this question, it is necessary to take a brief detour into the history of the two subjects.

This history has been well documented elsewhere[1] so it will suffice to provide a brief outline of the major phases which have been identified. While there are different versions of both subjects which derive from particular historical periods, it would be false to suggest that 'new' approaches have simply supplanted 'older' ones. On the contrary, at any one time there is often a variety of approaches, which may co-exist in a state of tension or uneasy harmony.

The 'cultural heritage' definition of English is typically identified with the work of Leavis and Thompson.[2] Here, the fundamental aim is to defend a culture which is seen as morally worthwhile against the perceived threat of an alien, commercial culture identified particularly with the mass media. Education, by offering a training in 'taste' and 'discrimination', seeks to enable the individual to resist moral and cultural decline. This approach is centrally concerned to preserve the status of a specific group of texts, a 'literary heritage', which is assumed to possess inherent quality, value or moral worth. Yet is is also concerned to develop critical skills which will enable students to discriminate these texts from those of lesser quality.

In the 1950s and 1960s, however, this fundamentally hostile approach towards media texts was supplanted by a more egalitarian approach. Rather than automatically discriminating *against* media texts, there was a move towards discriminating *within* them. Thus, for example, distinctions were made[3] between 'great' films and popular films, or between film and television. In the case of media texts which possessed artistic 'quality', it was argued, 'it was part of an educational process to transmit these aspects of a cultural heritage'.[4]

During the same period, a further approach emerged which sought to offer a more 'relevant' education, in particular for 'the Newsom child'. The widely used materials of the Schools Council Humanities Curriculum Project and books like the Penguin *Connexions* series testify to the new cross-curricular emphasis on 'social themes'. In this context, films were seen as more accessible than literary texts and could be used as an attractive 'way into' a theme, and as a stimulus for discussion. Particularly within English teaching, films were also increasingly being used as a stimulus for creative writing, with an emphasis on 'feeling' as a prerequisite for 'self-expression'.

By the late 1960s, the notion of 'personal growth' had emerged as one of the most dominant rationales for English teaching. While the emphasis on transmitting a 'literary heritage' was reduced, the view of literature as a means of promoting students' moral and emotional development remained. In the 1970s *The Bullock Report*[5] reflected this approach, with its rationale for the study of literature which involved terms such as insight, tolerance, sensitivity and personal and social growth. Literature was regarded as a means of enabling students to seek moral standards, confront issues, entertain a variety of viewpoints and show sympathetic identification. Despite conflicting versions of what constituted appropriate texts — traditional classics or the recent fiction favoured by more progressive teachers — the vast majority of English teachers accepted this view that literature could make the individual a better person. When confronted with a text, students might ask themselves: 'What would I do if I found myself in that situation? Do I or do I not care for people like that? Is there a part of me that understands them?'

The use of literary texts, and of certain 'approved' media texts, was thus related to a number of central aims: the transmission of 'culture'; developing appreciation and discrimination; developing an awareness of 'social issues' through abstracting the content of texts; 'personal growth'; and creative and practical expression. To these, one might add more instrumental approaches to texts, where the development of students' mechanical skills with language was the major aim.

Andy Freeman

During the 1970s the introduction of new critical theories provided a rather different rationale for studying film and other media texts. Description and analysis of popular cultural products began to replace approaches based on taste and evaluation. More 'objective' critical and ideological analysis of a broadly structuralist variety, with an emphasis on the formal properties of texts, effectively made questions about 'quality' and 'personal response' redundant. While these approaches were slow to make an impact on English teaching in schools[6] they were adopted comparatively quickly by teachers concerned with film and media texts, at least at the secondary level.

The emergence of this new theoretical basis for media teaching led to an increasing divergence from the traditional approaches of English. While most media teachers remain English teachers, there has been a considerable degree of antagonism between the two areas. Len Masterman,[7] the most influential advocate of media education, is certainly highly dismissive of what he terms the 'liberal humanist' approach of mainstream English teaching.

If we consider the relationship between English and Media Studies on this broad theoretical level, then, there are undeniably significant differences between them. From the perspective of Media Studies, English is often accused of being individualistic and depoliticized. The emphasis on language as a means of giving shape to students' thoughts and feelings effectively abstracts 'personal' values and qualities from any broader social context. The reader is defined as an individual subject, free to confront the text openly and to produce a personal response as a result. As critics have argued, mainstream English teaches individuals to be 'sensitive, imaginative, responsive, sympathetic, creative, perceptive... receptive... about nothing (or anything) in particular':[8] subjectivity is seen as an end in itself.

On the face of it, then, we might expect an opposition between English and Media Studies in terms of their relative emphasis on 'objective' and 'subjective' readings. We might expect Media Studies to be concerned with an analytical, 'objective' approach to texts, and to require relatively 'closed' responses from students. English on the other hand might be expected to be more 'subjective', inviting more open responses to texts and being more concerned with the expression of 'feeling'.

In practice, however, English teaching is rarely as wholly 'subjective' as this would suggest. The 'quality' of response — as manifested in certain 'approved' forms like the 'well-structured essay' — is often given at least as much significance as the content of the response. Students are tested not just on their level of personal interaction with the text, but on whether or not they can be 'critics'. Students' notion of what counts as an 'authentic' response will depend upon their understanding of what the teacher expects: implicitly, some kinds of responses will come to be seen as acceptable, while others will not. In a number of English teaching contexts, personal responses to the moral and political content of texts are subordinated to a notion of 'objective' reading. Thus, whilst a personal response or evaluation may be explicitly sought in the title of an assignment, students get to know that expressions of their opinions and experience are not necessarily the way to obtain high grades. Apparently 'open' assignments may in fact be much more closed than they seem at first sight.

This emphasis on 'objective' reading is much more explicit in accounts of media teaching. As a variety of writers have argued,[9] the aim of 'analysis' in media teaching is to enable students to go beyond their initial subjective responses, and to produce a more rigorous, objective reading — which, as other contributors to this book have argued, is often simply the one preferred by their Media Studies teacher. As the account which follows will suggest, there may be a good deal of common ground shared between English and Media Studies on this question of 'objective' reading.

Underlying this concern, one may detect further similarities between English and Media Studies in terms of their model of the relationship between texts and readers. Dominant definitions of both areas tend to be based on an assumption that texts exert powerful influences on students both in terms of the production of their own work and in terms of their attitudes and behaviour. Both subjects may share the view that it is only through the acquisition of critical skills, which encourage distance from the text, that students will be able to perceive its true meaning and assess the nature of its influence. While this view has been challenged in some recent work on English teaching[10] and by many of the accounts of media teaching contained in this book, this has been a comparatively recent development. Nevertheless, as I shall argue, the distinction between English and Media Studies may be much less clear-cut in practice than it would appear to be in theory.

* * * * *

The research reported in this chapter concentrates upon the use of texts, both written and audio-visual, in GCSE English and Media Studies lessons. While this obviously excludes a whole range of activities which may take place in each area, it does enable us to concentrate on the differences and similarities in one central aspect of both subjects.

In particular, I want to examine the kinds of activities relating to texts which students are asked to engage in. From the range of activities and written assignments I observed in both subjects, I drew up a list of eight categories, listed below. These are arranged firstly in terms of the degree of openness or closure available to the student in his or her reading of the text; and secondly in terms of the extent to which teacher expectation can be seen to determine or to limit the range of possible responses to a text.

1   Reading only: this would include on-going private reading/viewing where the only response is to record the texts read, perhaps with oral reports to other students. This type is most open in both respects.

2   Personal response to a text: for example, a piece of writing of any genre produced after reading a poem or viewing a film. This equally open in terms of reading, if slightly more specific in terms of response.

3   Using a text as stimulus for 'creative' writing. Here the writing is essentially more important than the reading of the stimulus text.

4   Reading and consideration of a text in relation to issues or a theme. Attributes of the text (often the 'content') are being used as material to form the basis of, for example, a discussion or a piece of transactional writing.

5   Response to a text in relation to its audience or production context. Here, students are invited to hypothesize about a range of possible readings, or about the potential target audiences of, for example, an advertisement.

6   A structured critical essay. Here, the student is required to choose a critical position and to argue it in an objective way, with reference to the text. This is limited in the possible style of responses, but there may be room for a restricted range of possible readings.

7   Identification and analysis of formal features. The form of response here is effectively closed, although there is some limited space for individual reading.

8   Evaluative response to a text on the basis of content analysis. Here, preferred readings and closed responses are required. Students are expected to reconstruct a single meaning: there is effectively one 'right' answer.

While there is inevitably some overlap between these categories, they do nevertheless embody quite different criteria by which students' work might be assessed. The difficulty, of course, is that these criteria may not always be made apparent to students. In many instances, there may be a 'hidden agenda' — a set of perceptions about what earns high grades — which students may have to discover by trial and error, and which they develop from one assignment to the next.

*   *   *   *   *

The research was carried out in a six-form-entry comprehensive, the only secondary school serving a small town. The catchment area includes affluent commuters, new housing estates, some older council houses and the demographic mix connected with farming. Within the English department, which is responsible for Media Studies, all students are taught in a mixed-ability groups, including at GCSE level.

The four assignments I want to consider in detail here were set by an experienced teacher of English and Media Studies to students in both her fourth-year GCSE groups. Both groups were following an English Language syllabus which specified that of the ten coursework units one must be 'related to study of the media', while another was to be based on a 'complete literary text'. Additionally, in the same lesson blocks as English Language, one group was working towards Media Studies GCSE, others towards English Literature GCSE, the groupings being based on student option choices in the third year. In considering responses to the assignments, I will examine the work of two students, one from each group.

The three syllabuses involved were predominantly coursework-based. The

English Language assessment is wholly by means of a course work folder containing ten units of work. For English Literature students were also required to submit ten units of work of which one must 'show evidence of close and detailed reading of a poem or a passage from a text' and another must be written in response to independent reading. A minimum of five individual texts must be studied, ensuring coverage of poetry, prose and drama.

The Media Studies syllabus required students to produce six pieces of coursework, including at least one cross-media piece and one piece based upon photographic image analysis. A practical project, accompanied by a written evaluation, makes up 30 per cent of the assessment, which is through moderation. The field of study is defined in terms of five 'core elements': institutions, conventions and modes, production, representation and construction, and audience.

* * * * *

The teacher with whom I collaborated had been teaching both English and Media Studies for some years, and in certain respects was concerned to question the traditional distinctions between them. Yet at the same time, her work in both areas was inevitably inflected by the different requirements of the syllabuses.

In an interview recorded at an early stage in the research, she argues that one of the major benefits of teaching about media texts is their relevance and accessibility for students:

> ... adolescents certainly, I think, get more pleasure and more interest out of ... using material in the classroom that they would personally choose to read or watch in their private lives.

She argues that the students she teaches are much more 'screen-wise than word-wise', whilst in matters literary, the teacher is irretrievably the expert. In the English Language/Literature group some students 'struggle with words', and may not reach the point where they can attempt analysis or deconstruction. When the English/Media Studies group were shown *Fort Apache: The Bronx* [11] however,

> I didn't have to make them feel confident with the material, we were able to make a fairly objective exercise out of it straight away ... you can bring them into being objective about Media Studies texts much sooner than you do about word texts.

By contrast, with poetry,

> ... you actually have to warm them up by letting them be seen to make personal choices about it before you can get them to look at it more objectively ....

At the same time, she notes that media texts are not automatically 'accessible' in this way: for example, ' . . . some of the kids found *Missing*[12] quite hard to follow', when the film was shown to the English Language/Literature group as part of a theme on South America.

Overall, however, this teacher regards using media texts as a more effective means of achieving an aim shared by both subjects, namely the development of objective responses by students. An objective approach implies a quest for a meaning which is independent of personal involvement — an aim which is perhaps common to both 'analytical' Media Studies work and formal literary critical assignments. This approach implies that there are neutral criteria against which texts can be judged, and that these are ultimately more valid than merely subjective responses.

Thus, the teacher also argues that Media Studies is not about making value-judgments of any sort:

> I think you're on very difficult ground if you start loading that exposé [of the workings of ideology] with value-judgments. I think in a way you've criticized it enough to look at the insidiousness of the way that ideology is promoted . . . I don't see myself saying this is right or wrong.

Here at least, the teacher claims that her perceptions of the ideology of texts do not determine whether they are selected for classroom use. Since she finds student pleasure helpful to her teaching, she justifies the inclusion of any text on this basis: any text is worth studying, not in itself, but because of the critical skills that may be developed through analyzing it.

At the same time, the teacher does identify differences between English and Media Studies in this respect. While she claims that the distinction between them is 'false', she also argues that 'personal response' is more appropriate to English:

> . . . it wouldn't be what I mean by Media Studies to get a kid to write a personal response to a film. I would see that as more appropriate to the Language folder or Literature folder.

The tensions and contradictions apparent here are, I would maintain, by no means unique to this teacher. While she retains a 'principled' commitment to the notion of dissolving the subject boundaries, she also has to work within the constraints of GCSE syllabuses which dictate otherwise. The tensions surrounding the notions of 'personal response' and 'objective reading' which are apparent here, and in the assignments discussed below, are precisely those which, I have argued, characterize the relationship between the two subject areas.

*   *   *   *   *

The analysis which follows is based on a small number of assignments and teacher responses to them. They have been selected, partly because they are representative of the kinds of assignments typically set at GCSE level, and partly because they illustrate a number of the different types of activity identified above.

In addition to the assignments themselves, reference is also made to the examining board's unit top sheet, which is submitted with each piece of English coursework. On this sheet, the candidate is required to enter the title and date of the assignment and to complete a section labelled 'Context and Conditions of Writing'. An opportunity for self-assessment is given in a 'Student's Comments' section. The sections for teacher's comment and grade are used both in external moderation and to provide feedback to the student. Reference may be made here to grade descriptions or marking criteria and the level of address may be more formal in tone than in generally the case with non-examination work.

By examining these forms of guidance and assessment, we may begin to identify the ways in which students perceive teacher expectations which may not be made explicit in the assignment itself. Whilst accumulating from assignment to assignment, these expectations may remain more or less hidden. For example, we may detect discrepancies between the guidelines offered in advance and the evaluative comments made afterwards. Certain terms, such as 'perception' and 'insight', may be used universally, transcending individual items of work and, as we shall see, crossing subject boundaries, yet they may never be defined. In examining these comments, we will be witnessing a process of negotiation between teacher and student — albeit one which may be much less than explicit.

*   *   *   *   *

Assignment one is a compulsory coursework unit on 'a complete literary text' in GCSE English, set after study of a contemporary novel, *Talking in Whispers*, about the life of a teenage boy in Chile under the Pinochet regime.[13] It carries the title 'What impressions do you get of life in Chile under a military regime? How do you think it would affect you as a teenager?'

The first part of this title, in seeking 'impressions', would appear to allow for a variety of readings. Yet, as I shall argue, the range of responses acceptable from the student in this type of assignment (type six) is pre-determined by a number of limiting factors. The explicit guidance offered to students in the section 'context and conditions of writing' relates only to the 'technical' aspects of the assignment:

> High grades will be awarded for:
> 1   A well organized essay;
> 2   Good illustrations from the text when making points.

Previous lessons dealing with the characteristics of 'good organization' in essays are this implicitly cited, reminding students of particular conventions. Whilst 'impressions' may be couched in personal terms, it is made clear that they are only to be valued highly if, for example, supported by illustrations from the text.

These 'technical' concerns are reinforced by the teacher's comments in the margins of the essay itself — for example, 'I like the use of the title in the conclusion' and 'I'd have liked a slightly longer introductory paragraph'. However, the teacher's comment on the cover sheet suggests that further criteria may be in operation:

> This goes from strength to strength. You have covered most of the ground and show a clear appreciation of the issues involved.
> Sentences tend to be too long and superficially confusing, although the structure when looked at is sound.

Again, there are some 'technical' considerations here, but there is also an implication that there is a certain set of 'issues' which are involved, and a certain amount of 'ground' to be covered. Furthermore, it is clear that these 'issues' refer not to the book itself — for example, its structure or style — but to the situation in Chile. In effect, a shift has taken place from 'impressions' to 'issues' — an indication that this assignment is more closed than might appear at first sight. While a subjective, personal response is apparently invited, a good student will refer to impressions formed on a pre-determined range of topics.

That a favourable impression of the Chilean Junta, extolling the virtues of, let us say, discipline, respect and anti-communism — not one of the preferred readings of the text itself — is unlikely to be assessed highly, is clear from the agenda implicitly set by the teacher. This may also have been evident to the student from the other work which formed the context of the assignment. Work on the film *Missing*, about an American killed by the army during the Chilean coup of 1973, together with a newspaper assignment in which students examined pro-government bias in the press, would serve to alert the student to particular 'preferred' readings.

Thus despite the overt invitation to provide personal 'impressions', there is a clear sense in which the text is being elevated to the role of guarantor of truth. Views established about the text during study and discussion are apparently open to debate by the student, yet the status of the text as a source of evidence about Chile is not questioned. The student's essay effectively treats material in the text as equivalent to historical statements: for example, 'under the military regime there is no freedom of speech in the streets' and 'another restriction was curfew'. There is little sense in which the status of the text itself has been open to question. Material is simply selected and extracted to be used as evidence and thereby to support ostensibly personal readings of the text.

Several issues are discussed by the student in this way, also drawing on her viewing of the film *Missing*. Here again, the major focus is on the 'content' of the text, which is being used to inform discussion of particular issues (activity type four). Yet the high status given to the novel through the process described above has resulted in a number of difficulties. 'So America is split. Just like Chile', writes the student. Such an assertion is based on the actions and attitudes of individual characters in the book towards the Chilean Junta, including members of the military. Yet the use of material from two such fictional sources is clearly insufficient for the assessment of major historical and political issues. While the texts chosen have been used to open issues, they have also been used to close them, in a rather limiting way. The student adopts this even-handed view of the political situation, refusing the ideological positioning suggested by the author. Such readings consistently condemn both the military regime and the American Government, as perpetrators of an injustice to be righted through struggle.

Ultimately, the ideological concerns which underlie the activity effectively preclude any questioning of the 'evidence' or of the point of view of the texts concerned. Despite the apparent openness, the activity is in fact quite closed. The teacher isolates preferred readings of the texts and devises activities which privilege questions raised in those readings. The results of these activities then find their way back into students' further work on the texts.

The speculation and empathy demanded by the second part of the title — 'How do you think it would affect you as a teenager?' — could be seen to work in a similar, if perhaps less constricting, way. The emphasis on 'relevance' and 'issues' in English teaching does not allow limitless scope, but privileges 'acceptable' responses which show the student to be confronting the issues in an apt manner. In particular, students are required to use a frame of reference related to their own life experience, although this again has to be defined in particular ways. The words 'as a teenager' are in a sense redundant since all those addressed are teenagers. However, I would suggest that the phrase serves to alert the student to a particular agenda of 'teenage' issues. In this case, the student selects, from the range of horrific acts of military repression described, two cliches of adolescence — about going out at night and about dressing as one chooses.

Clearly, a student seeking high grades is likely to be very receptive to teacher definitions of 'important issues'. In a variety of implicit ways, in the assignment title, in the evaluation and in the work surrounding the assignment, we may detect the existence of a 'hidden agenda' of issues which is nowhere explicitly stated.

* * * * *

Assignment two, entitled *Family Reunion*, consists of work on the Sylvia Plath poem of the same name. It was set as part of a sequence of activities which was to culminate in the students producing poetry coursework for their GCSE English Language folders.

The interview with the teacher provided an outline of how the group's work on poetry had developed. Initially the students were asked to choose half a dozen poems they liked:

> . . . just personal choice and trying to describe why they had chosen. And I
> then asked them to choose a particular poem and write about it, still not

having given them a structure or told them how to do a standard poetry appreciation . . .

The open readings available to students in the first instance (activity type one) are followed by a move towards a response which is limited by 'formal' features (type six).

> And from that I picked up two or three poems I felt were particularly useful as teaching tools. I picked Sylvia Plath's *Family Reunion* . . . as it had a very nice clear structure . . . But it was with the Sylvia Plath one where I took them through if you like the structure of a poem, starting off from feelings, how those feelings were produced, how the language produced those feelings . . . and so on. So I gave them a fairly standard piece of poetry appreciation and I asked them to write that one up, so they've all done one poem.

The plan for the remainder of the half term was that alongside their literature projects, students would produce six or eight pieces of poetry appreciation of which the two or three best ones would be submitted as coursework.

The first two paragraphs of the student's essay give reasons why the student likes the poem, reasons based on empathy, personal identification with the character in the poem and recognition of a situation from the student's experience. 'I like' and 'you really feel' introduce these ideas, 'feeling' occurring three times. Since it was made clear that the teacher guided responses only in general terms, it can be assumed that such terms represent the student's acquired agenda of aims when confronted with a poem.

The student does not appear to feel constrained by the notion of a specific preferred reading. A personal, subjective response to the text (activity type two) is evident at many points in the piece. On the other hand, there are at least two ways in which the student has interpreted the assignment in a more conventional, restricted manner: she uses the poem as a starting point for consideration of a topic, a visit by relatives (a type three activity); and she deals more formally with the language of the poem, selecting features which she likes:

> I like the metaphor 'the doorbell rends the noon-day heat with copper claws' indicating that the visitors are really tearing away at her personality and peace.

Thus at the same time as describing the meaning of the text for her, she is also passing judgment upon the process by which that meaning is produced:

> I like the alliteration 'the dull drum of my pulses beat' saying she is quite happy just to sit in the silence and listen to herself being herself.

> In this assignment, then, the student feels in a position to assess the text in terms

of personal pleasure, whilst simultaneously analyzing its formal features, effectively combining a more open activity (type two) with a more closed one (type seven). She perceives a relatively unrestricted space for responding to the text, yet she also draws on her implicit agenda to define the limits of areas in which to respond. It may be that this degree of space owes something to the fact that this assignment is not destined to be submitted as GCSE coursework. Significantly, the teacher comments at the end of the piece: 'Clear and well-expressed awareness of how language is used. Good'. An alert student would be encouraged by this to prioritize analysis over the expression of personal feelings in future work.

An extract from the transcript of a follow-up poetry lesson illustrates the kind of advice given to students about writing poetry appreciations:

> You spend some time finding individual bits and pieces, like for example we did with the Sylvia Plath one . . . I would pick out for example 'copper claws'. 'Copper claws', why 'copper', why 'claws', why alliteration of the two c's? It's harsh, it's scratchy, it gets over the invasion of her privacy. So, rather than just list all this that produced that feeling, choose three or four examples and go to town on them, using technical terms if you like . . . . Look at how the language, the choice of sounds, the choice of individual words produces these moods . . . and that really is what an appreciation is. Analyzing how the poet has used language to produce these feelings in you and then you need some sort of concluding paragraph . . . where maybe you say something you don't like about the poem. For example, the Sylvia Plath poem, one or two of you found it over the top, found it too exaggerated, too hysterical, which is an understandable reaction . . . and you might like to put that down in the last paragraph, that although you felt generally in sympathy with it, there were times when you felt she was too hysterical, too dramatic, too exaggerated . . .

Such an approach, without being completely prescriptive, is clearly guiding students towards a fairly circumscribed form of response, which is perhaps no less restricted than that of assignment one. Significantly, however, what you feel and how you feel are not as important here as being able to offer a more analytical account of *why* you feel. In effect, the student is being schooled in becoming a critic. Whilst it must be acknowledged that this teacher is also a teacher of Media Studies, she has the demands of the GCSE English syllabus firmly in mind. From a brief study of this unit of work, it is difficult to sustain the view that English is about feeling while analysis is the domain of Media Studies.

*   *   *   *   *

Assignment three, set to the English/Media Studies group, is an analysis of the opening sequence of the film *Fort Apache: The Bronx*, in the form of a storyboard. The unit of work began with a revision of earlier work on the 'codes' of expression, gesture, background clothing, lighting and camera angle, drawn from Andrew Bethell's *EyeOpener One*.[14] The opening sequence of *Fort Apache: The Bronx* was shown to the group at normal speed, followed by a freeze-frame analysis of the first six shots led by the teacher. The students then produced a drawn storyboard frame for each of the remaining shots with an analytical commentary written under each frame. They had access to the video player and were able to study each shot on more than one occasion. The student whose work I will focus on here used four sheets of A3 paper and drew thirty still images, writing approximately ten lines under each.

Whilst the syllabus allows for more open-ended activities, this exercise is comparatively closed, and fits into category seven above. The teacher introduced the assignment to the class emphasizing certain ideas and concepts which constituted the explicit agenda for work on this particular text. Evident also from this piece is the awareness that no single aspect of the construction of the text is accidental. Every component in every image is regarded as capable of interpretation: the teacher urged students to interrogate the images — 'Why that face? Why that shot? Why that angle? Why that lighting? Why don't we see the face there?' — and to refer to the 'codes' identified above.

A 'storyboard analysis' of the opening sequence of a film could take a number of forms, but the student has already internalized an agenda of what is important about the text and restricted his comments largely to two inter-related areas. He refers firstly to the technical properties of each shot, and then to the potential readings of an imagined audience whom he refers to as 'you'. His comments on the first eight frames each deal with the establishment of expectation. For example, under his drawn representation of the third shot in the sequence, he has written:

> Long shot. Camera tracking to get to this shot. Name of film fades onto screen. As the camera tracks, more light comes in and you know [sic] find out more about the place it's set. The title tells you a bit about what it will be about also. This shot makes you think and wonder what the film is going to be like so you will want to keep watching to find out.

That expectation and generic knowledge comprise one focus of work on an opening sequence is confirmed by a teacher comment on this frame, 'What sort of story line would you expect from this sort of setting?' The aims of this assignment are manifested further in the teacher comments, some of which refer to lost opportunities to make points. For example, 'Why do we not really see their faces in any detail?'. Similarly, under one frame, the student has written 'the low-cut dress establishes the woman as a prostitute', while the teacher has added 'the revealed cleavage also implies harmlessness'. The existence of a 'right answer' and a 'correct reading' required by the assignment is also confirmed through comments such as 'I'd have liked more detail: hairstyle, face, clothes, body language of these two central groupings' and 'I think this shows that these people saw what was happening'. If students have not achieved it on this occasion, the teacher is trying to lead them towards certain modes of responding in future assignments which she believes will be assessed highly on GCSE criteria.

The student's work for this assignment also refers to other 'core elements' not explicitly identified in the teacher's assignment briefing. A concern with representation, for example, is evident in comments like 'these men are "good-looking" and this is a very positive image of them'. Similarly, experience of previous assignments cues the student to use technical terms to describe aspects of the sequence, and to display knowledge of the process of production — although there is no reference to the institutional context in which the text was produced and circulated. A simple notion of audience is employed, in which an imaginary 'you' is postulated, the student commenting on 'your' reactions and expectations. Thus, for example, under one frame the student writes:

> Cut. Close up.
> Woman reaches into her bag. You wonder what she's getting out, so keep looking. Her bag is a gold colour which is attractive to look at. If it was a dull drab colour, it would put you off watching it.

This teacher would firmly reject the view that children learn through passive imitation. Her classroom is one in which students actively discuss and share ideas and produce their own texts, as well as engaging in analytical work. However, in common with many Media Studies teachers, an apparently progressive pedagogy exits alongside an inherently behaviourist view of meaning. Certainly in this assignment, there is a clear sense in which the text is seen to contain a single meaning, which can be uncovered through rigorous analysis: the possibility that different viewers might make sense of the text in different ways is effectively ignored.

We have seen the importance the teacher attaches to objective responses in English. While the form in which the responses are invited is clearly very different, are the assignments set in English in fact any more 'open' than those in Media Studies? Had the student written, not 'You wonder what she's getting out' but '*I* wonder what she's getting out', would the exercise have become, instead of 'objective analysis', a 'personal response'?

* * * * *

Assignment four, set to the English Language/Literature group as the compulsory unit of coursework 'related to a study of the media', is a similar exercise, in this case relating to the opening sequence of the feature film *Three Days of the Condor*.[15] Like assignment three, this is an example of a relatively closed activity (type seven). Initially, what is required is a set of drawings copied from freeze-frame video. 'High grades will be awarded' for three qualities listed in the 'context and conditions of writing' section of the unit top sheet. 'Detailed observation of what is on the screen' is the first of these, although it is not observation as such that is being assessed, so much as the reproduction through drawing and writing of the consequences of that observation. The assignment rests on the assumption that the connotative and analytical work demanded later can only exist on the foundation of sound observation.

The second guideline, 'Detailed analysis of the director's intentions', invites students to use the text as the basis for speculation. The conditions of production, institutional, economic and political factors are not held to be pertinent here. As in traditional literary approaches to *auteur* study, the text is regarded as a mirror into the mind of the author. Furthermore, it seems to be assumed that the director has complete control over the production of the text, and possesses a single, unambiguous intention. Through 'detailed analysis' the student is expected to reconstruct this preferred or dominant reading.

The third guideline to students is 'appreciation of the narrative importance of the opening sequence of a film'. 'Appreciation', a term full of Leavisite resonances, has little force here beyond that of 'recognition' or 'acknowledgment'. Interestingly, the teacher's comment commends the student in similar terms:

> You have clearly understood the overall constuction between good, bad. A
> lot of detail in this which shows a high degree of personal perception and
> appreciation of media constructs.

In fact, despite the Leavisite terminology, this is clearly not an exercise designed to invite the expression of a deeply-felt personal response. On the contrary, it would again seem to be premissed on the notion of the text somehow containing a single, dominant meaning. Thus, a binary opposition between good and bad is inherent in the dominant reading to which the teacher subscribes and this has been recognized by the student. Use of the word 'understand' suggests that students may be assessed according to the degree to which they have recovered or reproduced this reading.

To what extent can we identify what the student assumes to be the aims of the assignment? She writes in the student's comments section:

> This was a good piece of work to do as it made me think about how
> characters are set up and it's much the same in books as it is on TV. I
> thought it would be quite difficult to do but as I began to think about it
> some bits as to why they were put on the screen became quite obvious.
> Character analysis was difficult.

Having completed the exercise, the student is attempting to reconstruct its aims, in particular those she has not already been told. Thus, while 'character analysis' is not mentioned in the title or guidelines of the assignment, and is rarely a central aspect of media teaching, it occurs frequently in literary studies, and has effectively been 'imported' by the student here in an attempt to specify the 'hidden agenda' of the assignment. However, the student appears to acknowledge that the aim of the exercise is to develop a skill, an analytic tool, which she can apply to any text and consequently clarify a previously obscure aspect of its construction. The student does not, in her statement, regard knowledge of this specific text or its meaning as major priorities of the exercise beyond what is required for analysis.

The assignment itself begins with a piece of continuous writing which summarizes some of the conclusions the student has reached during the storyboarding section. She points out a number of formal aspects or 'codes' which are apparent in the sequence — lighting, dress, faces, body stances, camera angle — and identifies in some detail generic oppositions between 'goodies' and 'baddies'. The exercise is competently managed, revealing some knowledge of iconographic characteristics of the genre. There are, however, difficulties with a simple binary reading. 'The baddy in this film wore the classic trench coat, almost for camouflage and the hat to shadow his face'. These items of dress belong, in another branch of the crime genre, not to the baddy, but to the goody, the detective.

At the same time the student notes that the film leaves 'the viewer using his [sic] imagination, as to what you are not shown'. The role of generic elements and the suggestive power of the imagination are clearly acknowledged, whilst underpinned by the notions that meaning is univocal and that we all share a common imagination. The piece ends, however, with remarks about the appearance of the secretary. 'It looks from the secretary as though she has been with the business a long time and is trustworthy so that is why she stays' — an altogether more speculative statement of a personal reading, in contrast to previous firm statements.

The importance of visual 'codes', as in assignment three, had been emphasized by the teacher and this is reflected in the student's comments on specific frames. Camera position, lighting and iconography, are selected by the student as evidence of the way in which an imaginary viewer might respond:

> Cut. This shot immediately gives the watcher doubts and raises questions as to just how normal and respectable everything is. The camera is in a shadow showing secrecy.

Knowledge of camera angle and movement is demonstrated together with readings of the power these techniques are seen to possess: 'Tracking shot. Close up of gun. This shows that the woman thinks she needs help to back up the security system.' The student comments on those areas which her agenda of aims dictates to her and at the same time produces readings which are not her own, but are phrased in terms of a more generalized notion of 'the viewer' — albeit, as in the example quoted above, a male viewer.

Ultimately, this activity depends upon a pre-existing form of cultural knowledge on the part of the student, and in particular upon the student deriving certain types of generic expectation from certain images. In effect, what is being assessed is not a personal response, but an ability to identify the use of generic 'codes' which are assumed to exist objectively, and to be comparatively fixed. Furthermore, the assignment is based on a concept of audience in which one viewer, abstracted from any context, can be said to have fixed responses to certain stimuli. The assignment assumes that the responses of 'the viewer' correspond to the intentions of the director, and that both can be specified simply on the basis of internal textual information.

This approach reinforces the notion of the text as containing a single, valid meaning. The possibility that different viewers in different contexts might make sense of the text in different ways is effectively ignored. This impression that there is one single reading which the student should attempt to unravel is reinforced by teacher comment. For example, under one frame, the student has written, 'This shows a perfectly respectable business man'. 'Business man' has been underlined and superscribed are the words 'He's clearly a security guard'. Another example of this occurs where the student writes in relation to a further frame, 'He is dressed scruffy/casual' to which has been added the comment, 'There's nothing scruffy about Turner'. This example confirms two of my main points: that different students will make sense of the text in different ways, and yet that the fundamental aim of the exercise is to reproduce the 'correct' reading which has been determined by the teacher.

* * * * *

Theoretical accounts of English and Media Studies might lead us to expect significant differences between the two subjects, particularly in terms of how they deal with texts. Yet, as I have indicated, many of these differences may be less important in practice. While the assignments I have examined would appear to invite very different kinds of responses from students, they share a concern with developing critical and analytical skills, and with recovering a 'meaning' which is seen to be contained within the text. Although 'impressions' and 'feelings' were seen as more appropriate for English, and Media Studies appeared to be more concerned with describing the 'construction' of texts, all the assignments were premised on the notion of 'objective' reading. In both subjects, subjective readings were seen as a necessary and desirable preliminary — hence the emphasis on 'personal response' in English and accessibility and pleasure in Media Studies — but ultimately students were expected to move beyond them.

In the case of the English assignments, an apparent openness in the titles disguised the fact that the activities were comparatively closed, both in terms of the emphasis on a single 'correct' interpretation of the text, and in terms of the form in which that interpretation was to be expressed. While the media assignments were overtly more closed, and appeared to display a much more mechanistic approach to analysis, there was ultimately little difference between them in terms of the spaces available for students to construct their own readings.

As I have implied, dominant versions of both English and Media Studies would appear to operate with a very limited definition of 'reading', which effectively neglects the social contexts in which the meanings of a text are established. While Media Studies has always argued against the view that texts can 'objectively' represent the world, it often seems to accept the possibility, and indeed argue for the necessity, of 'objective' reading. Likewise, although English has increasingly asserted the importance of 'personal response', the form of reading which possesses highest status — namely, 'literary criticism' — is clearly a social practice which is far from being merely personal.

Recent developments in literary and media theory have begun to suggest an alternative to this approach, which avoids the notion that reading can ever be either purely objective or purely subjective.[16] While the implications of this theoretical approach have yet to be fully realized in terms of classroom practice, they do suggest that teachers should begin by validating and exploring the differential readings which students produce. This is not to suggest a return to the notion that reading is a purely individual process, and that any one reading is as valid as any other — a notion which is implicit in some versions of 'reception theory'. On the contrary, it suggests that we need to consider reading as a fully social process, which takes place in specific institutional contexts, of which the classroom is certainly one. It would also imply that we need to offer a greater plurality of possible forms of response. What is needed is an area in which students can transform texts without an externally imposed gulf between reading and responding. Such an approach to reading would lead towards a situation in which many of the distinctions often drawn between the two subjects will indeed be rendered 'false'.

Notes

1 See Cook and Hillier (1982); Masterman (1980, 1985); Alvarado, Gutch and Woolen (1987).
2 Leavis and Thompson (1933)
3 For example, Thompson (1964); Hall and Whannell (1964).
4 Knight (1972) p.17
5 Department of Education and Science (1974)
6 Though see, for example, Exton (1983)
7 Masterman (1985), pp. 254—256.
8 Eagleton (1985).
9 Bethell (1983), Masterman (1980), pp. 19—20.
10 West (1987), Moss (1989).
11 Directed by Paul Newman, USA, 1981.
12 Directed by Costa-Gavras, USA, 1981.
13 Watson (1984).
14 Bethell (1981).
15 Directed by Sydney Pollack, USA, 1975.
16 For example, Eagleton (1983).

Conclusion

Chapter 10

Making It Explicit:
Towards a Theory of Media Learning

David Buckingham

Debates about teaching and learning, both within media education and beyond it, have often been reduced to an unproductive confrontation between 'traditional' and 'progressive' pedagogies. Thus, it is argued that 'traditional' pedagogies are subject-centred and fundamentally hierarchical, while 'progressive' pedagogies are child-centred and egalitarian. 'Traditional' pedagogies are concerned with content, 'progressive' pedagogies with process. 'Traditional' pedagogies regard learners as passive, 'progressive' pedagogies regard them as active. And so on.

There are a number of problems with this debate. The two available options come to be seen as mutually exclusive: to attack one is automatically to espouse the other. More crucially, these 'positions' on pedagogy remain distanced from classroom practice itself. When one looks at detailed, ethnographic accounts of classrooms of the kind contained in this book, it is clear that the realities of teaching and learning are much less straightforward. Not only do teachers consciously adopt negotiated positions: it is also that the conditions of classrooms, and the often contradictory constraints on teachers, make it impossible simply to implement 'progressive' or 'traditional' pedagogies.

Thus, in the case of 'traditional' pedagogies, there is a wealth of sociological research looking at the way in which many working-class students in particular actively resist the imposition of hierarchical teaching methods, and create their own counter-culture which effectively inverts the values of the school.[1] Likewise, in the case of 'progressive' pedagogies, there are a number of studies which point to the gap between rhetoric and reality: 'learning by discovery' is often simply a matter of arriving at 'right answers' which have already been determined by the teacher, and so-called 'progressive' methods can serve as a more effective, less visible, means for teachers to exert control.[2] While they may possess a certain rhetorical power, these notions of 'traditional' and 'progressive' pedagogy do not simply describe or indeed determine what takes place in practice.

In the case of media education, as many of the contributions here illustrate, we are often caught between a principled commitment to 'progressive' methods and a belief in the necessity of students gaining access to a body of knowledge, skills or concepts.

We often pay lip-service to the idea that 'there are no right answers', while clearly believing that there are. As our account of teaching about advertising in Chapter 2 suggests, 'analysis' may often be little more than an exercise in guessing what's in teacher's mind. Likewise, Andy Freedman's contribution indicates that apparently open agendas — both in English and in Media Studies — are often more closed than they might seem at first sight.

Similarly, with practical work, there remains a particular anxiety around more 'open-ended' assignments. While we have increasingly come to acknowledge the sophistication of students' existing knowledge of the media, we often remain unwilling to allow them to give full expression to this. There is a persistent fear that letting students loose with video cameras will result in them simply 'mimicking' professional practice in an unthinking, and perhaps also 'ideologically unsound', manner. As a result, we often rely on strategies which in various ways attempt to police this process — and which, as Jenny Grahame argues, may often be superficial or ineffective. As Roy Stafford's contribution also suggests, much of this anxiety surrounding 'creative' practical work may well be misplaced.

Unlike many other subject areas, media education is one to which students bring an enormous amount of prior knowledge: they are already, in a certain sense, 'experts'. Many of the contributions to this volume bear ample witness to this. Julian Sefton-Green's account of his students' debates around *The Cosby Show*, for example, or Pete Fraser's discussion of his students' use of popular discourses about television, point to the complexity and the flexibility of students' existing understanding of the medium. As they argue, it is crucial that teachers come to recognize, and to validate, the knowledge students already have.

Yet at the same time, our aim as teachers is to enable students to build upon this knowledge, to develop new insights and understandings. We do not want simply to leave students where they are, or to enable them to express what they already know, but to give them access to different discourses, to new and hopefully productive ways of making sense of their own experience of the media.

The crucial difficulty, of course, is how we manage this process. In the past, media education has tended to neglect students' existing knowledge, or to regard it as merely inadequate or invalid. The central aim has been to replace this false, 'ideological' knowledge with true, 'objective' knowledge, largely deriving from academic research. In questioning this position, we have sought to develop a less hierarchical, but also more practically effective, approach. Yet the dilemma remains: how do we find ways of validating what students already know, while at the same time enabling them to move beyond this?

* * * * *

In recent years, particularly with the advent of GCSE, there has been a growing consensus about the kind of learning which should be taking place in media education.

GCSE syllabuses — and indeed those aimed at much younger children[3] — have increasingly come to define media education in terms of a set of 'key concepts' which students should master. These typically include terms such as 'media language' (or 'codes and conventions'), 'representation', 'institution' (or 'agency') and 'audience' — although the extent to which these can all be seen as 'concepts' is perhaps debatable.

Nevertheless, in many respects, this has been a valuable development: media education is no longer defined, as it was for some in the 1970s, in terms of a 'body of knowledge' or a set of facts to be learnt and then reproduced. The account of media education across the curriculum contained in Chapter 8 suggests a number of ways in which these conceptual understandings can be extended to apply, not simply to the media, but to the production of knowledge itself in a number of other subject areas. Yet at the same time, this emphasis on conceptual learning creates further problems, many of which have been addressed in this book.

Perhaps the most fundamental question here, both for teachers and researchers, is what we take as *evidence* of conceptual learning. One recent GCSE examination paper in Media Studies asked students to define the word 'representation' — although apparently only one candidate was awarded the full three marks. This is, certainly, one kind of evidence, although it is one which most teachers would probably regard as pretty inadequate. Yet it points to the way in which a set of 'concepts' can easily be reduced to a body of 'content', which can be ingested and then regurgitated. In evaluating students' production logs, as Jenny Grahame asks, are we simply looking for the use of 'academic' terminology as evidence of conceptual learning? And if not, what are we looking for?

This in turn raises further questions. To what extent to students already possess *conceptual* understandings about the media, and how do the concepts we are concerned with relate to these? For example, Julian Sefton-Green's students clearly do under-stand the notion of 'realism' — although, as he demonstrates, their use of the term 'realistic' is diverse and in certain instances quite contradictory. Yet the relationship between their 'commonsense' judgments about the realism (or lack of it) of *The Cosby Show* and our more 'academic' concern with the concept of representation is likely to be problematic — not least because the term 'representation' does not refer to a single, fixed position, but to an on-going debate, a debate which also underlies the students' discussions.

So how does conceptual learning take place, and how can it be encouraged? In this concluding chapter, I shall examine one attempt to answer these questions, which is largely derived from the work of the Soviet psychologist Vygotsky. Although it is hardly a complete answer, it does provide some elements of a theory of teaching and learning which gets beyond the rather sterile debate about 'traditional' and 'pro-gressive' pedagogy, and which might usefully inform media education in the future.

* * * * *

David Buckingham

In his book *Thought and Language* Vygotsky is particularly concerned with the ways in which children develop conceptual understandings, and with the contribution teachers might make to this process.[4] Vygotsky argues that the 'direct teaching of concepts is impossible and fruitless':

> A teacher who does this usually accomplishes nothing but empty verbalism,
> a parrotlike repetition of words by the child, simulating a knowledge of the
> corresponding concepts but actually covering up a vacuum. (p. 83)

He goes on to distinguish between what he terms 'spontaneous' and 'scientific' concepts. Spontaneous concepts are those developed mainly through the child's own mental efforts, while scientific concepts are decisively influenced by adults, and arise from the process of teaching. Scientific concepts — which include social scientific concepts — are distinct from spontaneous concepts in two major respects. Firstly, they are characterized by a degree of distance from immediate experience: they involve an ability to generalize in systematic ways. Secondly, they involve self-reflection — that is, attention not merely to the object to which the concept refers, but also to the thought process itself.

Vygotsky argues that these two kinds of concepts develop in different ways, but come to influence each other's evolution. Spontaneous concepts evolve 'upwards', gradually becoming more systematic, while scientific concepts evolve 'downwards' to a more elementary and concrete level:

> The child becomes conscious of his spontaneous concepts relatively late; the
> ability to define them in words, to operate with them at will, appears long
> after he has acquired the concepts. He has the concept (i.e. knows the object
> to which the concept refers), but is not conscious of his own act of thought.
> The development of a scientific concept, on the other hand, usually *begins*
> with its verbal definition and its use in non-spontaneous operations — with
> working on the concept itself. It starts its life in the child's mind at the level
> that his spontaneous concepts reach only later. (p. 108)

As the child gradually takes scientific concepts on board, they transform the structure of existing spontaneous concepts, and help to organize them into a system.

Vygotsky illustrates this argument by desribing the process whereby children learn to write. Unlike speech, writing is relatively 'non-spontaneous': it differs from speech in both structure and mode of functioning, and requires a high level of abstraction. Writing 'requires deliberate analytical action' in order to turn sounds into written symbols; and the motives for writing are 'more abstract, more intellectualized, further removed from immediate needs' than those for speech. It is through instruction in writing and grammar, he argues, that children become aware of what they are doing with language and learn to use their skills consciously.

Here and elsewhere, Vygotsky consistently argues that the acquisition of scientific concepts involves 'discipline' and 'strenuous mental activity'. Teaching must precede development, constantly seeking to move children on to higher developmental levels, rather than waiting until they are 'ready'. Teaching is not a matter of simply allowing children to 'discover' things, but rather of enabling them to take on, to internalize, external knowledge.

On one level, Vygotsky's argument clearly supports some of the basic principles of 'progressive' pedagogy — and it is largely in this way that he has been used, for example in a good deal of work on English teaching.[5] Thus, he emphasizes the importance of children being active users of language, and the role of interaction among the peer group as an important aid to learning.

Yet, on another level, he displays a much more 'traditional' emphasis on education as a means of enabling the child to take on, and participate in, the dominant culture — and in particular, to develop a familiarity with academic discourse and knowledge. He fully acknowledges the unequal power relationship between teachers and students, and sees this as a crucial aspect of the learning process.

In many ways, however, Vygotsky enables us to transcend the limitations of both 'traditional' and 'progressive' positions. The crux of his theory is the view of knowledge and thought as *social* phenomena: he thus escapes both the individualism of 'progressive' pedagogy and the belief in the objective validity of academic knowledge proposed by 'traditional' pedagogy. Instead, we have a view of learning as a process of socialization, yet one in which learners are active participants, not merely passive receptacles for an existing cultural heritage.

* * * * *

Vygotsky's broad arguments about the teaching of scientific concepts have considerable relevance to media education, particularly if we extend his notion of language to include signification more broadly. To begin with, they help to specify what the characteristics of conceptual understanding might be. To a certain extent, we might consider children's existing understanding of the media as a body of 'spontaneous' concepts. While these concepts will develop as they mature, gradually becoming more generalized and systematic, media education offers a body of 'scientific' concepts which will enable them to think, and to use language, in a much more conscious and deliberate way. The aim of media education, then, is not merely to enable children to 'read' — or make sense of — media texts, or to enable them to 'write' their own: it must also enable them to reflect systematically on the processes of reading and writing themselves, to understand and to analyze their own activity as readers and writers.

The emphasis on self-evaluation, particularly in relation to practical work, which is discussed in a number of contributions here, might well be seen as one significant means of encouraging this process. The aim of this kind of reflection is to enable students to make their implicit knowledge about language explicit, and to relate their specific experiences of media production to broader conceptual understandings. Nevertheless, as Jenny Grahame indicates, there remains a debate about the most effective methods of self-evaluation, and a need to ensure that it is more than merely another examination requirement.

Perhaps inevitably, Vygotsky's general theory fails to provide a clear indication of the ways in which this connection between students' existing 'spontaneous' concepts and the 'scientific' concepts provided by the teacher is to be forged. As we have seen, he argues against the 'direct teaching' of concepts — a practice which is common enough in media education. At the same time, he implies that students will need to encounter unfamiliar terminology, and that they will not fully understand this to begin with. Yet if we are to avoid the 'empty verbalism' Vygotsky describes, we need to think seriously about the purpose of the academic terminology of media education, and the ways in which this is introduced to students. To what extent does this specialist discourse actually assist students in reflecting on their own practice as readers and writers, or does it serve merely to exclude and intimidate?

As Pete Fraser's contribution suggests, 'adult' discourses about the media may fundamentally neglect children's experience, or at least seek to account for this in reductive ways. Giving children access to privileged discourses is obviously vital, but students must be encouraged to interrogate these, rather than simply reproduce them on demand.

Vygotsky's emphasis on the role of writing in developing children's conscious understanding of language is also important here. In particular, it suggests that the potential importance of practical work in media education may be much greater than has often been assumed. Far from regarding practical work as simply a poor relation of theory, it should be seen as a crucial means of enabling students to make explicit their existing knowledge, and to begin to organize it into a system. Teaching the 'grammar' of the media would be much more effective if it built on this experience of 'writing', rather than being based simply on 'readings' of media texts.

Likewise, Vygotsky's description of the role of play in development[6] points to the importance of children creating 'imaginary situations' as a means of developing abstract thought. Crucially, however, Vygotsky argues that it is through play that the child learns self-control and the significance of rules:

> . . . in play [the child] adopts the line of least resistance — she does what she most feels like doing because play is connected with pleasure — and at the same time she learns to follow the line of greatest resistance, by subordinating herself to rules and thereby renouncing what she wants, since subjection to rules and renunciation of impulsive action constitute the path of maximum pleasure in play. (p. 99)

Although Vygotsky's discussion of play refers primarily to pre-school children, he is also concerned to demonstrate the continuity between play and the 'complex, mediated form of thought' more characteristic of school learning. Here again, we might regard practical work in media education as an area in which play might usefully contribute to more abstract conceptual learning.

Again, many of the contributions here illustrate this. Roy Stafford's account of his students' video productions, for example, indicates the ways in which students can use relatively open-ended assignments as an opportunity to explore popular cultural forms and make them their own. While such projects are partly a celebration of the students' own culture, they also involve a highly specific consideration of 'conceptual' issues such as media forms and conventions, and the relationships between producers and their audiences. In the process, students may be adopting a very different, and more powerful, position in the institutional context of the school or college.

* * * * *

The specific implications of Vygotsky's theory for teachers have been developed by a number of subsequent writers. The work of Bruner is particularly important here, although there is a sense in which at least some of Bruner's work tends to play down the broader social aspects of Vygotsky's theory.[7] Nevertheless, Bruner's argument about the 'spiral curriculum' — his oft-quoted notion that it should be possible to teach concepts to children in an 'intellectually honest' form at any age — has significant implications for our understanding of conceptual learning in media education.

According to Bruner, self-reflection, achieved through interaction with the teacher and with other learners, is vital to learning:

> I suspect that much of growth starts out by our turning around and recoding in new forms with the aid of an adult tutor what we have been doing or seeing, then going on to new modes of organisation with the new products that have been formed by these recodings.[8]

In his more recent work, Bruner refers to this process of distanced reflection on what one knows as 'metacognition', and argues that it can be fostered most effectively through a debate, through the expression of 'stance and counter-stance', rather than by relying on 'the so-called uncontaminated language of fact and "objectivity"'.[9]

Bruner's notions of 'scaffolding' and 'handover' are both attempts to describe the process whereby children take on knowledge and conceptual understanding, and make it their own. This is accomplished through a dialogue with the teacher, or with more competent peers: children do not simply 'discover' concepts, but are guided and assisted by the systematic interventions of teachers. As for Vygotsky, the teacher has a crucial, and powerful, role in this process: teaching is not just a matter of creating 'natural' environments in which children can express themselves, but on the contrary of leading students onwards from 'apprenticeship' to 'mastery'.

In a recent study of British primary school classrooms, Edwards and Mercer have applied some of these ideas in an attempt to identify the importance of 'shared understandings' between teachers and students.[10] One particular problem they identify is the failure of teachers to make the 'ground rules' of teaching and learning explicit — in effect, to explain to students the purpose of the activities they are engaged in.

In discussing a simulation exercise, in which students were invited to imagine themselves as castaways on a desert island, Edwards and Mercer suggest that the theoretical principles or concepts underlying such activities are often not understood by pupils. In this instance, what was primarily intended to be an experiential lesson about a set of social science concepts (for example, cooperation, the division of labour and the organization of society) was understood by students as a kind of training exercise in how to survive as a castaway. The teacher's commitment to 'learning by discovery', and her fear of 'putting words into the children's mouths' meant that the relationship between the general and the particular was not made clear.

Edwards and Mercer also draw attention to the way in which 'ritual knowledge' — doing things correctly because they appear to please the teacher — can stand in for 'principled knowledge' — understanding why certain procedures or conclusions are valid. Students are very good at learning *what* to do, but this does not necessarily mean they know *why* they are doing it. Likewise, teachers may effectively stage-manage things so that pupils 'discover' what they are supposed to, but in many cases all they are doing is guessing what the teacher wants them to say — a practice Edwards and Mercer call 'cued elicitation'.

* * * * *

Here again, these ideas have a number of implications for media education. While they point to the central importance of active learning, and in particular of children being active users of language — and, by extension, of 'media language' — they also suggest that activity in itself does not necessarily result in learning. In the case of media education, it is often very easy to generate 'busywork' for students — activities which keep them occupied, but whose underlying theoretical rationale they rarely understand. Edwards and Mercer's analysis of the 'castaway' simulation could be applied to many similar exercises in media education. In the case of the *Playtime* simulation discussed by Jenny Grahame, or the advertising simulation described in Chapter 2, the relationship between theory and practice — and in effect, the purpose of the exercise — tended to get lost as students engaged in the detailed process of decision-making and production. While students clearly learnt a great deal from these activities, the underlying concepts were rarely made explicit.

At the very least, this points to the importance of providing sufficient opportunities, both during and after the simulation, for students to reflect on what has taken place, with the assistance of the teacher. This is not to suggest that practical work is simply 'unthinking', as some critics have argued: but it is to argue for the importance of systematic reflection, or what Bruner terms 'metacognition'. Indeed, Bruner's notion of 'recoding' may be particularly relevant to media education, where students are inevitably moving back and forth between verbal and visual forms of symbolic representation.

Similarly, Edwards and Mercer's argument about the limitations of 'ritual knowledge' may apply particularly to the kinds of textual analysis which take place in media education. In Chapter 2 for example, we identify some of the limitations of 'cued elicitation', and demonstrate how it can be used simply to impose the teacher's reading. Likewise, Andy Freedman's account of the ways in which teachers assess and respond to students' work in both English and Media Studies suggests that teachers may often present their own readings of texts as objective and incontrovertible. As he implies, textual analysis of this kind is far from being a neutral or indeed a natural process. Despite the rhetoric of 'personal response' in English and 'objective analysis' in Media Studies, students are effectively being 'schooled' in particular ways of reading texts which are neither purely 'personal' nor purely 'objective'.

Textual analysis needs to move beyond the notion that there are single meanings inherent in texts, and to acknowledge the fact that meaning is a negotiation between text and reader. Rather than seeking to arrive at definitive, objective interpretations of texts, we should encourage a debate over meaning, between 'stance and counter-stance'. The point of textual analysis is not to determine once and for all what a text means, but to examine how it comes to have a meaning in the first place — a process which involves acknowledging, rather then repressing, the different meanings it will have for different readers. As Julian Sefton-Green's contribution shows, the ways in which a given text represents the world can be judged according to a diverse, and potentially contradictory, range of criteria: yet it is vital that these criteria are made explicit, and their aesthetic and political implications are debated. Ultimately, what is important is not the 'answer', but understanding how we arrive at the answer.

This would suggest that, as with practical work, we should be attempting to encourage students to reflect on the processes by which they generate meaning. Textual analysis often produces the response 'so what?' — largely because students often perceive it as an exercise in stating what to them is merely obvious. Yet the central question we should be addressing is surely: how does it come to be 'obvious'? To ask the question in this way implies that 'saying what it means' is only the beginning of the process: it should be followed by a much more self-reflective understanding of the reading process, in which the teacher is likely to take a prominent role. We need to have good answers to the question 'so what?' — although they are answers which will perhaps inevitably be abstract.

*   *   *   *   *

While this kind of analysis of conceptual learning does have considerable relevance to media education, it also has its limitations. Two issues in particular are suggested by the contributions included here.

The first of these concerns the 'affective' dimensions of learning — an area which

Vygotsky himself admits he tends to neglect.[11] While there are certainly aspects of his theory that do acknowledge the question of pleasure, in particular his essay on play (quoted above), there is nevertheless a tendency to focus largely on the cognitive aspects of learning. This is also a limitation in many discussions of media education, which have tended to marginalize pleasure and subjectivity, and to focus exclusively on cognitive understanding.[12] For some critics, media education has been seen as an attempt to 'police' the potentially subversive elements of popular pleasures, and to impose a highly rationalistic approach to texts.[13]

A number of contributions to this book indicate the limitations of this tendency. Both Chris Richards' and Julian Sefton-Green's contributions point to the considerable emotional investments students may have in particular texts, and the limitations of 'analysis' as a means of accounting for these. In both cases, questions about subjectivity, about students' sense of their own identity, are inextricable from the ways in which they read and use the media. If we are concerned to address this dimension of students' experience, it is vital that media education is not reduced to a mere academic exercise, or a purely instrumental activity. We need to provide opportunities for students to explore their emotional investments in the media *in their own terms*, rather than attempting to replace these by rigorous 'rational' analysis.

Likewise, those contributions concerned with practical work point to the necessity of allowing students the opportunity to give voice to their own pleasures in popular texts, and to their broader social experience. To ignore these aspects of learning on the grounds of a reaction against 'liberal progressivism' — as a number of media educationists have done[14] — is both misguided and potentially counter-productive.

The implication of these studies is that we need to acknowledge the central role of pleasure, both in students' use of the media, and in the learning process itself. Theoretical work on the media has often proceeded from a basic distinction between ideology and pleasure, or between the rational and the emotional[15] — a distinction which is itself highly problematic. Likewise, it is vital to avoid any superficial opposition between affective and cognitive processes in learning. The view, adopted by some advocates of media education, that subjective responses can simply be put to one side in favour of objective analysis, is clearly simplistic, as many of the contributions here indicate.[16]

*   *   *   *   *

The second issue here concerns the significance and function of language. As we have seen, Vygotsky and his followers have emphasized the central role of language in learning: in this theory, language performs functions which are not merely social or interpersonal, but also cognitive. It is through the use of language, for example, that implicit understandings are made explicit: language serves as a fundamental tool in developing thought and understanding.

Many of the contributors to this book have taken a more sceptical — or perhaps more thoroughly social — view of language, which is partly derived from recent developments in discourse analysis.[17] According to this view, what children say does not simply reflect what they think or believe. On the contrary, the language individuals produce is crucially determined by the social and interpersonal context. Thus, for example, in Pete Fraser's contribution, the children and teachers employ different discourses about television at least partly in order to define themselves in relation to others in the group, or to the interviewer. These discourses already contain within them certain definitions of 'self' and 'other'.

Classrooms are obviously not neutral contexts: the ways in which both teachers and students use language will clearly depend upon the power relationships which obtain there. As our account of teaching about advertising demonstrates, what students say should not necessarily be taken at face value. For example, language can be used by students as a means of 'doing power' against the teacher: particular positions can be adopted, not as a result of deeply held convictions, but simply as a way of subverting or playing with existing power relationships. The discussion analyzed at the end of Julian Sefton-Green's chapter demonstrates the way in which the social context of the classroom can exert quite contradictory pressures, often with problematic results.

As these analyses suggest, such power relationships are inherent in classrooms, and cannot simply be abolished. We cannot hope to create 'natural' spaces in which students can 'say what they really think'. Furthermore, there is also a recognition here that language does not in itself produce learning: indeed, it can constrain or actively prevent it. There are only limited linguistic resources available to us which might help us understand and indeed transform our experience of the media.

Yet in a sense it is precisely here that the great potential of media education lies. It builds upon an existing knowledge of language in all its forms which is both complex and sophisticated. By enabling students to make that knowledge explicit, it gives them the ability to manipulate and control it. To enable students to use language is clearly to empower them. Yet to enable them to understand language itself is to empower them still further.

Notes

1 For example, Willis (1977); Corrigan (1979).
2 For example, Sharp and Green (1975); Edwards and Mercer (1987).
3 Bazalgette (1989b).
4 Vygotsky (1962), particularly Chapters 5 and 6. See also Vygotsky (1978), Chapter 6.
5 For example, the work of Barnes (1976) and Britton (1970).
6 Vygotsky (1978), Chapter 7.
7 Bruner (1985, 1986).
8 Bruner (1966), quoted in Barnes (1976), p. 24.
9 Bruner (1986), p. 129.
10 Edwards and Mercer (1987).
11 Vygotsky (1962), p. 8.
12 See Buckingham (1986).
13 Walkerdine (1986), Buckingham (1989).
14 For example, Alvarado (1981).
15 For example, Ang (1985).
16 See Masterman (1980), Bethell (1983).
17 See Potter and Wetherell (1987).

Bibliography

ADLER, B. (1986) *The Cosby Wit: His Life and Humour*, New York, Robson Books.
ADLER, R. P. *et al.* (1980) *The Effects of Television Advertising on Children*, Lexington, Mass., Lexington Books.
ALLEN, R. (ed.) (1987) *Channels of Discourse*, London, Methuen.
ALTHUSSER, L. (1971) 'Ideology and ideological state apparatuses', in *Lenin and Philosophy and Other Essays*, London, New Left Books.
ALVARADO, M. (1977) 'Class, culture and the education system', *Screen Education*, no. 25.
ALVARADO, M. (1981) 'Television Studies and pedagogy', *Screen Education*, No. 38.
ALVARADO, M. GUTCH, R. and WOLLEN, T. (1987) *Learning the Media: An Introduction to Media Teaching*, London, Macmillan.
ANG, I. (1985) *Watching 'Dallas': Soap Opera and the Melodramatic Imagination*, London, Methuen.
ARTHURS, J. (1987) 'Production projects for GCSE', *In the Picture* (Yorkshire Arts), Autumn.
BARNES, D. (1976) *From Communication to Curriculum*, Harmondsworth, Penguin.
BARNES, D. and TODD, F. (1977) *Communication and Learning in Small Groups*, London, Routledge and Kegan Paul.
BARTHES, R. (1977) 'The rhetoric of the image', in S. Heath (ed.) *Image-Music-Text*, Glasgow, Fontana.
BAZALGETTE, C. (1986) 'Making sense for whom?', *Screen*, vol. 27, no. 5.
BAZALGETTE, C. (1989a) 'Putting the children first', *Times Educational Supplement*, 24 April.
BAZALGETTE, C. (ed.) (1989b) *Primary Media Education: A Curriculum Statement*, London, British Film Institute.
BENNETT, T. (1979) *Formalism and Marxism*, London, Methuen.
BERNSTEIN, B. (1971) 'On the classification and framing of educational knowledge', in M. F. D. Young (ed.) *Knowledge and Control*, London, Collier Macmillan.
BETHELL, A. (1981) *EyeOpeners One and Two*, Cambridge, Cambridge University Press.
BETHELL, A. (1983) 'Media Studies', in J. Miller (ed.) *Eccentric Propositions*, London, Routledge and Kegan Paul.
BETHELL, A. (1985) 'Negative images, positive talk' in *Education and the Afro-Caribbean Child* (eds unidentified), London, Afro-Caribbean Education Project.
BLANCHARD, T., GREENLEAF, S. and SEFTON-GREEN, J. (1989) *The Music Business: A Teaching Pack*, London, Hodder and Stoughton.
BLEWITT, J. (1988) 'History, political science and media education', *Teaching Politics*, vol. 17, no. 1.
BRANSTON, G. (1987) *Teaching Media Institutions*, London, British Film Institute Education Department, mimeo.
BRITISH FILM INSTITUTE EDUCATION DEPARTMENT (n.d.) *Selling Pictures*, London, British Film Institute.
BRITISH FILM INSTITUTE WORKING PARTY ON PRIMARY MEDIA EDUCATION (1987) *Working Papers Three*, London, British Film Institute, mimeo.
BRITISH FILM INSTITUTE WORKING PARTY ON PRIMARY MEDIA EDUCATION (1988) *Working Papers Four*, London, British Film Institute, mimeo.
BRITTON, J. (1970) *Language and Learning*, Harmondsworth, Allen Lane.

BRUNER, J. (1966) *Toward a Theory of Instruction*, Boston, Belknap Press.

BRUNER, J. (1985) 'Vygotsky: a historical and conceptual perspective', in J. V. Wertsch (ed.) *Culture, Communication and Cognition: Vygotskian Perspectives*, Cambridge, Cambridge University Press.

BRUNER, J. (1986) *Actual Minds, Possible Worlds*, Cambridge, Mass., Harvard University Press.

BUCKINGHAM, D. (1986) 'Against demystification', *Screen* vol. 27, no. 5.

BUCKINGHAM, D. (1987a) *Unit 27: Media Education* (EH207 Communication and Education), Milton Keynes, Open University Press.

BUCKINGHAM, D. (1987b) *Public Secrets: 'EastEnders' and its Audience*, London, British Film Institute.

BUCKINGHAM, D. (1989) 'Television literacy: a critique', *Radical Philosophy*, No. 51.

BUSCOMBE, E., GLEDHILL, C. LOVELL, A. and WILLIAMS, C. (1976) 'Why we have resigned from the board of *Screen*', *Screen*, vol. 17, no. 2.

BUTTS, D. (1987) 'Zooming out: the widening concept of media education for teachers', *Educational Media International*, vol. 27, no. 4.

CHODOROW, N. (1978) *The Reproduction of Mothering: Psychoanalysis and the Sociology of Gender*, San Francisco University of California Press.

CLARKE, M. (1987) *Teaching Popular Television*, London, Heinemann.

COHEN, P. (1988) 'The perversions of inheritance', in P. Cohen and H. S. Bains (eds) *Multi-Racist Britain*, London Macmillan.

CONNELL, I. (1983) '"Progressive" pedagogy?' *Screen*, vol. 24, no. 3.

CONNELL, I. (1984) 'Fabulous powers: blaming the media', in L. Masterman (ed.) *Television Mythologies*, London, Comedia.

COOK, J. and HILLIER, J. (1982) *The Growth of Film and TV Studies, 1949-1975*, London, British Film Institute, mimeo.

CORNISH, T. (1987) 'From art to zoology', *Times Educational Supplement*, 20 November.

CORRIGAN, P. (1979) *Schooling the Smash Street Kids*, London, Macmillan.

COWARD, R. and ELLIS, J. (1977) *Language and Materialism*, London, Routledge and Kegan Paul.

CULLINGFORD, C. (1984) *Children and Television*, Aldershot, Gower.

DEPARTMENT OF EDUCATION AND SCIENCE (1974) *A Language for Life* (The Bullock Report), London, HMSO.

DEPARTMENT OF EDUCATION AND SCIENCE (1983) *Popular Television and Schoolchildren: The Report of a Group of Teachers*, London, Department of Education and Science.

DEPARTMENT OF EDUCATION AND SCIENCE (1989), National Curriculum Council, National Curriculum English Working Group *English for Ages 5–16: Proposals to the Secretary of State for Education and Science and The Secretary of State for Wales*, (The Cox Report), London, Department of Education and Science.

DEWDNEY, A. and LISTER, M. (1988) *Youth, Culture and Photography*, London, Macmillan.

DRUMMOND, P. (1977) 'Reply to critics of *Screen Education* 20 'The Sweeney', *Screen Education*, no. 23.

DURKIN, K. (1985) *Television, Sex Roles and Children*, Milton Keynes, Open University Press.

DYER, R. (1985) 'Male sexuality in the media', in A. Metcalf and M. Humphries (eds.) *The Sexuality of Men*, London, Pluto Press.

EAGLETON, T. (1983) *Literary Theory*, Oxford, Blackwell.

EAGLETON, T. (1985) 'The subject of literature', *The English Magazine*, no. 15.

EDWARDS, D. and MERCER, N. (1987) *Common Knowledge: The Development of Understanding in the Classroom*, London, Methuen.

EXTON, R. (1983) 'The poststructuralist always reads twice', *The English Magazine*, no. 10.

EXTON, R. *et al.* (1977) 'Statement: *Screen Education* and 'The Sweeney', *Screen Education*, no. 23.

FERGUSON, B. (1969) *Group Film Making*, London, Studio Vista.

FERGUSON, B. (1977) 'Liberal education, Media Studies and the concept of action', *Screen Education*, no. 22.

FERGUSON, B. (1977/78) 'Media education: discussion or analysis?', *Screen Education*, no. 25.

FERGUSON, B. (1981) 'Practical work and pedagogy', *Screen Education*, no. 38.

FISKE, J. (1987) *Television Culture*, London, Methuen.
FURTHER EDUCATION UNIT (FEU) (1979) *A Basis for Choice*, London, FEU.
FURTHER EDUCATION UNIT (FEU) (1982a) *Basic Skills*, London, FEU.
FURTHER EDUCATION UNIT (FEU) (1982b) *Curriculum Styles and Strategies*, London, FEU.
FURTHER EDUCATION UNIT (FEU) (1985) *Creative and Arts Activities in Further Education*, London, FEU.
GARDNER, C. and YOUNG, R. (1981) 'Science on TV: A Critique', in T. Bennett *et al.* (eds) *Popular Television and Film: A Reader*, London, British Film Institute/Open University Press.
GLASGOW UNIVERSITY MEDIA GROUP (1982) *Really Bad News*, London, Writers and Readers.
GRAHAME, J. (1985) 'Media education across the curriculum', *The English Magazine*, no.15.
GRAHAME, J. (1990) 'The production process', in D. Lusted (ed.) *The Media Studies Book: A Guide for Teachers*, London, Routledge.
GREALY, J. (1975) 'Film teaching and the ideology of the education system', *Screen Education*, no. 15.
GREALY, J. (1977) 'Notes on popular culture', *Screen Education*, no. 22.
HALL, S. (1980) 'Encoding/decoding', in S. Hall *et al.* (eds.) *Culture, Media, Language*, London, Hutchinson.
HALL, S. and WHANNEL, P. (1964) *The Popular Arts*, London, Hutchinson.
HAMMERSLEY, M. and ATKINSON, P. (1983) *Ethnography: Principles in Practice*, London, Tavistock.
HART, A. (1987) 'Making sense of TV science', *Media Education Journal*, no. 6.
HARTLEY, J., GOULDEN, H. and O'SULLIVAN, T. (1985) *Making Sense of the Media*, London, Comedia.
HEATHCOTE, G. *et al.* (1980) 'Integration or co-ordination', *NATFHE Journal*, February.
HOBSON, D. (1982) *'Crossroads', The Drama of a Soap Opera*, London, Methuen.
HODGE, B. and TRIPP, D. (1986) *Children and Television: A Semiotic Approach*, Cambridge, Polity Press.
HORNSBY, J. (1984) *The Case for Practical Studies in Media Education*, London, British Film Institute Education Department, mimeo.
JENKINS, T. and STEWART, D. (n.d.) *The Film Industry*, Bracknell, The Media Centre.
KNIGHT, R. (ed.) (1972) *Film in English Teaching*, London, Hutchinson/British Film Institute.
LARGE, M. (1980) *Who's Bringing Them Up?*, Gloucester, Alan Sutton.
LAWRENCE, E. (1982) 'In the abundance of water the fool is thirsty: sociology and black "pathology"', in Centre for Contemporary Cultural Studies (ed.) *The Empire Strikes Back: Racism in 70s Britain*, London, Hutchinson.
LEAVIS, F. R. and THOMPSON D. (1933) *Culture and Environment*, London, Chatto and Windus.
LEGGETT, J. and HEMMING, J. (n.d.) *Comics and Magazines*, London, ILEA English Centre.
LORAC, C. and WEISS, M. (1981) *Communications and Social Skills*, London, Wheaton.
LUSTED, D. (1982) 'Media education and the secondary/FE curriculum', in *Media Education Conference 1981: A Report*, London, British Film Institute Education Department/University of London Goldsmiths College.
LUSTED, D. (1985) 'Media Studies and media education', in *Papers from the Bradford Media Education Conference*, London, Society for Education in Film and Television.
LUSTED, D. (1986) 'Why pedagogy?', *Screen*, vol. 27, no. 5.
LUSTED, D. and DRUMMOND, P. (1985) *TV and Schooling*, London, British Film Institute.
McKIERNAN, D. (1988) 'Media education: learning from history', *Teaching History*, no. 53.
MARLAND, M. (ed.) (1977) *Language Across the Curriculum: The Implementation of the Bullock Report in the Secondary School*, London, Heinemann.
MASTERMAN, L. (1980) *Teaching About Television*, London, Macmillan.
MASTERMAN, L. (1981/2) 'TV Pedagogy', *Screen Education*, no. 40.
MASTERMAN, L. (1983) 'Media education: theoretical issues and practical possibilities', *Prospects*, vol. 13, no. 2.
MASTERMAN, L. (1985) *Teaching the Media*, London, Comedia/MK Media Press.
MASTERMAN, L. (1986) 'Reply to David Buckingham', *Screen*, vol. 27, no. 5.

Bibliography

MASTERMAN, L. (1989) 'Illumination', *Times Educational Supplement*, 24 April.

MORLEY, D. (1980) *The 'Nationwide' Audience*, London, British Film Institute.

MORLEY, D. (1986) *Family Television: Cultural Power and Domestic Leisure*, London, Comedia.

MOSS, G. (1989) *Un/Popular Fictions*, London, Virago.

MURDOCK, G. and PHELPS, G. (1973) *Mass Media and the Secondary School*, London, Macmillan.

PACKARD, V. (1957) *The Hidden Persuaders*, London, Longman.

PALMER, E. L. and DORR, A. (eds.) (1980) *Children and the Faces of Television: Teaching, Violence, Selling*, London, Academic Press.

POSTMAN, N. (1983) *The Disappearance of Childhood*, London W. H. Allen.

POTTER, J. and WETHERELL, M. (1987) *Discourse and Social Psychology*, London, Sage.

PRING, R. (1976) *Unit 12: The Integrated Curriculum*, (E203 Curriculum Design and Development), Milton Keynes, Open University Press.

REID, I. (1987) 'Integrated practice', *Media Education Journal*, no. 6.

ROOT, J. (1986) *Open the Box*, London, Comedia.

SCREEN EDITORIAL BOARD (1976) 'Reply', *Screen*, vol. 17, no. 2.

SECONDARY EDUCATION JOURNAL, (1985) Special issue, 'Teaching about the media', vol. 1 no. 2.

SHARP, R. and GREEN, A. (1975) *Education and Social Control*, London, Routledge and Kegan Paul.

SIMONS, M. and BETHELL, A. (n.d.) *The Visit*, London, ILEA English Centre.

STAFFORD, R. (1983) 'Media Studies or Manpower Services?', *Screen*, vol. 24, no. 3.

TAYLOR, L. and MULLAN, B. (1986) *Uninvited Guests*, London, Chatto and Windus.

THOMPSON, D. (ed.) (1964) *Discrimination and Popular Culture*, Harmondsworth, Penguin.

TRELEASE, J. (1984) *The Read-Aloud Handbook*, Harmondsworth, Penguin.

VYGOTSKY, L. (1962) *Thought and Language*, Cambridge, Mass., MIT Press.

VYGOTSKY, L. (1978) *Mind and Society*, Cambridge, Mass., Harvard University Press.

WALKERDINE, V. (1985) 'Developmental psychology and the child-centred pedagogy: the insertion of Piaget into early education', in J. Henriques *et al. Changing the Subject*, London, Methuen.

WALKERDINE, V. (1986) 'Video replay: families, films and fantasy', in V. Burgin, J. Donald and C. Kaplan (eds) *Formations of Fantasy*, London, Routledge and Kegan Paul.

WATNEY, S. (1987) 'People's perception of the risk of AIDS and the role of the mass media', *Health Education Journal*, vol. 146, no. 2.

WATSON, J. (1984) *Talking in Whispers*, London, Fontana.

WAUGH, C. (1985) 'Integration, policies and priorities', *Liberal Education*, no. 54.

WEEKS, J. (1981) *Sex, Politics and Society: The Regulation of Sexuality Since 1800*, London, Longman.

WEST, A. (1987) 'The limits of a discourse', *The English Magazine*, no. 18.

WILLIAMSON, J. (1981/2) 'How does girl number twenty understand ideology?', *Screen Education*, no. 40.

WILLIAMSON, J. (1985) 'Is there anyone here from a classroom? And other questions of education', *Screen*, vol. 26, no. 1.

WILLIS, P. (1977) *Learning to Labour: How Working Class Kids Get Working Class Jobs*, London, Saxon House.

WILLIS, P. (1980) 'Notes on method', in S. Hall *et al.* (eds.) *Culture, Media Language*, London, Hutchinson.

WINN, M. (1977) *The Plug-In Drug*, New York, Viking.

YOUNG, B. (1986) 'New approaches to old problems: the growth of advertising literacy', in S. Ward, T. Robertson and R. Brown (eds.) *Commercial Television and European Children*, Aldershot, Gower.

Notes on Contributors

David Buckingham is a Lecturer in the Department of English and Media Studies at the Institute of Education, London University. He is currently Director of a research project on 'The Development of Television Literacy', funded by the Economic and Social Research Council. His publications include a course unit on *Media Education* (Open University Press, 1987) and *Public Secrets: EastEnders and its Audience* (British Film Institute, 1987).

Pete Fraser teaches Media Studies and English in an outer London secondary school. He is an examiner for the WJEC Film Studies 'A' level, and a committee member of Teaching Media in London. He has contributed to *Media Education Initiatives*.

Andy Freedman is Education Officer at Media Arts, Swindon. He formerly taught English and Media Studies in secondary schools in Bristol, and devised the Southern Examining Group Mode 3 GCSE Media Studies syllabus. He contributed to the County of Avon Media Education Guidelines, and is co-author of *Who is this Woman?* (RLDU, 1985), a teaching pack on gender representation.

Jenny Grahame is Advisory Teacher for Media Education at the ILEA English Centre, and an examiner for City and Guilds and LEAG GCSE Media Studies courses. She formerly taught in London comprehensive schools and in the Youth Service. She is co-author of *Criminal Records* (British Film Institute), and has contributed to *The English Magazine*, *Teachers Weekly* and *Media Education Initiatives*.

Netia Mayman teaches English and Media Studies in an inner London comprehensive, and has also been visiting lecturer on PGCE courses at the Institute of Education and King's College, London. Her publications include *TV Sitcom* (ILEA English Centre) and, as co-author, *Criminal Records* (British Film Institute). She has contributed to *The English Magazine*, *Media Education Initiatives* and *English in Education*.

Chris Richards is currently a Lecturer in the Department of English and Media Studies at the Institute of Education, London University. He has taught English and

Media Studies in inner London secondary schools and in Further Education colleges in outer London. He has contributed to *Teaching London Kids*, *Screen Education* and *Screen*.

Jocelyn Robson is a Lecturer in Education at Thames Polytechnic (formerly Garnett College), where she has particular responsibility for training teachers of Media Studies and Communications for the post-compulsory education sector. She has taught in both Adult and Further Education, and on the Open University module 'Representations of Women in Film'.

Julian Sefton-Green teaches English and Media Studies in a comprehensive school in Tottenham, North London. He is co-author of *The Music Business: A Teaching Pack* (Hodder and Stoughton, 1989) and also contributed to *Wham Wrapping: Teaching the Music Industry* (British Film Institute, 1989). He was an active member of the Haringey Education Media Project.

Jonathan Simmons is a Lecturer in Education at Thames Polytechnic (formerly Garnett College), where he is responsible for training teachers of General Education for the Further Education sector. He has taught Film, Media and General Studies in Further and Adult Education, and has contributed to *Media Education Initiatives*.

Martin Sohn-Rethel formerly taught English and Media Studies in London secondary schools, most recently at North Westminster School, where he was also responsible for implementing a whole school policy on media education across the curriculum. He is currently based in Dorset, freelancing in cross-phase media education advisory work and engaged in research into teaching about media institutions.

Roy Stafford taught General Studies and Media Studies for many years in a Further Education College in South London. He is currently a Media Education Advisor, part-funded by the British Film Institute and based at Trinity and All Saints' College in Leeds. He has contributed to *Screen* and *Screen Education*.

Index